THE DAILY TELEGRAPH BOOK OF HYMNS

Ian Bradley

Continuum

The Tower Building
11 York Road
London SE1 7NX

15 East 26th Street
New York
NY 10010

www.continuumbooks.com

First published 2005

British Library Cataloguing-in-Publication Data
A catalogue record for this book is available from the British Library.

ISBN 0-8264-8678-9

Typeset by BookEns Ltd, Royston, Herts.
Printed and bound by MPG Books Ltd, Bodmin, Cornwall

CONTENTS

This book is dedicated to the memory of my brother
David William Bradley (11 June 1952–27 May 1987)
(*'We may not know, we cannot tell, what pains he had to bear'*)

INTRODUCTION

The first gramophone record that I owned was an EP of songs and sketches written and performed by the original *Private Eye* team in 1962. Squeezed in between extracts from a speech by Harold Macmillan made to sound like a pop song, irreverent reflections on the Common Market and dramatic readings from the personal columns of *The Times* was a section entitled 'Lift Up Your Parts' which included the following parody of 'Eternal Father, strong to save', intoned in suitably parsonical voices to John Bacchus Dykes's wonderful tune Melita:

> When I am feeling like a laugh,
> I read the *Daily Telegraph*,
> And all my troubles disappear
> When I am reading Peterborough.

> O hear us, when we cry to thee,
> For those in peril in the BBC!

I begin with this somewhat inconsequential little item not just because it introduces the only hymnodic reference that I know of to the newspaper which is sponsoring this volume but also because it shows the extraordinary power that hymns have exerted on the British, even in their most iconoclastic and irreverent moments. When the soldiers stuck in the trenches of Flanders in the First World War sought an escape mechanism through song, it was to hymns as much as music hall favourites that they turned to provide tunes for their heart-felt expressions of frustration and yearning. 'What a friend we have in Jesus' was transmogrified into 'When this lousy war is over', 'Holy, holy, holy' into 'Raining, raining, raining' and 'The Church's one foundation' into 'We are Fred Karno's Army'.

Parodies of hymns are not so common now as they were in the twentieth century. Hymns are a less pervasive and ubiquitous part of our national landscape and consciousness. They are not much sung at school, and attendance at Sunday schools – where so many hymns were first learned never to be forgotten – has plummeted in recent decades. Yet the British love affair with hymns continues, even if it is not quite as fervent and universal as it once was. More people, I suspect, would be able to quote the first line of a hymn than a verse from the Bible or a prayer. Communal hymn-singing may take place less often than it used to on the football terraces, but it is still an important ingredient of national occasions such as the British Legion Festival of Remembrance.

It is no coincidence that the flagship programme of the BBC's religious broadcasting department, screened at tea-time every Sunday on BBC1 to an audience of around three million, is based around communal hymn-singing. *Songs of Praise*, now in its fifth decade, has changed subtly in format to reflect changing cultural mores – more celebrities, more soft-focus shots, more soloists and more songs from shows and films. Yet its core remains the singing of hymns by congregations gathered in churches up and down the country. There is no other television programme like it anywhere in the world. Together with its Radio 2 companion, *Sunday Half Hour*, it continues to celebrate and promote the British love and legacy of hymn-singing.

Hymns have, indeed, been Britain's particular and most distinctive contribution to Christian literature, worship and witness. Other nations have produced more profound theologians and more fervent saints, but nowhere else has produced a pantheon of hymn-writers of the calibre of Isaac Watts, Charles Wesley and their successors.

This book does not just contain the work of British writers. There are several hymns by North American authors and there are translations of verses from various European languages. Its core, however, is the rich and solid tradition of hymnody which comes from England, Scotland, Wales and Ireland – a tradition which is very much alive and still continuing to bear much good fruit. This is a personal selection of my own favourite hymns, ancient and modern, which also takes account of polls indicating the most popular hymns in the country as a whole. In particular, I have drawn on the extensive poll undertaken among *Songs of Praise* viewers in 2002, the latest available when this volume went to press.

The texts of the hymns in this collection are, for the most part, given in their original form so that readers can see how their authors originally intended them to read. We have included the original titles for those hymns that have them, as well as the first-line titles. Modifications and alterations to make the versions that we now sing and find in our hymnbooks are described and printed in the introductory notes which accompany each hymn.

I am very conscious that a collection of hymns without tunes is a somewhat incomplete and imperfect entity. It would have greatly added to the cost and complexity of producing this book to have included music, and I hope readers will excuse this words-only version. Many, like me, will be unable to read through the verses that follow without having the melody that invariably accompanies them going round in their heads. (Indeed, some will probably find it impossible not to burst into song when they come to their favourite hymns!) But it is perhaps no bad thing to treat hymns as poems to be read off the printed page. A good number were never intended to be sung at all. Most stand as devotional texts which repay reading, rereading and savouring in a way that is not possible when they are being sung. Hymns provide a wonderful treasury of spiritual riches, and I hope that the readers of this volume will find them aids to personal devotion and meditation as well as striking examples of a branch of English literature which is only now being taken as seriously by scholars and critics as it deserves.

A SAFE STRONGHOLD
OUR GOD IS STILL

This great work by Martin Luther is an appropriate first entry in an anthology of well-loved and much-sung hymns, for it is from the German Reformation that the whole tradition of congregational hymn-singing comes. Although, as we shall see, there are several verses dating from medieval times which are regularly sung today they were not written for congregational use.

Martin Luther (1483–1546), the German monk who is generally regarded as the instigator of the Reformation, deplored the largely passive and silent role played by the congregation in traditional Roman Catholic worship. He wrote a total of 37 hymns for congregational use, mostly to be sung at important points during the Mass. Instead of being in Latin for chanting by choirs they were in the language of the people.

'*Ein' feste Burg ist unser Gott*', to give this one its original German first line, is not, in fact, a liturgical hymn. Rather it is a defiant song of battle against the forces of evil in the world and maybe also against the power of the Roman Catholic Church. Certainly many commentators have interpreted the 'ancient priest of Hell' in the fifth line of the first verse as referring to the Pope as well as the Devil. The opening of the hymn is based on Psalm 46: 'God is our refuge and strength, a very present help in trouble.' But Luther soon departs from the language of the psalmist to create his own powerful imagery.

For a long time it was thought that the hymn was written shortly before Luther's celebrated appearance in front of the Emperor Charles V at the Diet of Worms in 1521 to account for his published attacks on the Roman Catholic Church, and that he sang it as he entered the town. But in fact he almost certainly wrote it eight years later for the Diet of Speyer. It was at that diet that a number of German princes protested to the Emperor at the suppression of religious liberty and so gained the name 'Protestants'.

'*Ein' feste Burg*' was first published in 1529 in Wittenberg, the town where, twelve years earlier, Luther had nailed up his famous 95 theses attacking such practices as the sale of indulgences. It rapidly became not only, in Heinrich Heine's words, 'the Marseillaise of the Reformation' but also the anthem of German nationalism. During the Thirty Years War it was sung to the accompaniment of trumpets by the massed forces of Gustavus Adolphus as they prepared to take on the Catholic forces at the Battle of Leipzig. Frederick the Great called it 'God Almighty's Grenadier March', and it was taken up by the German forces during the Franco-Prussian war of 1870.

Although the hymn was first translated into English by Miles Coverdale in 1538 (as 'Oure God is a defence and towre'), it was not much sung in the English-speaking world until the nineteenth century. The translation printed here, by Thomas Carlyle (1795–1881), the Scottish historian and essayist, was first published in *Fraser's Magazine* in 1831, and is probably the best known in Britain. It has been described by the distinguished hymnologist Erik Routley as 'the greatest translation in the whole field of hymnody'. Carlyle himself said of the hymn: 'There is something in it like the sound of Alpine avalanches or the first murmur of earthquakes: in the very vastness of which dissonance a higher unison is revealed to us.'

In his massive *Dictionary of Hymnology* John Julian★ lists no less than 47 different English translations of Luther's humn. Others still regularly used include 'God is a stronghold and a tower' (Elizabeth Wordsworth, 1891), 'A fortress sure is God our King' (Godfrey Thring, 1882) and 'A mighty fortress is our God' (F.H. Hedge, 1852), a version particularly popular in the United States. Altogether '*Ein' feste Burg*' has been translated into more than 50 languages.

★ John Julian (ed.), *A Dictionary of Hymnology* (London: John Murray, 1907).

The tune, known as *Ein' feste Burg*, or sometimes Worms, was also written by Martin Luther. Mendelssohn included it in the last movement of his 'Reformation' symphony, and Wagner incorporated its theme in his '*Kaisermarsch*' written to celebrate the triumphal entry of German soldiers into Berlin after the Franco-Prussian war.

Der XXXXVI Psalm. Deus noster refugium et virtus

A safe stronghold our God is still,
A trusty shield and weapon;
He'll help us clear from all the ill
That hath us now o'ertaken.
The ancient prince of hell
Hath risen with purpose fell;
Strong mail of craft and power
He weareth in this hour;
On earth is not his fellow.

2   With force of arms we nothing can,
Full soon were we down-ridden;
But for us fights the proper Man
Whom God Himself hath bidden.
Ask ye who is this same?
Christ Jesus is His Name,
The Lord Sabaoth's Son;
He, and no other one,
Shall conquer in the battle.

3   And were this world all devils o'er,
    And watching to devour us,
    We lay it not to heart so sore;
    Not they can overpower us.
    And let the prince of ill
    Look grim as e'er he will,
    He harms us not a whit;
    For why his doom is writ;
    A word shall quickly slay him.

4   God's word, for all their craft and force,
    One moment will not linger,
    But, spite of hell, shall have its course;
    'Tis written by His finger.
    And, though they take our life,
    Goods, honour, children, wife,
    Yet is their profit small;
    These things shall vanish all:
    The city of God remaineth.

ABIDE WITH ME: FAST
FALLS THE EVENTIDE

Although not quite as popular as it used to be, this Victorian hymn is still in the *Songs of Praise* Top Twenty, coming fourteenth in the latest viewers' poll, and remains a favourite choice for funeral services and cremations.

The author, Henry Francis Lyte (1793–1847), was born in Scotland and educated at Trinity College, Dublin, where he won the prize for English poetry three times. He was ordained in 1815 and served as a curate in churches in Ireland and the West of England. In 1823 he became perpetual curate of the parish of Lower Brixham, a seaside and fishing village in Devon. There he remained for the rest of his life, increasingly dogged by illness.

Lyte wrote a large number of sacred poems and hymns, most of which were published in two books, *Poems chiefly Religious* (1833) and *The Spirit of the Psalms* (1834). 'Abide with me' was not, however, published until after his death. For a long time it was thought that he had written it in his study on his last evening in Lower Brixham, 4 September 1847, after he had preached a farewell sermon to his congregation. The following day he sailed for Italy where he died of consumption just over two months later.

It now seems more likely, however, that the verses were composed in 1820 when Lyte was just 27 and still in good health. The inspiration for the hymn seems to have come from a visit that he paid to an old friend, Augustus le Hunte, who was in his last illness. The dying man kept repeating the phrase 'Abide with me', and these words so impressed the young curate that he constructed a set of verses around them. When Lyte came to the end of his time at Lower Brixham and knew himself to be close to death, his mind went back to the hymn that he had written more than a quarter century earlier and he gave the manuscript to a relative who subsequently secured its publication.

The scriptural inspiration for the hymn comes from Luke 24.29 where the disciples journeying on the road to Emmaus beseech Christ: 'Abide with us: for it is toward evening, and the day is far spent.' It is printed here in its full original form. In most modern hymnbooks the third, fourth and fifth verses are omitted.

Lyte composed his own tune for 'Abide with me', and it was also sung in its early days to the Old 124th, St Saviour and a tune called Troyte's Chant. However when *Hymns Ancient and Modern* was being compiled, the editors felt that none of these was satisfactory and the musical editor, William Henry Monk (1823–89), organist of St Matthias, Stoke Newington, was asked to write a new melody. His tune, Eventide, accompanied the hymn in the first edition of the new hymn-book which was published in 1861, and has been its inseparable companion ever since.

The story goes that Monk wrote the tune for 'Abide with me' in ten minutes following a committee meeting of the compilers of *Hymns Ancient and Modern* and while a piano lesson was going on in the same room. But his widow recalled: ' "Abide with Me" was written at a time of great sorrow. Hand in hand we were silently watching the glory of the setting sun (our daily habit) until the golden hue had faded … then he took paper and pencilled the tune which has gone all over the world.' In fact, these two versions of the circumstances in which the tune was written are not totally incompatible. Several of the compilers' meetings took place at Monk's house and it is quite possible that he wrote Eventide after such a meeting and after a walk with his wife.

'Abide with me' was much parodied by soldiers in the First World War. The most common version, heard more in training camps in England than in the trenches of Flanders, was 'We've had no beer, we've had no beer today'. In its original version the hymn gave much comfort to Edith Cavell, the British nurse imprisoned and condemned to death by the Germans in 1915 for helping wounded soldiers to escape. On the night before she was shot she sat in her cell singing it with a British chaplain.

The practice of singing 'Abide with me' at the FA Cup Final

at Wembley Stadium before the arrival of the opposing teams on the pitch began in 1927 at the suggestion of Sir Alfred Wall, the secretary of the Football Association, with the strong approval of King George V who shared with his wife Queen Mary a particular affection for Lyte's hymn. It is still regularly used at state and solemn public occasions on both sides of the Atlantic, remaining a favourite at the annual British Legion Festival of Remembrance at the Albert Hall and being memorably played by a Salvation Army band at Ground Zero in the aftermath of the terrorist attack on the World Trade Center, New York, on 11 September 2001.

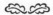

Abide with me: fast falls the eventide;
The darkness deepens; Lord, with me abide:
When other helpers fail, and comforts flee,
Help of the helpless, O abide with me.

2 Swift to its close ebbs out life's little day;
Earth's joys grow dim, its glories pass away;
Change and decay in all around I see;
O thou who changest not, abide with me.

3 Not a brief glance I beg, a passing word;
But as thou dwell'st with thy disciples, Lord,
Familiar, condescending, patient, free,
Come not to sojourn, but abide with me.

4 Come not in terrors as the King of Kings,
But kind and good, with healing in thy wings,
Tears for all woes, a heart for every plea –
Come, Friend of sinners, and thus bide with me.

5 Thou on my head in early youth didst smile;
And, though rebellious and perverse meanwhile,
Thou hast not left me, oft as I left thee,
On to the close, O Lord, abide with me!

6 I need thy presence every passing hour;
What but thy grace can foil the tempter's power?
Who like thyself my guide and stay can be?
Through cloud and sunshine, O abide with me.

7 I fear no foe, with thee at hand to bless;
Ills have no weight, and tears no bitterness.
Where is death's sting? where, grave, thy victory?
I triumph still, if thou abide with me.

8   Hold thou thy Cross before my closing eyes;
     Shine through the gloom, and point me to the skies:
     Heaven's morning breaks, and earth's vain shadows flee;
     In life, in death, O Lord, abide with me.

3

ALL CREATURES OF OUR
GOD AND KING

This fine hymn of praise for God's creation is based on the *Cantico di frate sole* (Canticle of Brother Sun) composed by St Francis of Assisi (1182–1226) towards the end of his life. It derives much of its imagery from Psalm 148 ('Praise ye the Lord, Praise ye the Lord from the heavens').

Francis was the son of a wealthy merchant. At the age of 25 he renounced all earthly possessions and, in his phrase, wedded Lady Poverty. He founded the order of poor brothers known by his name which became one of the largest religious orders in Christendom.

There are conflicting stories about the precise circumstances in which his poem, which is also known as the 'Canticle of the Creatures', was written. It seems probable, however, that it was composed over a period of time. The first four verses seem to have come to St Francis during an hour of ecstasy after he had been engaged in vigils for 40 nights in his rat-infested hut at San Damiano. The fifth verse, with its strong call for the spirit of forgiveness, is said to have been added after a quarrel between the Bishop of Assisi and the local magistrates had caused division in the community. The sixth verse, welcoming death, was composed when, wracked with pain and almost completely blind, Francis had a vision indicating that his own sufferings on earth would soon be over.

St Francis' Canticle was regarded by the nineteenth-century French philosopher Ernest Renan as 'the most perfect utterance of modern religious sentiment'. The most faithful translation into English, which preserves the metre of the original, was made by Matthew Arnold in 1865. It begins:

O most high, almighty, good Lord God,
To thee belong praise, glory, honour and all blessing.
Praised be my Lord God, with all his creatures;
And specially our brother the sun, who brings us the day and
who brings us the light.
Fair is he and shines with a very great splendour:
O Lord, he signifies to us Thee!

The version printed here is a rather freer and more singable translation by W.H. Draper (1855–1933). He wrote the hymn while he was rector of Adel in Yorkshire for a Whitsuntide festival of schoolchildren in Leeds.

Educated at Keble College, Oxford, and the translator of many hymns from the Greek and Latin, Draper was a product of the Oxford Movement, the Catholic revival that swept through the Church of England in the mid-nineteenth century. It is because of that movement that translations of many of the great canticles and hymns of the Early Church are now found in English-language hymnals. The Tractarians, as those involved in the Oxford Movement were called, sought to restore all that was best in patristic and medieval liturgy.

The tune *Lasst uns erfreuen*, to which 'All creatures of our God and King' is almost invariably sung, first appeared in a German tune-book called *Geistliche Kirchengesang*, published in Cologne in 1623. Its first appearance in a British hymnbook was in 1906 in the first edition of the *English Hymnal* where it was set to the hymn 'Ye watchers and ye holy ones'. It was first used for 'All creatures of our God and King' in the *Public School Hymn Book* of 1919.

Laudato sia Dio mio Signore

❧❧

All creatures of our God and King,
Lift up your voice and with us sing
    Alleluia, Alleluia!
Thou burning sun with golden beam,
Thou silver moon with softer gleam,

> *O praise him, O praise him,*
> *Alleluia, Alleluia, Alleluia!*

2   Thou rushing wind that art so strong,
Ye clouds that sail in heaven along,
    O praise him, Alleluia!
Thou rising moon, in praise rejoice,
Ye lights of evening, find a voice:

3   Thou flowing water, pure and clear,
Make music for thy Lord to hear,
    Alleluia, Alleluia!
Thou fire so masterful and bright,
That givest man both warmth and light:

4   Dear mother earth, who day by day
Unfoldest blessings on our way,
    O praise him, Alleluia!
The flowers and fruits that in thee grow,
Let them his glory also show:

5   And all ye men of tender heart,
Forgiving others, take your part,
    O sing ye, Alleluia!
Ye who long pain and sorrow bear,
Praise God and on him cast your care:

6   And thou most kind and gentle Death,
     Waiting to hush our latest breath,
        O praise him, Alleluia!
     Thou leadest home the child of God,
     And Christ our Lord the way hath trod:

7   Let all things their Creator bless,
     And worship him in humbleness,
        O praise him, Alleluia!
     Praise, praise the Father, praise the Son,
     And praise the Spirit, Three in One:

ALL GLORY, LAUD, AND HONOUR TO THEE, REDEEMER, KING

This popular Palm Sunday hymn is another translation of verses dating from the early Middle Ages. The Latin original on which it is based, '*Gloria, laus et honor tibi sit, rex Christe redemptor*', was the work of St Theodulph of Orleans (c. 750–821).

Born in Italy, St Theodulph became abbot of a monastery in Florence and was then brought to France by Charlemagne and consecrated Bishop of Orleans around 785. He retained this position for more than 30 years until he was suspected by the Emperor Louis of plotting against him and imprisoned in Angers in 818.

It was almost certainly during his imprisonment that St Theodulph wrote his hymn which celebrates Christ's entry into Jerusalem on a donkey as described in Matthew 21.1–17. It ran to 39 verses and was designed to be sung during the long processions which many churches organized on Palm Sunday. Legend has it that Theodulph himself sang it from the window of his cell as the king, Louis the Pious, went past in a procession on Palm Sunday, 821. The king is said to have been so moved by the hymn that he ordered the release of its author. St Theodulph was to have only a brief taste of liberty, however, since he died later that year.

From an early stage of its history the hymn was incorporated into Palm Sunday processions throughout Western Europe. The opening verses were often assigned to seven boys who were posted at a high spot on the processional route, perhaps to commemorate the imprisoned bishop.

The English version printed here was the work of John Mason Neale (1818–66), a prominent member of the Oxford Movement who translated many early Latin and Greek hymns into

English in an effort to restore the medieval and Catholic heritage of the Church of England. (See no. 22 for notes on his life.)

Neale first translated 'Gloria, laus et honor' for his book *Mediaeval Hymns* in 1852 and it is that version which is printed here, except for the first line which was originally 'Glory, and laud and honour'. The compilers of *Hymns Ancient and Modern* altered the fifth verse of the hymn, with Neale's permission, to the form which appears in all modern hymnals:

> To thee before thy passion
> They sang their hymns of praise;
> To thee now high exalted
> Our melody we raise.

'All glory, laud, and honour' uses only a small part of St Theodulph's original hymn. Neale noted that 'another verse was usually sung until the seventeenth century, at the quaintness of which we can scarcely avoid a smile'. It went:

> Be thou, O Lord, the rider,
> And we the little ass,
> That to God's holy city
> Together we may pass.

The usual tune for the hymn, known as St Theodulph, Melchior or Kronstadt, was written by Melchior Teschner, cantor and pastor at Fraustadt in Germany, and first published in Leipzig in 1615. J.S. Bach incorporated the melody into the *St John Passion*.

Gloria, laus et honor

All glory, laud, and honour
To thee, Redeemer, King,
To whom the lips of children
Made sweet hosannas ring.

2   Thou art the King of Israel,
     Thou David's royal Son,
     Who in the Lord's name comest,
     The King and Blessed One.

3   The company of angels
     Are praising thee on high,
     And mortal men and all things
     Created make reply.

4   The people of the Hebrews
     With palms before thee went;
     Our praise and prayer and anthems
     Before thee we present.

5   In hastening to thy Passion,
     They raised their hymns of praise;
     In reigning 'midst thy glory,
     Our melody we raise.

6   Thou didst accept their praises:
     Accept the prayers we bring,
     Who in all good delightest,
     Thou good and gracious King.

ALL HAIL THE POWER OF
JESUS' NAME

This hymn should have a broad appeal. Its author, Edward
Perronet (1724–92), went through no fewer than four different
denominations, passing from Anglicanism by way of Methodism
to membership of the Countess of Huntingdon's Connection
and ending up an Independent.

Perronet's grandfather was a French Huguenot who had come
over to England to escape persecution after the revocation of the
Edict of Nantes in 1685. His father was the vicar of Shoreham in
Kent for 57 years and was deeply influenced by the Evangelical
Revival in the Church of England. He was a close friend of the
Wesleys and earned the title of the 'Archbishop of Methodism'.
Edward shared his father's evangelical faith and became an
itinerant preacher in the style of John Wesley. In 1757 he
published *The Mitre*, a bitter satire on the Church of England
which greatly offended the Wesleys who were not prepared to
break completely with Anglicanism. He parted company with
the Methodists and became minister of the Canterbury chapel of
the Countess of Huntingdon's Connection. However, even the
Countess became annoyed with the violence of his anti-Anglican
feelings and he ended up as the pastor of a small Independent
congregation in Canterbury.

Perronet wrote a large number of hymns, but this is the only
one which is remembered and used today. It is printed here as it
first appeared in the April 1780 issue of the *Gospel Magazine*. It
has been called 'The Coronation Hymn' for obvious reasons and
its clear purpose is to affirm the kingship of Christ. Much of its
imagery is drawn from the Book of Revelation (the morning star
and martyrs calling from under the altar) and from the
Lamentations of Jeremiah (the wormwood and the gall).

As sung today, the hymn differs in several ways from

Perronet's original and broadly follows an amended version that appeared in a selection of hymns which appeared in 1787 edited by Dr John Rippon (1751–1836). A Baptist minister who spent all his working life in London, Rippon omitted the original second verse, changed the wording of the eighth (which has subsequently been further altered by different hands) and added a new last verse:

> O that, with yonder sacred throng,
> We at His feet may fall,
> Join in the everlasting song,
> And crown Him Lord of all!

Rippon also provided titles for the various verses as follows:

All hail the power of Jesus' name	Angels
Crown him, ye morning stars of light	The Created Order
Crown him ye martyrs of your God	Martyrs
Ye seed of Israel's chosen race	Converted Jews
Hail Him, ye heirs of David's line	The Church, the New Israel
Sinners, whose love can ne'er forget	Redeemed Sinners
Let every tribe and every tongue	All Mankind
O that, with yonder sacred throng	Ourselves

Three different tunes, all specially written for this hymn, are in regular use today. Anglicans tend to favour the oldest, Miles Lane or Scarborough, composed by William Shrubsole (1760–1806), which appeared in the *Gospel Magazine* for November 1779 with the first verse only of 'All hail the power'. Shrubsole grew up in Canterbury where he was a chorister at the cathedral and got to know Peronnet. He later became organist at Bangor Cathedral but was dismissed in 1784 for frequenting Dissenting Conventicles and he ended up at Spa Fields Chapel, London, one of the main places of worship of the Countess of Huntingdon's Connection. Nonconformists have generally preferred to use the jaunty tune Diadem, which was written in 1838 by James Ellor, an 18-year-old hat-maker who ran the Wesleyan chapel choir in the village of Droylsden near Manchester. More recently, W.H. Ferguson (1874–1950) has provided Ladywell, which appears in several modern hymnbooks.

On the Resurrection: The Lord is King

All hail the power of Jesus' Name;
Let Angels prostrate fall;
Bring forth the royal diadem
To crown Him Lord of all.

2   Let highborn seraphs tune the lyre,
And as they tune it, fall
Before His face Who tunes their choir,
And crown Him Lord of all.

3   Crown Him, ye morning stars of light,
Who fix'd this floating ball;
Now hail the strength of Israel's might,
And crown Him Lord of all.

4   Crown Him, ye martyrs of your God,
Who from His altar call;
Extol the stem-of-Jesse's rod,
And crown Him Lord of all.

5   Ye seed of Israel's chosen race,
Ye ransom'd of the fall,
Hail Him Who saves you by His grace,
And crown Him Lord of all.

6   Hail Him, ye heirs of David's line,
     Whom David Lord did call,
     The God Incarnate, Man Divine,
     And crown Him Lord of all.

7   Sinners, whose love can ne'er forget
     The wormwood and the gall,
     Go spread your trophies at His feet,
     And crown Him Lord of all.

8   Let every tribe and every tongue
     Before Him prostrate fall,
     And shout in universal song
     The crownèd Lord of all.

6

ALL MY HOPE ON GOD IS FOUNDED

This is a good example of a hymn which has only become really popular because of a particular tune. Until Herbert Howells composed Michael for it in 1930, 'All my hope on God is founded' was sung comparatively little. Since then it has been a favourite, particularly in public school chapels, although it is still not found in as many hymnbooks as it ought to be considering the quality of both its words and music and the renewed interest in the theology of hope to which it testifies so strongly.

It is loosely based on a German hymn, '*Meine Hoffnung stehet feste*', by Joachim Neander (1650–80). Neander was born in Bremen, became a Christian pastor following a dramatic conversion after a youth devoted to riotous living, and at the age of 24 was appointed headmaster of the Latin School at Dusseldorf. His highly independent and unorthodox views caused some trouble with the authorities and he was forced to sign a declaration that he would not engage in extreme religious fervour. Although he died of consumption at the age of 30, he left around 60 hymns (including no. 110 in this collection) many of which are still sung by reformed congregations in Germany.

'*Meine Hoffnung stehet feste*', which appeared in Neander's hymn collection, *Alpha and Omega*, published in 1680, was originally intended to be sung as a grace after a meal. It was based on the passage in 1 Timothy 6.17 where the rich are charged not to 'trust in uncertain riches, but in the living God, who giveth us richly all things to enjoy'.

In the last decade of the nineteenth century Robert Bridges (1844–1930) freely adapted Neander's original to create the hymn printed here. Educated at Eton and Corpus Christi College, Oxford, he studied medicine at St Bartholomew's Hospital, London, and qualified as a doctor. After eight years in practice, however, he retired to the village of Yattendon in Berkshire to devote himself to writing. For many years he was the village choirmaster and it was his frustration at the poor quality of many hymns that led him to assemble a collection of a hundred new hymns, some based on translations and others entirely his own work. These were published as a collection in 1899 under the title the *Yattendon Hymnal*. Several have found their way into modern hymnbooks, perhaps the most popular apart from this one and 'O sacred head sore wounded' (no. 90 in this collection) being 'Thee will I love, my God and King' and 'Happy are they, they that love God'.

Originally, 'All my hope' was set to the tune which Joachim Neander had himself written for '*Meine Hoffnung*'. That tune is still used today, but much more popular is Herbert Howells' sprightly Michael, written in response to a request from the director of music at Charterhouse School and named after the composer's son who had died in infancy. Howells later said that on receiving the request he had written the tune there and then at the breakfast table where he was opening his mail. There is also a very serviceable Welsh tune, Groeswen, by J. Ambrose Lloyd (1815–74). Founder of the Welsh Choral Union of Liverpool, Lloyd was a prolific composer, producing a number of good hymn tunes, a cantata, *The Prayer of Habakkuk* and a part-song, 'Bloedeuyn Olef'.

All my hope on God is founded;
He doth still my trust renew,
Me through change and chance he guideth,
Only good and only true.
　　God unknown,
　　He alone
Calls my heart to be his own.

2　Pride of man and earthly glory,
　　Sword and crown betray his trust;
　　What with care and toil he buildeth,
　　Tower and temple, fall to dust.
　　　　But God's power,
　　　　Hour by hour,
　　Is my temple and my tower.

3　God's great goodness aye endureth,
　　Deep his wisdom, passing thought:
　　Splendour, light, and life attend him,
　　Beauty springeth out of naught.
　　　　Evermore
　　　　From his store
　　New-born worlds rise and adore.

4　Daily doth th' Almighty Giver
　　Bounteous gifts on us bestow;
　　His desire our soul delighteth,
　　Pleasure leads us where we go.
　　　　Love doth stand
　　　　At his hand;
　　Joy doth wait on his command.

5 Still from man to God eternal
  Sacrifice of praise be done,
  High above all praises praising
  For the gift of Christ his Son.
    Christ doth call
    One and all:
  Ye who follow shall not fall.

ALL PEOPLE THAT ON
EARTH DO DWELL

This simple but majestic paraphrase of Psalm 100 ('Make a joyful noise unto the Lord, all ye lands') has the distinction of being the earliest hymn written in the English language which is still in general use today. It is one of the first of the many metrical versions of the Psalms which were made in the early days of the Reformation and which have been particularly dear to Scottish hearts.

Most of the metrical psalms were written by followers of John Calvin, who believed that these were the only form of hymn which ought to be sung in churches. This one is the work of William Kethe (?–1594), a native of the Scottish borders who, like many Puritans, left Britain during the reign of the Catholic queen, Mary Tudor (1553–58). He went first to Frankfurt and then to the Calvinist stronghold of Geneva where he helped to translate the Bible into English and to compile a book of metrical psalms. 'All people that on earth do dwell' was first published in Geneva in 1561 in the *Fourscore and Seven Psalms of David*. Later that year the *Geneva Psalter*, as it was called, was published in London. Kethe's version of Psalm 100 also appeared in the first Scottish Psalter, published in 1564. He returned to Britain and was chaplain to the forces under the Earl of Warwick in 1563 before becoming rector of Childe Okeford in Dorset where he seems to have remained until his death.

The first four verses of the paraphrase were written by Kethe. The doxology that forms the fifth verse was sung in the early days of the Methodist movement following the conversion of any member of the congregation. It was also traditionally sung by inhabitants of the fenlands of East Anglia as a thanksgiving following the end of a period of danger of flooding and high tides.

Certain modern hymnals render the third line of the first verse 'Him serve with mirth', following a change that was first made in the Scottish Psalter to bring the hymn more in line with the second verse of Psalm 100 which says: 'Serve the Lord with gladness'. One cannot help feeling that Kethe was a little severe in his paraphrasing at this point but he does at least allow us 'a cheerful voice' in the line before.

For a long time the third line of the second verse was thought to begin 'We are his flock'. This was because when the hymn was first published in England the word 'folk' was spelt in its old English form 'folck'. This was thought to be a misprint for 'flock', to which not long afterwards the word was changed. The mistake persisted for nearly three centuries and when efforts were finally made to rectify it and restore 'folk' (which is closer to the original third verse of the psalm: 'We are his people and the sheep of his pasture') there was a considerable outcry. The *Daily Mirror*, for example, described it as an abomination when the 1904 edition of *Hymns Ancient and Modern* substituted 'folk' for the time-honoured 'flock'. Most modern hymnals now have the correct 'folk'.

The tune which invariably accompanies these verses, known as the Old Hundredth, is also from the *Geneva Psalter* although it predates Kethe's version of Psalm 100 and is first found in the French-language 1551 edition accompanying Psalm 134. It is by Louis Bourgeois (1510–61), who was born in Paris and followed Calvin to Geneva where he was appointed cantor of one of the churches and given the job of providing the music for the metrical psalter then in preparation. For some time after 1700 the tune was known as Savoy because of its frequent use by a congregation worshipping in the Savoy Chapel, just off the Strand.

Psalm C

All people that on earth do dwell,
Sing to the Lord with cheerful voice;
Him serve with fear, his praise forth tell,
Come ye before him, and rejoice.

2   The Lord, ye know, is God indeed;
Without our aid he did us make;
We are his folk, he doth us feed,
And for his sheep he doth us take.

3   O enter then his gates with praise,
Approach with joy his courts unto;
Praise, laud, and bless his name always,
For it is seemly so to do.

4   For why? the Lord our God is good;
His mercy is for ever sure;
His truth at all times firmly stood,
And shall from age to age endure.

5   To Father, Son, and Holy Ghost,
The God whom heaven and earth adore,
From men and from the angel-host
Be praise and glory evermore.

ALL THINGS BRIGHT
AND BEAUTIFUL

This Victorian children's hymn has shown remarkable staying power, standing at no. 13 in the 2002 *Songs of Praise* Top Twenty, despite the fact that it has been the subject of strong criticism for its inegalitarian sentiments. The third verse was banned from use in all schools run by the Inner London Education Authority in 1982 and described in 1995 by David Konstant, the Roman Catholic Bishop of Leeds, as 'one of the most dreadful, even unintentionally wicked commentaries on society'.

In fact, the authoress, Cecil Frances Alexander, *née* Humphreys (1818–95), penned the offending words about 'the rich man in his castle' and 'the poor man at his gate' not in order to suggest that class distinction was divinely ordained but rather to point to the equality of all people before God – the comma after the 'them' is crucial. But it is understandable that this verse jars on modern ears and has been excised from hymnbooks. The hymn as a whole is heard much less often at school assemblies and children's services than it used to be and is something of a period piece, although its message of praise and wonder at the beauty of creation is still relevant in our ecologically conscious age. It remains popular for weddings, presumably because of its childhood associations for many brides. It also supplied the author James Herriot with the title for his books, and the highly successful BBC television series based on them, about his life as a vet in North Yorkshire, *All Creatures Great and Small*.

Mrs Alexander, whose prolific output is represented by two other items in this collection (nos 54 and 63) was born in Dublin, the daughter of a former army officer who managed the estates of the Earl of Wicklow. She developed an early love of poetry and was also strongly influenced while young by the

religious teachings of the leading figures in the Oxford Movement. She was extremely attractive and was courted by two
leading clergymen in the Irish Church, Professor William Archer
Butler and the Revd William Alexander. Her dilemma as to
which of these two suitors she should marry was ended by the
death of the former, and she married the latter in 1850 when he
was a curate. He went on to become Bishop of Derry and
Raphoe, and later Archbishop of Armagh and Primate of all
Ireland. Like his wife, he was a talented poet.

Many of Mrs Alexander's religious poems and hymns were
written before her marriage. They were nearly all designed for
the children in the Sunday Schools where she taught and were
used to illustrate and explain the basic doctrines of Christianity,
and in particular the meaning of the Apostles' Creed. Her well-
known carol, 'Once in Royal David's city', for example, was
written to illuminate the phrase 'Born of the Virgin Mary'.

'All things bright and beautiful' was designed to explain to
children the meaning of the opening words of the Creed: 'I
believe in God the Father Almighty, Maker of heaven and earth.'
It was almost certainly written at Markree Castle at Collooney
near Sligo. It first appeared in Frances Humphreys' *Hymns for
Little Children*, published in 1848 with a preface by John Keble.
The book went into a hundred editions and the profits were
devoted to a school for deaf mutes in Londonderry.

Bishop Konstant's denunciation of this hymn provoked some
spirited defences of Mrs Alexander in the correspondence
columns of *The Times*. It also inspired Bel Littlejohn to produce
a new version of the verse in the spirit of New Labour: 'God
made them high and lowly and vowed that through an ongoing
consultative process He would eventually adopt a dynamic new
policy agenda to iron out the very real divisions in our society
whilst still making proper provision for the rewarding of hard
work and initiative.' Auberon Waugh reflected in the *Daily
Telegraph*:

The rich man almost certainly no longer lives in his castle. He has lost
his money – at Lloyd's, or through some imprudent investment, or sold

the castle to the daughter of a local bus conductor. If he still lives in his castle, he is reduced to penury by the cost of maintaining it. He has sold the lodge at his gate to a much richer man who uses it at weekends … The new arrangement, of poor man in his castle, rich man at his gate, was not ordained by God but by Mrs Thatcher and the Tory radicals. It offers nothing to sing about.

An earlier parody of the hymn by the *Monty Python* team is worth quoting in full:

> All things dull and ugly,
> All creatures short and squat,
> All things rude and nasty,
> The Lord God made the lot.
> Each little snake that poisons,
> Each little wasp that stings,
> He made their brutish venom,
> He made their horrid wings.

The tune generally associated with the hymn – which, though light and lively, has suffered from over-use and rather verges on the trite – is Royal Oak, an adaptation of a traditional English melody by Martin Shaw (1875–1958). Alternatives are the rather similar sounding All Things Bright by William Henry Monk (1823–89), a tune of the same name by Sir Frederick Ouseley (1825–89) and Greystone by W.R. Waghorne.

All things bright and beautiful,
All creatures great and small,
All things wise and wonderful,
The Lord God made them all.

2   Each little flower that opens,
     Each little bird that sings,
     He made their glowing colours,
     He made their tiny wings.

3   The rich man in his castle,
     The poor man at his gate,
     God made them, high or lowly,
     And ordered their estate.

4   The purple headed mountain,
     The river running by,
     The sunset and the morning,
     That brightens up the sky;

5   The cold wind in the winter,
     The pleasant summer sun,
     The ripe fruits in the garden,
     He made them every one;

6   The tall trees in the greenwood,
     The meadows for our play,
     The rushes by the water,
     To gather every day;

7   He gave us eyes to see them,
     And lips that we may tell
     How great is God Almighty,
     Who has made all things well.

ALLELUIA, SING TO JESUS

This communion hymn was written in 1866 by William Chatterton Dix (1837–1898), a devout High Churchman who felt that the Church of England was lacking in eucharistic hymns.

Dix was born in Bristol, the son of a surgeon with literary leanings and who wrote a life of the poet Thomas Chatterton – hence William's second name. After attending Bristol Grammar School he went into business and became manager of a marine insurance company in Glasgow.

In his spare time Dix was a prolific hymn-writer and published four volumes of his own hymns as well as translating Ethiopian (then Abyssinian) hymns and Offices of the Eastern Orthodox Church. Among other hymns written by him which are still sung today are 'As with gladness men of old', 'To thee, O Lord, our hearts we raise' and 'Come unto Me, ye weary, and I will give you rest'.

'Alleluia, sing to Jesus' first appeared in Dix's *Altar Songs*, published in 1867. It was intended to be sung principally at Ascensiontide and has several references to Christ's ascension, most notably in the lines 'Though the cloud from sight received him' and 'Thou within the veil hast entered'. It is also interesting in referring to Christ as the 'bread of angels', picking up the reference in John 6.32 to 'the true bread from heaven' which also features so prominently in 'Guide me, O Thou Great Jehovah' (no. 45 in this collection).

For a long time the first verse of the hymn was repeated at the end to give a total of five stanzas. Nowadays only the four verses printed here are sung and the second is sometimes left out.

When Dix's hymn appeared in the appendix to the first edition of *Hymns Ancient and Modern* in 1868, it was accompanied by a tune specially written for it by Samuel Sebastian Wesley (1810–76) and called Alleluia. For the 1909 edition a new tune called Adoration was composed by B. Luard Selby, but it is not found in any modern hymnbook. The tune to which the hymn is now nearly always sung, and to which it is admirably suited, is the majestic Hyfrydol by R.H. Prichard (1811–87). Prichard was a loom-tender's assistant in the works of the Welsh Flannel Manufacturing Company in Holywell, North Wales. He was only 20 when he wrote this lovely tune which is also much used for 'Love divine, all loves excelling' (no. 82) and 'I will sing the wondrous story of the Christ who died for me'.

Redemption by the Precious Blood

Alleluia! sing to Jesus,
His the sceptre, his the throne;
Alleluia! his the triumph,
His the victory alone:
Hark! the songs of peaceful Zion
Thunder like a mighty flood;
Jesus, out of every nation,
Hath redeemed us by his blood.

2   Alleluia! not as orphans
Are we left in sorrow now;
Alleluia! he is near us,
Faith believes, nor questions how;
Though the cloud from sight received him
When the forty days were o'er,
Shall our hearts forget his promise,
'I am with you evermore'?

3   Alleluia! bread of angels,
Thou on earth our food, our stay;
Alleluia! here the sinful
Flee to thee from day to day:
Intercessor, friend of sinners,
Earth's Redeemer, plead for me,
Where the songs of all the sinless
Sweep across the crystal sea.

4   Alleluia! King eternal,
Thee the Lord of Lords we own;
Alleluia! born of Mary,
Earth thy footstool, heav'n thy throne:
Thou within the veil hast entered,
Robed in flesh, our great High Priest;
Thou on earth both priest and victim
In the Eucharistic feast.

10

AMAZING GRACE

Thirty or so years ago this hymn by John Newton (1725–1807) was hardly to be found in a single British hymnbook. Long popular in the USA as a gospel song, it is now well ensconced in the UK hymnological hit parade being put in 32nd place in the 2002 *Songs of Praise* poll and sixth in the 2004 poll of readers of the Roman Catholic weekly, *The Tablet*. Its popularity in Britain was boosted in the mid-1970s by a recording of the tune by the pipes and drums of the Royal Scots Dragoon Guards which was No. 1 for nine weeks and remained in the charts for several months. The hymn has also been recorded by several leading vocalists and gospel singers.

John Newton was one of the most remarkable figures in the Evangelical Revival that swept through Britain in the eighteenth century. His father was a sailor and his mother died when he was 7. After only two years of schooling, he was sent to sea at the age of 11. His early life was by his own account godless and dissolute. Flogged for deserting from the navy, at the age of 22 he became captain of a ship engaged in the slave trade between Britain, West Africa and the West Indies. Three years later he underwent a dramatic conversion to Christianity which seems to have started while he was reading Thomas à Kempis's book *The Imitation of Christ* on a voyage across the Atlantic. A violent storm blew up, and Newton spent nine hours manning the pumps and a further seventeen hours at the ship's wheel as the waves crashed around him. Several times he found himself crying aloud to God for protection. The storm eventually abated, and Newton later traced the first stirrings of the 'great change' that was to turn him towards evangelical religion to his sense of deliverance after this terrible experience.

Forsaking the slave trade and the seafaring life, he became friendly with John Wesley and George Whitefield, the two leading figures in the Evangelical Revival, and spent nine years training for the Anglican ministry. In 1764 he was ordained and became curate at Olney in Buckinghamshire. There he collaborated with William Cowper, the poet and a fellow Evangelical, to produce a collection of hymns which includes 280 of his own compositions, including such favourites as 'Glorious things of thee are spoken' (no. 39 in this collection) and 'How sweet the name of Jesus sounds' (no. 53). He remained at Olney for sixteen years and then went to London as rector of St Mary Woolnoth where he remained until his death.

'Amazing grace' first appeared in *Olney Hymns*, which was published in 1779. It reflects Newton's own intense conversion experience and his profound sense that it was only the overwhelming grace of God which had saved one as wretched as himself from eternal damnation. The great nineteenth-century hymnologist John Julian says with some justice that it is 'far from being a good example of Newton's work'.*

Some versions of the hymn contain an additional verse written by an unknown hand and apparently first attached to Newton's hymn in E.O. Excell's *Coronation Hymns*, published in Chicago in 1910:

> When we've been there ten thousand years,
> Bright shining as the sun,
> We've no less days to sing God's praise
> Than when we first begun.

The tune Amazing Grace is based on an American folk melody which seems to have been first published in 1831 in a tune-book entitled *Virginia Harmony*. It is very likely Scottish in origin and was probably brought across the Atlantic by colonists in the eighteenth century.

---

* John Julian (ed.), *A Dictionary of Hymnology* (London: John Murray, 1907).

Amazing grace! how sweet the sound
That saved a wretch like me!
I once was lost, but now am found,
Was blind, but now I see.

2 'Twas grace that taught my heart to fear,
And grace my fears relieved;
How precious did that grace appear
The hour I first believed.

3 Through many dangers, toils and snares
I have already come;
'Tis grace hath brought me safe thus far,
And grace will lead me home.

4 The Lord has promised good to me,
His word my hope secures;
He will my shield and portion be
As long as life endures.

5 Yes, when this heart and flesh shall fail,
And mortal life shall cease,
I shall possess within the veil
A life of joy and peace.

6 The earth shall soon dissolve like snow,
The sun forbear to shine,
But God, who called me here below,
Will be for ever mine.

AND CAN IT BE, THAT I SHOULD GAIN

This powerful hymn by Charles Wesley (1707–88) has much the same intensely personal message as John Newton's 'Amazing grace'. Both are about the conversion of an individual soul to faith in the atoning death of Christ. But there is also a sense of mystery and universality in this great hymn which lifts it far above the mainstream of 'born again' Christian experience. Wesley's is altogether a nobler and more edifying treatment of the central theme of God's wonderful and limitless grace.

Charles Wesley has rightly been described as the prince of English hymn-writers. More of his hymns are sung today than those of any other writer, and no fewer than 11 of them appear in this book. He was born at Epworth in Lincolnshire, where his father Samuel was rector. Charles was the eighteenth child in the family; his brother John, commonly regarded as the founder of Methodism, was four years his senior. Educated at Westminster School, Charles went on to Christ Church, Oxford, where in 1729 he became a tutor. He was ordained in 1735, and joined his brother who was evangelizing in the British colony of Georgia. But Charles found the work there uncongenial and he returned to England where he came under the influence of Peter Böhler, a Moravian missionary, and underwent a conversion to the 'vital religion' of evangelicalism. For the rest of his life he was an itinerant preacher in Britain.

Opinions vary as to exactly how many hymns Charles Wesley wrote, but his total known output amounted to 8,989 religious poems, of which over 6,000 can properly be classified as hymns. All of them were written after his conversion to vital religion which took place on 21 May 1738. 'And can it be' was one of the first, being composed together with 'Where shall my wondering soul begin' a matter of hours after he had made 'the great change'. The scriptural passage which he had in mind when he wrote it was Galatians 2.20: 'I live by the faith of the Son of God, who loved me, and gave himself for me.' It was first published in his brother John's *Psalms and Hymns* in 1738, and then in his *Hymns and Sacred Poems* the following year. The *Wesleyan Hymn Book* of 1780 dropped the fifth verse and it has continued to be omitted in subsequent hymnbooks.

There is a strong probability that John Wesley sang this hymn on the evening of his own conversion to vital religion, which took place in Aldersgate, London, three days after his brother Charles had had a similar experience. We know that he sang a hymn that evening to the tune 'Crucifixion' by Samuel Akeroyd. In John Wesley's first tune-book, published in 1742 and known as the *Foundery Tune Book*, that tune is set to 'And can it be' although in later Methodist hymnals it is set to another of Charles Wesley's hymns, 'Where shall my wondering soul begin'.

From the mid-nineteenth century onwards 'And can it be' has generally been sung to Thomas Campbell's soaring tune Sagina. Campbell (1800–76), who came from Sheffield, published a book of 23 hymn tunes in 1825 entitled *The Bouquet*. He gave botanical names to all his tunes. *Sagina*, the Latin name for the pearlwort, is the only one which is generally sung nowadays.

Free Grace

And can it be, that I should gain
An interest in the Saviour's blood?
Died He for me, who caused His pain –
For me, who Him to death pursued?
Amazing love! How can it be
That Thou, my God, shouldst die for me?

2   'Tis mystery all! The Immortal dies:
Who can explore His strange design?
In vain the first-born seraph tries
To sound the depths of love divine.
'Tis mercy all! let earth adore,
Let angel minds inquire no more.

3   He left His Father's throne above –
So free, so infinite His grace –
Emptied Himself of all but love,
And bled for Adam's helpless race:
'Tis mercy all, immense and free;
For, O my God, it found out me!

4   Long my imprisoned spirit lay
Fast bound in sin and nature's night;
Thine eye diffused a quickening ray, –
I woke, the dungeon flamed with light;
My chains fell off, my heart was free,
I rose, went forth, and followed Thee.

5   Still the small inward voice I hear,
That whispers all my sins forgiven;
Still the atoning Blood is near,
That quenched the wrath of hostile heaven.
I feel the life His wounds impart;
I feel my Saviour in my heart.

6 No condemnation now I dread;
  Jesus, and all in Him, is mine!
  Alive in Him, my living Head,
  And clothed in righteousness divine,
  Bold I approach the eternal throne,
  And claim the crown, through Christ my own.

12

AND DID THOSE FEET IN
ANCIENT TIME

Does William Blake's mystical poem really constitute a hymn? Compilers of hymnbooks have often been understandably coy about including it – in the *English Hymnal*, for example, it for long appeared unnumbered at the very end of the appendix and without a tune. But there is no doubt that set to Sir Hubert Parry's majestic tune Jerusalem it has attained the status of a national hymn, if not even a second national anthem. It is no longer the invariable accompaniment to Women's Institute meetings, but continues to be sung with gusto on the last night of the Proms and is regularly heard in churches and school chapels.

William Blake (1757–1827) was born in London, the son of a hosier. He had no formal schooling but was apprenticed to an engraver. From an early age he was a seer of visions and a dreamer of dreams. Most of his literary works, which were illustrated by his own engravings, had a highly mystical flavour. A constant theme in them is the exaltation of love and imagination against the restrictive codes of conventional morality. But in his later works a new element enters in – the revelation of forgiveness through Christ.

The four verses which make up the hymn first appeared in the preface to one of Blake's last poems, 'Milton', which was written in 1804. Underneath them he wrote 'Would to God that all the Lord's people were prophets', and gave the biblical source from which this quotation comes: Numbers 11.29. In the poem the seventeenth-century poet is depicted as returning from eternity and entering into Blake to preach the message of Christ crucified and the doctrines of self-sacrifice and forgiveness.

The imagery of these verses is complex. Some of it is borrowed from the Bible, for instance, the chariots of fire, which are taken from 2 Kings 2.11, but much is of Blake's own invention. In suggesting that Jesus may have set foot in England, Blake is resurrecting the old legend which told of Christ's wanderings as a young man with Joseph of Arimathea. The story goes that Joseph was a tin merchant and that Jesus went with him to Cornwall. A verse from Blake's long poem *Jerusalem*, which also dates from 1804, echoes this theme:

> She walks upon our meadows green;
> The Lamb of God walks by her side:
> And every English child is seen,
> Children of Jesus and his Bride.

There are two very different interpretations as to the main message in 'And did those feet'. One school of thought regards it as a plea for intuition and imagination in the face of scientific rationalism. On this interpretation, the 'dark, satanic mills' represent the cold logical approach of philosophers such as Locke and Bacon that Blake so much deplored, while Jerusalem represents the ideal life of freedom.

The other, more common, way of interpreting the poem is as a call for the rule of those values of social justice and freedom which will build a new Jerusalem in Britain. That is certainly how it was interpreted by the man who rescued it from relative obscurity and can claim the credit for turning it into a hymn. In 1916 Robert Bridges (then Poet Laureate) included 'And did those feet' in a patriotic anthology entitled *The Spirit of Man*. He subsequently asked the distinguished musician Sir Hubert Parry to set it to some 'suitable, simple music' so it could be sung at meetings of 'Fight for the Right', a crusading movement set up to build a better Britain for the millions of soldiers who would return home after the war.

Parry's setting of Jerusalem was also sung at a meeting held in March 1918 in the Albert Hall to celebrate the granting of votes to women. Afterwards, Mrs Millicent Fawcett, one of the leaders of the suffragette movement, suggested to the composer, 'Your "Jerusalem" ought to be made the Women Voters' Hymn.' Parry responded enthusiastically, 'I wish indeed it might become the women voters' hymn. People seem to enjoy singing it. And having the vote ought to diffuse a good deal of joy too. So they would combine happily.' As well as being sung by several women's organizations, Jerusalem has also been heard at Labour Party conferences. One of its greatest contemporary fans is the socialist singer and song-writer Billy Bragg, who said in a BBC Radio 4 programme devoted to the song in December 2004 that for him it asks the questions what would Jesus find if he came to modern Britain and how far have we built the kind of society based on the principles of social justice that he championed.

The first hymnbook to include Blake's verses set to Parry's tune was the *Student Hymnal* of 1923.

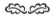

And did those feet in ancient time
Walk upon England's mountains green?
And was the holy Lamb of God
On England's pleasant pastures seen?

2   And did the countenance divine
Shine forth upon our clouded hills?
And was Jerusalem builded here
Among those dark satanic mills?

3   Bring me my bow of burning gold!
Bring me my arrows of desire!
Bring me my spear! O clouds, unfold!
Bring me my chariot of fire!

4   I will not cease from mental fight,
Nor shall my sword sleep in my hand,
Till we have built Jerusalem
In England's green and pleasant land.

13

AS PANTS THE HART FOR
COOLING STREAMS

For more than a century after the Reformation the only kind of congregational singing practised in British churches was the chanting of metrical versions of the Psalms. We have already come across one of these in William Kethe's paraphrase of Psalm 100 (no. 7). This is another.

A book containing metrical versions of all 150 Psalms which was published in 1562 may properly be regarded as the first hymnbook of the Church of England. Known as the 'Old Version', its proper title being *The Whole Booke of Psalmes, collected into English metre*, it was the work of Thomas Sternhold and John Hopkins, who came from Gloucestershire. Although it was to last for 134 years as the official book of praise of the Church, nothing in it is still sung today.

In 1696 this psalter was revised by Nahum Tate (1652–1715) and Nicholas Brady (1659–1726). It is from their revision, generally known as 'Tate and Brady' or 'the New Version' and much used by American Episcopalians during the eighteenth century, that this fine paraphrase of Psalm 42 comes. Tate and Brady were also responsible for 'Through all the changing scenes of life' (no. 137) and the well-known Christmas carol 'While shepherds watched their flocks by night'.

Psalm 42 (As the hart panteth after the water brooks) has inspired several notable paraphrases. Tate and Brady's version introduces the idea of a hunt, which is not found in the original but is otherwise fairly faithful to it. It is printed in its entirety here as it first appeared in their revised version of the Psalter. In modern hymnals the hymn is greatly reduced in length, often only including verses 1, 2 and 12 of the original, and with the following doxology added:

To Father, Son, and Holy Ghost,
The God whom we adore,
Be glory, as it was, is now,
And shall be evermore.

Both Tate and Brady were of Irish descent. Tate was the son of a Dublin clergyman called Faithful Teat. He came to England after graduating from Trinity College, Dublin, and changed his name to Tate. He became friendly with the leading English poet John Dryden, and was a distinguished versifier in his own right, producing the libretto for Henry Purcell's opera, *Dido and Aeneas*. He also rewrote Shakespeare's *King Lear* to give it a happy ending. In 1690 he was made Poet Laureate, but in later life he fell victim to excessive drinking and ended his days in a debtors' prison.

Brady was also a graduate of Trinity College, Dublin. He is said to have saved his native town of Bandon in County Cork from being burned down by rebel mobs and to have first come to England to petition William III on its behalf. The king subsequently appointed him as a personal chaplain and he ended up as vicar of Stratford upon Avon.

The tune to which this hymn is now universally sung, Martyrdom or All Saints, is by Hugh Wilson and was first published in R.A. Smith's *Sacred Music Sung in St George's Church, Edinburgh* (1825). Wilson (1766–1824) was an Ayrshire shoemaker who later became manager of a mill at Pollokshaws, near Glasgow.

Psalm XI

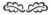

As pants the hart for cooling streams
When heated in the chase;
So longs my soul, O God, for thee
And thy refreshing grace.

2   For thee, my God, the living God,
My thirsty soul doth pine;
O when shall I behold thy face,
Thou Majesty divine?

3   Tears are my constant food, while thus
Insulting foes upbraid,
'Deluded wretch, where's now thy God,
And where thy promis'd aid?'

4   I sigh whene'er my musing thoughts
Those happy days present,
When I with troops of pious friends
Thy temple did frequent;

5   When I advanc'd with songs of praise
My solemn vows to pay;
And led the joyful sacred throng
That kept the festal day.

6   Why restless, why cast down, my soul?
Trust God, and he'll employ
His aid for thee, and change these sighs
To thankful hymns of joy.

7   My soul's cast down, O God, and thinks
On thee and Sion still;
From Jordan's banks, from Hermon's heights,
And Missar's humbler hill.

8 One trouble calls another on
  And, bursting o'er my head,
  Fall spouting down, till round my soul
  A roaring sea is spread.

9 But when thy presence, Lord of life,
  Has once dispelled this storm,
  To thee I'll midnight anthems sing,
  And all my vows perform

10 God of my strength, how long shall I,
  Like one forgotten, mourn?
  Forlorn, forsaken, and expos'd
  To my oppressors' scorn.

11 My heart is pierced as with a sword,
  Whilst thus my foes upbraid,
  'Vain boaster, where is now thy God?
  And where his promised aid?'

12 Why restless, why cast down, my soul?
  Hope still; and thou shalt sing
  The praise of him who is thy God,
  Thy health's eternal spring.

14

AT THE NAME OF JESUS

This is a hymn that can have a totally different impact depending on the tune to which it is sung. Some make it grand and confident, others quieter and more reflective, and there is one – John Michael Brierley's Camberwell – which makes it positively swinging.

It is the work of Caroline Maria Noel (1817–77), the first of a remarkable group of sickly Victorian spinsters whom we shall encounter at various points in this book and whose contribution to English hymnody was considerable. She belonged firmly to the evangelical wing of the Church of England. Her father, Canon Gerard Thomas Noel, for many years vicar of Romsey in Hampshire, was himself a hymn-writer. So was her uncle, the Hon. Baptist Wriothesley Noel, a colourful figure who after being ordained into the Church of England and appointed a chaplain to Queen Victoria became a believer in adult baptism and switched to the Baptist Church. His hymns, which were still sung in the Baptist Church until recently, include the intriguingly entitled 'There's not a bird with lonely nest'.

Caroline wrote her first hymn at the age of 17, but produced nothing more until she was 40, when illness sent her back to hymn writing. She hoped that her verse would cheer and comfort others who were sick. She wrote a large number of hymns in the last 25 years of her life, which were spent in almost constant pain and sickness. They were published in two volumes, *The Name of Jesus, and Other Verses for the Sick and Lonely* (1861) and *The Name of Jesus, and Other Poems* (published posthumously in 1878). She is buried outside the Abbey Church at Romsey, next to the grave of her father.

'At the name of Jesus' first appeared in the second of her two volumes of hymns, and was probably written in the early 1870s. It is based on the passage in Philippians 2.9–11:

Wherefore God also hath highly exalted him, and given him a name which is above every name; that at the name of Jesus every knee should bow, of things in heaven, and things in earth, and things under the earth; and that every tongue should confess that Jesus Christ is Lord, to the glory of God the Father.

In his book *A Panorama of Christian Hymnody*, Erik Routley has described 'At the name of Jesus' as 'the only objective theological hymn to come from the hand of a nineteenth-century woman writer'. Certainly it is completely free of the strongly personal and sentimental elements which characterize much of the work of Frances Crosby (nos 18 and 140 in this collection) and Anna and Susan Warner (nos 62 and 66). Caroline Noel wrote it with Ascension Day processions in mind, which may partly explain its length, but it is appropriate for congregational use at any point in the Church's calendar. The hymn is strongly biblically based, drawing clearly in addition to the text quoted above on the opening verses of St John's Gospel:

In the beginning was the Word, and the Word was with God, and the Word was God. The same was in the beginning with God. All things were made by him; and without him was not any thing made that was made. In him was life; and the life was the light of men.

'At the name of Jesus' has been set to an extraordinarily wide variety of tunes. The Baptists for long used Ashbury by Sir George Clement Martin (1844–1916) and the *English Hymnal* offered either King's Weston by Ralph Vaughan Williams (1872–1958) or *Laus tibi domini Christe* from a fourteenth-century German processional melody. Several tunes have been specially composed for the hymn. They include Evelyns written by William Henry Monk (1823–89) for the revised edition of *Hymns Ancient and Modern* in 1875, Cuddesdon, written by William Harold Ferguson (1874–1950) for the *Public School Hymnbook* and *In nomine Jesu*, written by Arthur Oldham for the third edition of the *Church Hymnary*.

The swinging tune Camberwell, which I mentioned earlier, first appeared in the album *Thirty Twentieth-Century Hymn Tunes*, which was published in 1960. It is in some ways a classic product of that decade: easy, catchy, confident and without any hidden depths or subtle shades. I was brought up on it in school chapel in the 1960s and have to confess to a great liking for it, although I can see its limitations and can understand why many churches have now returned to Evelyns or Cuddesdon. It certainly made singing this particular hymn fun – indeed, rather too much fun, I suspect.

Every knee shall bow

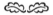

At the name of Jesus
Every knee shall bow,
Every tongue confess him
King of glory now;
'Tis the Father's pleasure
We should call him Lord,
Who from the beginning
Was the mighty word.

2   Mighty and mysterious
In the highest height,
God from everlasting,
Very light of light:
In the Father's bosom
With the spirit blest,
Love, in love eternal,
Rest, in perfect rest.

3   At his voice creation
Sprang at once to sight,
All the angel faces,
All the hosts of light,
Thrones and dominations,
Stars upon their way,
All the heavenly orders,
In their great array.

4   Humbled for a season,
To receive a name
From the lips of sinners
Unto whom he came,
Faithfully he bore it
Spotless to the last,
Brought it back victorious
When from death he passed:

5   Bore it up triumphant
With its human light,
Through all ranks of creatures,
To the central height,
To the throne of Godhead,
To the Father's breast;
Filled it with the glory
Of that perfect rest.

6   Name him, brothers, name him,
With love as strong as death,
But with awe and wonder,
And with bated breath;
He is God the Saviour,
He is Christ the Lord,
Ever to be worshipped,
Trusted, and adored.

7   In your hearts enthrone him;
There let him subdue
All that is not holy,
All that is not true:
Crown him as your captain
In temptation's hour;
Let his will enfold you
In its light and power.

8   Brothers, this Lord Jesus
Shall return again,
With his Father's glory,
With his Angel train;
For all wreaths of empire
Meet upon his brow,
And our hearts confess him
King of glory now.

15

AWAKE, MY SOUL, AND
WITH THE SUN

This stirring morning hymn was the work of Thomas Ken (1637–1711), one of the most saintly figures in the history of the Church of England.

Orphaned in early childhood, he was brought up by Izaak Walton, the author of *The Compleat Angler*. He was educated at Winchester and New College, Oxford, and ordained at the age of 26. Six years later he returned to his old school as a teacher and chaplain, becoming also a Prebendary of Winchester Cathedral.

Ken later achieved considerable fame as chaplain to King Charles II, whose amorous adventures he found impossible to sanction. On one celebrated occasion Charles found himself in Winchester with his mistress Nell Gwynn and asked Ken to put them up in his house. Ken refused, declaring 'Not for your kingdom would I allow such an insult on the house of a Royal Chaplain.' Despite the snub, the King held no grudge against Ken and appointed him to the bishopric of Bath and Wells in 1685. Later that year he attended at Charles's deathbed. He fell foul of his brother, James II, refusing to sign the Declaration of Indulgence which suspended penal laws against Roman Catholics and Dissenters. As a result, he was imprisoned in the Tower of London. Although reinstated in his see by William of Orange after the Glorious Revolution of 1688, he was soon again in trouble for refusing to take the oath of allegiance to the new monarch. He retired and spent his last days at Longleat House, the home of Lord Weymouth.

'Awake, my soul' was written while Ken was still at Winchester and before he had become embroiled in the world of politics. In 1674 he published a manual of prayers for the boys at the college, and in the 1695 edition of that work this hymn appeared together with hymns to be sung in the evening and at midnight. In the preface to the manual the young scholars were exhorted 'to sing the Morning and Evening hymns in your chamber devoutly', though it was not made clear whether they should also wake themselves up in the middle of the night to sing the midnight hymn. During Ken's own time as a pupil at Winchester the day began at 5 a.m. with morning prayers and a Latin hymn '*Iam lucis orto sidere*' ('Now the daylight fills the sky') which was sung before breakfast. Subsequent generations of boys had cause to thank him for producing something in English for their morning devotions, even it was on the long side.

The hymn as printed here is as Ken originally wrote it. He produced a revised version in 1709 in which the first two lines of verse 2 were changed to 'Redeem thy misspent time that's past, / And live this day as if thy last' and two new verses were added:

> Let all thy converse be sincere,
> Thy conscience as the noonday clear;
> Think how all-seeing God thy ways
> And all thy secret thoughts surveys.

> Awake, awake, ye heavenly choir,
> May your devotion me inspire,
> That I like you my age may spend,
> Like you may on my God attend.

Modern hymnbooks tend to print a shortened version. The hymn is generally sung to the tune Morning Hymn by François Hippolite Barthelemon (1741–1808). Also known as Hippolytus and Magdalene, it was specially written for 'Awake, my soul' at the request of the chaplain of a female orphan asylum in London and was first published in 1785. Previously the orphans had used the tune Uffingham by Jeremiah Clarke (1670–1707), famous as the composer of the Trumpet Voluntary. The hymn can also be sung to Tallis's Canon, normally associated with Ken's evening hymn, 'All praise to thee, my God, this night' (later changed to 'Glory to thee, my God, this night').

At his own request, Ken was buried at sunrise in the churchyard at Frome, Somerset, with his beautiful morning hymn being sung at his funeral service.

Morning Hymn

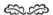

Awake, my soul, and with the sun
Thy daily stage of duty run,
Shake off dull sloth, and joyful rise
To pay thy morning sacrifice.

2　Thy precious time misspent, redeem,
Each present day thy last esteem,
Improve thy talent with due care,
For the Great Day thyself prepare.

3　By influence of the Light divine
Let thy own light to others shine.
Reflect all heaven's propitious ways
In ardent love, and cheerful praise.

4　Wake, and lift up thyself, my heart,
And with the angels bear thy part,
Who all night long unwearied sing
High praise to the eternal King.

5　All praise to thee who safe hast kept
And hast refreshed me while I slept.
Grant, Lord, when I from death shall wake
I may of endless light partake.

6   Heav'n is, dear Lord, where e'er thou art,
O never then from me depart;
For to my soul 'tis hell to be
But for one moment void of thee.

7   Lord, I my vows to thee renew,
Disperse my sins like morning dew.
Guard my first springs of thought and will
And with thyself my Spirit fill.

8   Direct, control, suggest this day
All I design, or do, or say,
That all my powers with all their might
In thy sole glory may unite.

9   Praise God, from whom all blessings flow,
Praise him, all creatures here below,
Praise him above, ye heavenly host,
Praise Father, Son, and Holy Ghost.

16

BE STILL, MY SOUL

This is a hymn which owes its popularity very largely to a tune which has been borrowed from a symphonic work by a major classical composer. Other examples of equally successful 'hijackings' of the classics include 'Thine be the glory, risen, conquering son' (no. 135) and 'I vow to thee, my country' (no. 58). But whereas in those two cases the classical melody was associated with the hymn from the beginning, it was nearly a century after the first appearance of 'Be still, my soul' that it was set to the tune from Sibelius's *Finlandia* to which it is now invariably sung.

The hymn is based on a German original, '*Stille, mein Wille; dein Jesus hilft siegen*', which was written in 1752 by Katharina von Schlegel (1697–?) She is said to have been head of the evangelical Lutheran nunnery in the city of Cothen, but it seems more likely that she was, in fact, attached to the ducal court there. The translation into English was made in 1855 by Jane Laurie Borthwick (1813–97). The elder daughter of the manager of the North British Insurance Company in Edinburgh, Miss Borthwick was a devout member of the Free Church of Scotland. With her sister Sarah Findlater she published a volume of translations of German hymns under the title *Hymns from the Land of Luther*, and it was there that 'Be still, my soul' first appeared.

In the book Miss Borthwick attached the text 'In your patience possess ye your souls' (Lk. 21.19) to this hymn. The opening words are based on Psalm 46.10: 'Be still, and know that I am God', while the last two lines of the second verse recall the words of Mark 4.41: 'What manner of man is this, that even the wind and the sea obey him?'

Altogether Jane Borthwick supplied 69 of the translations which went into *Hymns from the Land of Luther*, while her sister provided 53. She lived for a time in Switzerland and published a further book of translations under the title *Alpine Lyrics* in 1875. Like so many other Victorian spinster hymn-writers she was also a devoted doer of good works, being actively involved in the Edinburgh House of Refuge, the Moravian Mission in Labrador and the Home and Foreign Missions of her own church.

For a long time 'Be still, my soul' was sung to the tune St Helen, specially composed for it in 1868 by Walter Hately (1843–1907), a leading precentor and choirmaster in the Free Church in Edinburgh. It was first set to the chorale-like melody in the symphonic poem *Finlandia* in 1933, by the Presbyterian Board for Christian Education in the USA.

Jean Sibelius (1865–1957) was born in Finland and spent nearly all of his working life there after studying in Berlin and Vienna. It has been said of his orchestral compositions that 'they seem to have passed over black torrents and desolate moorlands, through pallid sunlight and grim primeval wet greys and blacks, relieved only by brightness, wan and elusive as the northern summer, frostily green as the polar light'.

Finlandia was written in 1899 for a great patriotic demonstration in favour of the freedom of the press at a time when the Finns were struggling against Russian domination. Interestingly, 'Be still my soul' is not the only well-known British hymn to have a tune from Finland. The popular carol 'Good King Wenceslas' is set to a melody from *Piae cantiones*, a Finnish tune-book of 1582.

Submission

Be still, my soul; the Lord is on thy side;
Bear patiently the cross of grief or pain;
Leave to thy God to order and provide;
In every change he faithful will remain.
Be still, my soul: thy best, thy heavenly Friend
Through thorny ways leads to a joyful end.

2 Be still, my soul: thy God doth undertake
To guide the future as he has the past.
Thy hope, thy confidence let nothing shake;
All now mysterious shall be bright at last,
Be still, my soul: the waves and winds still know
His voice who ruled them while he dwelt below.

3 Be still, my soul: when dearest friends depart,
And all is darkened in the vale of tears,
Then shalt thou better know his love, his heart,
Who comes to soothe thy sorrow and thy fears.
Be still, my soul; thy Jesus can repay,
From his own fullness, all he takes away.

4 Be still, my soul: the hour is hastening on
When we shall be for ever with the Lord,
When disappointment, grief and fear are gone,
Sorrow forgot, love's purest joys restored.
Be still, my soul: when change and tears are past,
All safe and blessèd we shall meet at last.

BE THOU MY VISION, O LORD OF MY HEART

This translation of an early Irish poem has established itself as one of the most popular hymns in Britain today. It came sixteenth in the 2002 *Songs of Praise* poll and second in the 2004 poll among readers of the Roman Catholic weekly *The Tablet*.

It derives from an eighth-century Irish poem, '*Rob tu mo bhiole, a Comdi cride*', which was translated from the original Gaelic into English in 1905 by Mary Byrne (1880–1931), an expert on the Irish language. In 1912 her translation was versified by Dr Eleanor Hull (1860–1935), the author of a number of books on the subject of Celtic folklore. The verses were published in her *Poem Book of the Gael* and first appeared as a hymn in the form printed here in the *Irish Church Hymnal* of 1919.

It is only relatively recently that most British hymnbooks have included 'Be thou my vision'. It appears in a number of different forms, with particularly significant variations occuring in the last verse. In the *New English Hymnal* this is given as:

> High King of heaven, thou heaven's bright Sun,
> O grant me its joys after vict'ry is won,
> Great Heart of my own heart, whatever befall,
> Still be thou my vision, O Ruler of all.

The third edition of the *Church Hymnary* offers the following alternative:

> High King of heaven, after victory won,
> May I reach heaven's joys, O bright heav'n's Sun!
> Heart of my own heart, whatever befall,
> Still be my Vision, O Ruler of all.

'Be thou my vision' is universally sung to a traditional Irish air, Slane, which was resurrected in Joyce's *Old Irish Folk Music and Songs*, published in 1920. The same tune is also often used for 'Lord of all hopefulness, Lord of all joy' and for 'Lord of creation, to thee be all praise' (see no. 80). In his book, *Hymns for Today Discussed*,★ Cyril Taylor makes a strong plea for Slane to be reserved for this hymn and not to have its impact weakened through overuse. It is such a strong and powerful tune that I am not sure it can be overused, but I would certainly agree with him that if it is to be reserved for one hymn alone, then 'Be thou my vision' should be the one.

★ Cyril Taylor, *Hymns for Today Discussed* (Norwich: Canterbury Press, 1984).

Be thou my vision, O Lord of my heart,
Naught be all else to me save that thou art;
Be thou my best thought in the day and night,
Waking of sleeping thy presence my light.

2   Be thou my wisdom, be thou my true word,
I ever with thee and thou with me, Lord;
Thou my great Father, and I thy true son;
Thou in me dwelling, and I with thee one.

3   Be thou my breast-plate, my sword for the fight,
Be thou my armour, and be thou my might,
Thou my soul's shelter, and thou my high tower,
Raise thou me heavenward, O Power of my power.

4   Riches I heed not, nor man's empty praise,
Thou mine inheritance through all my days;
Thou, and thou only, the first in my heart,
High King of heaven, my treasure thou art!

5   High King of heaven when battle is done,
Grant heaven's joy to me O bright heaven's sun,
Christ of my own heart, whatever befall,
Still be my vision, O Ruler of all.

BLESSED ASSURANCE,
JESUS IS MINE

This confident evangelical hymn is the work of one of the most prolific hymn-writers of all time, Mrs Frances Jane van Alstyne (1820–1915), better known by her maiden name, Fanny Crosby.

Born in New York, and totally blind from infancy, she went at the age of 14 to the first special school for the blind established in the USA. In later life she returned to teach there and met her future husband who was also a blind teacher at the school. Fanny Crosby wrote verse from an early age and was encouraged by William Cullen Bryant, the distinguished American poet and hymn-writer. At the age of 24 she published her first book of verse, *The Blind Girl and Other Poems*.

Fanny Crosby was converted to evangelical religion during the singing of Isaac Watts's hymn 'Here, Lord, I give myself away' at a meeting in a Methodist church in New York. Later she met the great evangelist and composer Ira D. Sankey who set many of her verses to music.

Altogether Fanny Crosby wrote more than 8,000 hymns and sacred songs. She had regular contracts with a number of evangelical publishers. One firm commissioned her to write three songs a week and for two firms alone she wrote 5,000 hymns. She used 216 different pen-names. Among her most popular hymns are 'To God be the glory' (no. 140), 'Safe in the arms of Jesus', 'Rescue the perishing', 'I am thine, O Lord; I have heard thy voice' and 'O my Saviour, hear me'.

It has to be admitted that many of her hymns do sound as though they have come off the production line and lack subtlety and imagination. No one would claim that 'Blessed assurance' is great poetry, but it expresses the heart of the Christian gospel of salvation simply and movingly, even if its language is rather too personal and possessive for many tastes. It has long been popular in evangelical circles and became the theme song of the Billy Graham evangelistic movement, being used in his 'Hour of Decision' broadcasts. Those who have some doubts about the approach adopted in these kind of evangelistic enterprises have penned a parody of the opening lines:

> Blessed assurance, Jesus is mine:
> I had an experience at a quarter to nine.

The tune for 'Blessed assurance' was the work of Mrs Phoebe Knapp (1839–1908), the wife of J.F. Knapp, founder of the Metropolitan Life Insurance Company of New York and one of the richest men in the city. It may well be that it preceded the words, since the story goes that in 1873 Mrs Knapp played the tune through on a visit to the blind poetess and asked her what it said to her. Fanny Crosby is said to have come up almost instantly with the words of the hymn.

> Blessèd assurance, Jesus is mine:
> O what a foretaste of glory divine!
> Heir of salvation, purchase of God;
> Born of His Spirit, washed in His blood.
>
> *This is my story, this is my song,*
> *Praising my Saviour all the day long.*

2   Perfect submission, perfect delight,
    Visions of rapture burst on my sight;
    Angels descending, bring from above
    Echoes of mercy, whispers of love.

3   Perfect submission, all is at rest,
    I in my Saviour am happy and blest;
    Watching and waiting, looking above,
    Filled with His goodness, lost in His love.

BREATHE ON ME,
BREATH OF GOD

The idea of breath has always had a central role in Christian theology. The creative function of God has often been conceived of as the action of breathing life into mankind, following the description in Genesis 2.7: 'And the Lord God formed man of the dust of the ground, and breathed into his nostrils the breath of life; and man became a living soul.'

Breath has also long been synonymous in Christian thought with the concept of the Holy Spirit. In both Greek and Latin one word is used for both spirit and breath (*pneuma* and *spiritus* respectively). Whereas to a physicist pneumatology means the science of air and gases, to a theologian it means the doctrine and study of the Holy Spirit.

It is the notion of the Holy Spirit as the breath of God breathed on and into his creatures that Edwin Hatch (1835–89) develops in this simple devotional hymn. It first appeared in 1878 in a privately printed pamphlet *Between Doubt and Prayer*.

Born of nonconformist parents, Hatch was educated at King Edward School, Birmingham, and Pembroke College, Oxford, where he was friendly with several future members of the Pre-Raphaelite brotherhood, including William Morris, Edward Burne-Jones and Algernon Swinburne. As an undergraduate he contributed articles to several magazines and reviews, but instead of following his friends into a literary or artistic career he was ordained into the Church of England and served for a period in a parish in the East End of London.

For most of his adult life Hatch held academic positions. From 1859 to 1867 he was Professor of Classics at Trinity College, Toronto. In 1867 he returned to Oxford as Vice-Principal of St Mary's Hall. He had a brief spell as Rector of Purleigh in Essex before ending his days as University Reader in Ecclesiastical

History (1885–9). Despite his academic eminence, Hatch was a man of deep and simple piety, as this hymn shows. It was said of his religion that it was as simple and unaffected as a child's.

'Breathe on me, Breath of God' is sung to a bewildering number of tunes. Perhaps the most effective are Aylesbury (also known as Wirksworth, Fetter Lane and Brentford), which was first found in John Chetham's *Book of Psalmody* in 1718 and harmonized by S.S. Wesley (1810–76), and Carlisle by Charles Lockhart (1745–1815). Despite being blind from infancy, Lockhart was a notable London church organist and particularly renowned for his training of children's choirs. Other tunes to which the hymn is sung include: *Veni Spiritus,* by Sir John Stainer (1840–1901); Hampton, which first appeared in 1770 in the *Universal Psalmodist,* compiled by Aaron Williams (1731–76); St George, by H.J. Gauntlett (1805–76); Boylston, by Lowell Mason (1792–1872), a bank clerk in Savannah who founded the Boston Academy of Music; and Trentham, by Robert Jackson (1842–1914). The use of this last tune comes in for something of a hammering from Donald Webster in his book, *Our Hymn Tunes, their Choice and Performance:*[*] 'One might conclude from it and the way it is sung', he writes, 'that the breath of God was an anaesthetic, not a "Giver of Life".' My own favourite is Carlisle.

[*] Donald Webster, *Our Hymn Tunes, their Choice and Performance* (Edinburgh: St Andrew Press, 1983).

The Breath of the Spirit

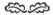

Breathe on me, Breath of God,
Fill me with life anew,
That I may love what thou dost love,
And do what thou wouldst do.

2   Breathe on me, Breath of God,
Until my heart is pure,
Until with thee I will one will,
To do and to endure.

3   Breathe on me, Breath of God,
Blend all my soul with thine,
Until this earthly part of me
Glows with thy fire divine.

4   Breathe on me, Breath of God;
So shall I never die,
But live with thee the perfect life
Of thine eternity.

20

BRIGHT THE VISION
THAT DELIGHTED

This bouncy and breezy hymn dates from 1837, the year of Queen Victoria's accession. It is the work of Richard Mant (1776–1848), a leading divine in the Church of Ireland.

Educated at Winchester and Trinity College, Oxford, Mant was ordained at the age of 26 and served as a curate at Buriton, Hampshire, Crawley, Sussex, and in his father's parish in Southampton. After holding livings in Essex, London and Surrey, he moved to Ireland in 1820 as Bishop of Killaloe and Kilfenoragh. In 1823 he was translated to the see of Connor and Down, and in 1833 the see of Dromore was added to his diocese. He wrote a substantial history of the Church in Ireland and two volumes of hymns. The only other one of his hymns which is still sometimes sung today has the following first verse:

> For all thy saints, O Lord,
> Who strove in thee to live,
> Who followed thee, obeyed, adored,
> Our grateful hymn receive.

The seer mentioned in the second line of 'Bright the vision that delighted' is the prophet Isaiah who lived in the kingdom of Judah during the eighth century BC. The hymn is, in fact, about the vision which he had around the year 740 and which led him to become a prophet. It is based on the account in Isaiah 6.1–4:

In the year that King Uzziah died I saw also the Lord sitting upon a throne, high and lifted up, and his train filled the temple. Above it stood the seraphims: each one had six wings; with twain he covered his feet, and with twain he did fly. And one cried unto another and said, Holy, holy, holy is the Lord of hosts: the whole earth is full of his glory. And the posts of the door moved at the voice of him that cried, and the house was filled with smoke.

The tune normally used for the hymn is known variously as Dresden, Redhead or *Laus Deo*. It was adapted from a German melody in 1853 by Richard Redhead (1820–1901), for 30 years organist at St Mary Magdalene's, Paddington. A strong supporter of the Oxford Movement, he wrote many other hymn tunes, including Petra for 'Rock of Ages' (113). 'Bright the vision' is sometimes also sung to the tune *Sanctus* by John Richards (1843–1908), a native of Bangor, North Wales, who is said to have regularly got up in the middle of the night with a good tune in his head and written it down using soap on the bedroom mirror in the absence of more conventional writing materials.

Bright the vision that delighted
Once the sight of Judah's seer;
Sweet the countless tongues united
To entrance the prophet's ear.

2   Round the Lord in glory seated
Cherubim and Seraphim
Filled his temple, and repeated
Each to each the alternate hymn:

3   'Lord, thy glory fills the heaven;
Earth is with its fullness stored;
Unto thee be glory given,
Holy, Holy, Holy, Lord.'

4   Heaven is still with glory ringing,
Earth takes up the Angels' cry,
'Holy, Holy, Holy,' singing,
'Lord of hosts, the Lord most high.'

5   With his seraph train before him,
With his holy Church below,
Thus conspire we to adore him,
Bid we thus our anthem flow:

6   'Lord, thy glory fills the heaven;
Earth is with its fullness stored;
Unto thee be glory given,
Holy, Holy, Holy, Lord.'

21

BRIGHTEST AND BEST OF
THE SONS OF THE
MORNING

Strange as it may seem now, this very popular hymn was for a long time excluded from many hymnals on the grounds that it involved the worship of a star. Objections were also raised to the fact that its metre was suggestive of a dance. In fact, it is a straightforward Epiphany hymn, telling the story of the three wise men coming to visit the infant Jesus in Bethlehem.

'Brightest and best' was the first hymn written by one of the greatest hymn-writers in the Church of England, Reginald Heber (1783–1826). Born into an aristocratic family in the village of Malpas on the Cheshire–Shropshire border, where his father was rector, he was educated at Whitchurch Grammar School and privately in Neasden, north London. He went on to Brasenose College, Oxford, where he won the University prize for Latin verse three years running. He was elected to a fellowship at All Souls College, and after an extensive grand tour of Europe, became rector of Hodnet in Shropshire. In 1823 he went to India as Bishop of Calcutta, but his time there was brief. One hot afternoon in April 1826, after preaching on the evils of the caste system before a large congregation at Trichinopoly, he went to cool off in the local swimming pool. He suffered a stroke in the water and drowned.

Heber spent sixteen years as a parish priest, and it was during this period that he wrote most of his 57 hymns, which include such favourites as 'Holy, Holy, Holy! Lord God Almighty' (no. 52), 'From Greenland's icy mountain', the once-popular missionary hymn which describes the heathen in his blindness bowing down to wood and stone and the wonderful 'By cool Siloam's shady rill', which is still popular in Scotland as a baptismal hymn. He wrote a hymn for nearly every Sunday and for each solemn day and feastday in the Church of England calendar. 'Brightest and best' was written for the Feast of the Epiphany. It was first published in 1811 in the *Christian Observer*, an evangelical periodical edited by Zachary Macaulay, the father of the writer and statesman Thomas Babington Macaulay. It was a curious choice for the High Church Heber, but he was determined to show that hymn-singing was not just a prerogative of the evangelical wing of the Church of England. The hymn first appeared between hard covers in his *Hymns written and adapted to the weekly Church Service* in 1827.

The phrase 'sons of the morning' which Heber uses to such spectacular effect in the first line of this hymn has its origins in Isaiah 14.12, where it is used to describe Lucifer. The first verse also has echoes of Job 38.7: 'When the morning stars sang together, and all the sons of God shouted for joy'. Edom (verse 3, line 2) was the mountainous land to the south of Moab, stretching down to the Gulf of Aqaba on the Red Sea. The Edomites were enemies of the Israelites and were spoken of bitterly by many of the Old Testament prophets. As far as I know, there is no particular reason to link Edom with the frankincense and myrrh which were brought by the three wise men to the infant Jesus.

The hymn was originally sung to the tune of an old Scottish ballad called 'Wandering Willie'. Since then it has been set to many different tunes. Perhaps the commonest, and the one I think is most suitable, although it seems to have gone out of fashion recently, is Epiphany by Joseph Francis Thrupp (1827–67), vicar of Barrington, Cambridge. It first appeared in his *Psalms and Hymns*, published in 1853, and is sometimes called Epiphany Hymn, possibly to distinguish it from another tune called Epiphany, by E.J. Hopkins (1818–1901), to which Heber's hymn has also been sung. Other melodies in contemporary use include Bede, adapted from Handel's *Athalaih* of 1733 by Sir John Goss (1800–80), Wallog by Walford Davies (1869–1941) and Crudwell by Walter Kendall Stanton.

Brightest and best of the sons of the morning,
Dawn on our darkness and lend us thine aid;
Star of the east, the horizon adorning,
Guide where our infant Redeemer is laid.

2　Cold on his cradle the dew-drops are shining,
Low lies his head with the beasts of the stall:
Angels adore him in slumber reclining,
Maker and Monarch and Saviour of all.

3　Say, shall we yield him, in costly devotion,
Odours of Edom and offerings divine?
Gems of the mountain and pearls of the ocean,
Myrrh from the forest or gold from the mine?

4　Vainly we offer each ample oblation,
Vainly with gifts would his favour secure;
Richer by far is the heart's adoration,
Dearer to God are the prayers of the poor.

CHRIST IS MADE THE
SURE FOUNDATION

This is another medieval hymn translated from the Latin by John Mason Neale (1818–66). It is to be found in the oldest extant hymnbooks of the Western Church, which date from the eleventh century, and is part of a regular monastic cycle of praise which probably goes back as far as the seventh century.

The original Latin cycle ran to nine stanzas, the last of which was a doxology. It was generally divided into two parts: the first four verses, which began '*Urbs beata Jerusalem*' and dealt with the heavenly city of Jerusalem, being sung at evensong and matins, while the last four were sung at lauds, the first service of the Daily Office normally celebrated at daybreak. Neale kept this division in his translation. He turned the first four stanzas into the hymn 'Blessed city, heavenly Salem' and took 'Christ is made the sure foundation' from the last four verses which began '*Angularis fundamentum lapis Christus missus est*'. Neale's two translations first appeared in his *Medieval Hymns*, published in 1851. An earlier and freer translation of *Angularis fundamentum*, which began 'Christ is our Corner Stone', made in 1837 by John Chandler (1806–76), vicar of Witley in Surrey, is still regularly sung today.

The imagery of the hymn is taken from 1 Peter 2.6: 'Behold I lay in Zion a chief corner stone, elect, precious' and from St Paul's words in Ephesians 2.20 that the household of God is 'built upon the foundation of the apostles and prophets, Jesus Christ himself being the chief corner stone'.

Neale, who was responsible for five of the hymns in this anthology (the others are nos. 4, 60, 91 and 125), was born in London and educated at Sherborne Grammar School in Dorset and at Trinity College, Cambridge. He was briefly fellow and chaplain of Downing College, Cambridge, and he won the University prize for sacred poetry eleven times. After holding a curacy in Guildford, Surrey, he was presented to the living of Crawley, Sussex, but never took up the charge as he was afflicted by a lung complaint and retired for a period to Madeira. In 1846 he was back in Britain as warden of Sackville College, a group of almshouses in East Grinstead, Sussex. There he founded the Society of St Margaret, an order of nursing sisters who tended the sick in local villages, and also an orphanage, a girls' school and an establishment in Aldershot for the reclamation of fallen women.

In his latter years Neale got into increasing trouble with the Church of England authorities for his extreme High Church views and closeness to Roman Catholicism. The only prefer- ment that he was offered was the provostship of St Ninian's Cathedral in Perth, Scotland, but the climate there was too cold for him to take this up. He was increasingly afflicted by ill health, but continued to work on long-forgotten books and manuscripts of Greek and Latin hymns and to produce superb translations of their lyrics. Altogether, he translated some hundred hymns.

For a long time 'Christ is made the sure foundation' was sung to a plainsong melody in keeping with its monastic origins. An alternative was *Urbs coelestis* by the Revd H.E. Hodson (1842– 1917). Hodson's tune, written in 1872 one peaceful evening by the River Dove at Ilam in the Derbyshire Peak District, was later incorporated in his cantata 'The Golden Legend'. Nowadays, Neale's words are generally sung to the stately and measured Westminster Abbey, adapted from an anthem by Henry Purcell (1659–95).

Angularis fundamentum

Christ is made the sure Foundation,
Christ the Head and Corner-stone,
Chosen of the Lord, and precious,
Binding all the Church in one,
Holy Zion's help for ever,
And her confidence alone.

2   All that dedicated city,
Dearly loved of God on high,
In exultant jubilation,
Pours perpetual melody,
God the One in Three adoring
In glad hymns eternally.

3   To this temple, where we call thee,
Come, O Lord of Hosts, today;
With thy wonted loving-kindness
Hear thy servants as they pray;
And thy fullest benediction
Shed within its walls alway.

4   Here vouchsafe to all thy servants
What they ask of thee to gain,
What they gain from thee for ever
With the blessèd to retain,
And hereafter in thy glory
Evermore with thee to reign.

5   Laud and honour to the Father,
Laud and honour to the Son;
Laud and honour to the Spirit;
Ever three and ever one;
Consubstantial, co-eternal,
While unending ages run.

CHRIST, WHOSE GLORY
FILLS THE SKIES

Charles Wesley (1707–88) wrote this morning hymn shortly after 'And can it be, that I should gain' (no. 11 – see notes there for biographical details). It was first published in a book entitled *Hymns and Spiritual Songs* which he produced with his brother John in 1740. For many years it was wrongly attributed to Augustus Montague Toplady, the author of 'Rock of ages', and, rather surprisingly, it did not appear in its complete form in the *Wesleyan Hymn Book* until 1875.

Like most of Wesley's hymns it draws strongly on metaphors and images from Scripture. The striking phrase 'Sun of Right-eousness', which occurs in the third line of the first verse, is taken from Malachi 4.2: 'But unto you that fear my name shall the Sun of Righteousness arise with healing in his wings.' Interestingly, Wesley used the phrase again in his fine poem entitled 'Wrestling with Jacob', which begins 'Come, O thou traveller unknown', and is still to be found in several hymnals although it is perhaps too personal and devotional for congregational singing.

The fifth line of the hymn echoes Luke 1.78: 'The dayspring from on high hath visited us to give light to them that sit in darkness and in the shadow of death.' The sixth line follows 2 Peter 1.19: 'We have also a more sure word of prophecy whereunto ye do well that ye take heed, as unto a light that shineth in a dark place, until the day dawn, and the day star arise in your hearts.'

The second and third verses of this hymn are quoted in Chapter 38 of George Eliot's novel, *Adam Bede*, which was first published in 1859. There they are put into the mouth of Seth Bede, the hero's brother and a devout Methodist, who sings Wesley's hymn (described as one of his favourites) as he is walking home one Sunday morning.

The hymn was originally sung to the German tune Heidelberg, which first appeared in a book of songs and psalms published in Berlin in 1653. There is some reason to think that it may have been the work of Princess Louisa Henrietta of Brandenburg though it was later ascribed to Johann Crüger (1598–1662). The tune more often used now is Ratisbon, another German melody, which first appeared in a book of chorales published in Leipzig in 1815 where it was set to the words, '*Jesu meines Lebens Leben*'.

⟨⟩⟨⟩

Christ, whose glory fills the skies,
Christ, the true, the only Light,
Sun of Righteousness, arise,
Triumph o'er the shades of night:
Dayspring from on high, be near;
Day-star, in my heart appear.

2 Dark and cheerless is the morn
Unaccompanied by thee;
Joyless is the day's return,
Till thy mercy's beams I see;
Till Thou inward light impart,
Glad my eyes, and warm my heart.

3 Visit then this soul of mine,
Pierce the gloom of sin and grief;
Fill me, Radiancy divine,
Scatter all my unbelief;
More and more thyself display,
Shining to the perfect day.

CITY OF GOD, HOW
BROAD AND FAR

The theology of this hymn is as broad as its description of the city of God – too broad, indeed, for some people who consider that it is not properly a Christian hymn at all. It was not included in *Hymns Ancient and Modern* until 1950 because earlier editors were unhappy about its doctrinal position.

It is quite understandable that 'City of God' has caused difficulties to some Christians. It avoids any mention of Christ or the Holy Spirit and prefers rather to dwell on such abstract ideals as 'freedom, love and truth'. Yet there is nothing in it that is incompatible with the Christian religion. The notion of the Kingdom of God as a city is a familiar one in the Bible, especially in the Psalms. It provides the basis for a number of hymns, including the more orthodox 'Christ is made the sure foundation' (no. 22), 'God, whose city's sure foundation' and 'Glorious things of thee are spoken, Zion, city of our God' (no. 39). There is also a strong emphasis on the unity of the Church in this hymn which is reminiscent of that in 'Onward, Christian soldiers' (no. 105) and 'The Church's one foundation' (no. 124).

The author, Samuel Johnson (1822–82), was an American radical who refused to join any established Christian denomination. He was probably closest to the Unitarians, sharing their refusal to accept the divinity of Christ or the doctrine of the Trinity. Educated at Harvard University, he established his own Free Church at Lynn in Massachusetts in 1853 where he ministered until 1870. He was active in movements of political reform, notably the anti-slavery crusade, and was also a scholar of comparative religion, publishing *Oriental Religions and their relation to Universal Religion*.

'City of God' was written in 1860 on a visit to Nice in the South of France which Johnson made with his friend and fellow-

Unitarian, Samuel Longfellow. Longfellow, a brother of the poet Henry Wadsworth Longfellow, also wrote hymns, and the two men collaborated in producing a book called *Hymns of the Spirit* which was published in 1864. The object of the book, its compilers wrote, was 'to exclude all hymns which by their traditional phraseology or out-of-date thought forms would offend the sensibilities of a cultured liberal Christian'. It was in this volume that 'City of God' first appeared.

It is interesting to note that in the first line of the fourth verse Samuel Johnson uses the same imagery of 'watchfires' (not found in the Bible) that Mrs Julia Ward Howe was to employ just a year later in her 'Mine eyes have seen the glory of the coming of the Lord' (no. 84).

The tune normally used for this hymn is Richmond, otherwise known as Haweis, or Spa Fields Chapel. It was written by Thomas Haweis (1734–1820) and adapted by Samuel Webbe (1770–1843). Haweis was a curate at St Mary Magdalen, Oxford, and then Vicar of Aldwinkle in Northamptonshire, before leaving the Church of England to become chaplain to Lady Huntingdon's Chapel in Bath. He originally wrote the tune in 1792 for the hymn 'O Thou, from whom all goodness flows'. It is also used for 'Praise to the Holiest in the height' (no. 109) 'O for a thousand tongues to sing' (no. 93) and 'O Jesu, king most wonderful'.

The Church, the City of God

City of God, how broad and far
Outspread thy walls sublime!
The true thy chartered freemen are
Of every age and clime.

2 One holy Church, one army strong,
One steadfast, high intent;
One working band, one harvest-song,
One King omnipotent.

3 How purely hath thy speech come down
From man's primeval youth!
How grandly hath thine empire grown,
Of freedom, love, and truth!

4 How gleam thy watch-fires through the night
With never-fainting ray!
How rise thy towers, serene and bright,
To meet the dawning day!

5 In vain the surge's angry shock
In vain the drifting sands:
Unharmed upon the eternal Rock
The eternal City stands.

COME DOWN, O LOVE
DIVINE

Like 'All creatures of our God and King' (no. 3), this hymn is a translation of a medieval poem originally written in Italian. It owes much of its popularity to the tune composed for it in the early years of this century by Ralph Vaughan Williams (1872–1958).

The author of the devotional verses on the subject of the Holy Spirit and its descent on man which form the basis of the hymn was Bianco da Siena (c. 1350–1434). Born in the upper Valdarno region of Tuscany, he spent his boyhood as an apprentice in the wool trade in Siena and at the age of 17 joined an order of mystics. Although he wrote a number of lyrics and hymns little more is known about him, other than that he spent the last part of his life in Venice.

Bianco's poem, which began '*Discendi, amor santo*' and ran to eight verses, was little known until 1851 when it was copied by an Italian from an ancient manuscript. Some years after this rediscovery, four of the verses were translated by Dr Richard Littledale (1833–90). They appeared in the form given here in his *People's Hymnal* which was published in 1867.

Littledale's translation retains much of the spirit of the original Italian verses. In particular it preserves Bianco da Siena's allusion to the monastic vocation, especially in the lines in the third stanza which talk of the vesture of holy charity and the inner clothing of lowliness.

Richard Littledale was a High Churchman who translated many hymns from Latin, Greek and other languages. Educated at Trinity College, Dublin, he was curate first at St Matthew's, Thorpe, Norfolk, and then at St Mary the Virgin, Soho. Although a Tractarian, he was strongly opposed to the Roman Catholic Church and did much by his writing to keep many of those influenced by the Oxford Movement within the Anglican fold.

'Come down, O Love divine' was very little sung in Britain until it was chosen as one of the entries for the *English Hymnal* in 1906. Percy Dearmer, the editor, chose the young and virtually unknown Vaughan Williams to be responsible for the musical side of the new book. On the whole where existing tunes were lacking or inadequate, Vaughan Williams tended to prefer settings of English folk-songs to new tunes. But 'Come down, O Love divine' was an exception. He wrote a new tune especially for it: Down Ampney, after his birthplace in Gloucestershire. It was one of only four new tunes that he wrote for the hymnal (the others being for 'God be with you till we meet again', 'For all the Saints' and 'Hail thee festival day'). Thanks largely to his tune, the hymn became extremely popular, especially at weddings.

Discendi, amor santo

Come down, O Love divine,
Seek thou this soul of mine,
And visit it with thine own ardour glowing;
O Comforter, draw near,
Within my heart appear,
And kindle it, thy holy flame bestowing.

2   O let it freely burn,
    Till earthly passion turn
    To dust and ashes in its heat consuming;
    And let thy glorious light
    Shine ever on my sight,
    And clothe me round, the while my path illuming.

3   Let holy charity
    Mine outward vesture be,
    And lowliness become mine inner clothing;
    True lowliness of heart,
    Which takes the humbler part,
    And o'er its own shortcomings weeps with loathing.

4   And so the yearning strong,
    With which the soul will long,
    Shall far outpass the power of human telling;
    For none can guess its grace,
    Till he become the place
    Wherein the Holy Spirit makes his dwelling.

COME, HOLY GHOST,
OUR SOULS INSPIRE

This hymn has had a continuous existence of more than a thousand years, though in its present form it is only 350 years old. The original on which it is closely based is a Latin hymn, *Veni, creator spiritus*, which almost certainly dates from the ninth century. The original plainsong melody to which it was sung is still used for the English version, giving an added sense of mystery and antiquity to its thrilling invocation to the Holy Spirit.

The precise origins and authorship of *Veni, creator spiritus* are unclear. It has been variously attributed to the Emperor Charles the Fat (grandson of Charlemagne), Gregory the Great, St Ambrose and Rhabanus Maurus, Archbishop of Mainz in the middle of the ninth century. There is clear evidence that it was sung at Whitsuntide in the tenth century and it was generally accompanied by much solemnity and ceremonial, including the ringing of bells, the lighting of candles and the use of incense. During the eleventh century it came to be used at ordination services and during the consecration of bishops. It continues to serve that function in many churches today.

The translation which is printed here, and which is to be found in most hymnals, was made by John Cosin (1594–1672) and was first published in his *Collection of Private Devotions in the Practice of the Ancient Church* in 1627. At that time, Cosin was rector of Brancepeth in County Durham. He later became Dean and Master of Peterhouse, Cambridge, but was driven out by the Puritans in 1641. After the Restoration he was successively Dean and Bishop of Durham.

Cosin intended his hymn to be sung every morning at nine in memory of the descent of the Holy Spirit upon the Church. His was not, in fact, the first English translation of *Veni, creator spiritus*

– the 1549 Prayer Book of the Church of England had contained a rather wooden version in common metre, which ran to sixteen verses and began 'Come, Holy Ghost, eternal God', for use at ordinations. The inclusion of Cosin's version in the 1662 Prayer Book, the only hymn to appear in the volume, has made it the best-known English version, although subsequent translators have produced more accurate renditions of the original Latin. They include John Dryden's 'Creator Spirit, by whose aid', Tate and Brady's 'Come Holy Ghost, Creator come', Robert Bridges' 'Come, O Creator Spirit, come' and J.D. Aylward's 'Creator Spirit, all-divine'. Julian identified more than 50 different English translations.

The reference in the last line of the first verse to 'sevenfold gifts' is taken from the frequent references in the book of Revelation to the seven spirits of God. Seven was a sacred number among the Jews and indicated perfection or completion.

The plainsong tune *Veni creator* seems to have been associated with this hymn since it was first sung. It may well be even older than the hymn itself. There is evidence that it was previously attached to an Easter hymn by St Ambrose which began *Hic est dies verus Dei*.

Veni, Creator Spiritus

Come, Holy Ghost, our souls inspire,
And lighten with celestial fire;
Thou the anointing Spirit art,
Who dost thy sevenfold gifts impart.

2   Thy blessed unction from above
Is comfort, life, and fire of love;
Enable with perpetual light
The dullness of our blinded sight.

3   Anoint and cheer our soilèd face
With the abundance of thy grace:
Keep far our foes, give peace at home;
Where thou art guide no ill can come.

4   Teach us to know the Father, Son,
And thee, of both, to be but One;
That through the ages all along
This may be our endless song:

  Praise to thy eternal merit,
  Father, Son, and Holy Spirit.   Amen.

COME, LET US JOIN OUR
CHEERFUL SONGS

This joyful hymn is the work of the man who is normally regarded as the father of English hymnody, and who must surely vie with Charles Wesley for the title of greatest hymn-writer in the English language.

Isaac Watts (1674–1748) was born in Southampton, the son of an elder in an Independent (Congregational) church. Educated at the local grammar school, he early showed himself a formidable scholar. Not being a member of the Church of England, he was unable to study at either Oxford or Cambridge, and he trained instead at one of the Dissenting academies. In 1702 he was appointed minister at Mark Lane Chapel in London, but after ten years his health broke down and for the last 36 years of his life he lived as the house-guest of Sir Thomas and Lady Abney, first in Hertfordshire and then in Stoke Newington, North London.

In the words of Erik Routley, 'Watts is the liberator of hymnody in English.' It was Watts who effectively broke the Calvinist tradition of using only metrical psalms in Christian worship. The story goes that at the age of 16 he complained to his father that what was sung in church was dull and profitless. His father replied, 'Then write something better.' He immediately took up the challenge and produced the first of nearly 700 hymns, many of which are still in regular use today. Watts broke out of the straitjacket of strict metrical paraphrases of biblical texts and wrote much freer verses in his own words; these lent themselves to more exciting tunes.

'Come, let us join our cheerful songs' was published in Watts's *Hymns and Spiritual Songs* in 1707. He attached it to the scriptural reference 'Revelations 5.11–13'. The verses referred to read:

And I beheld, and I heard the voice of many angels round about the throne and the beasts and the elders: and the number of them was ten thousand times ten thousand, and thousands of thousands; saying with a loud voice, Worthy is the Lamb that was slain to receive power and riches, and wisdom, and strength, and honour, and glory, and blessing. And every creature which is in the heaven and on the earth, and under the earth, and such as are in the sea, and all that are in them, heard I saying, Blessing, and honour, and glory, and power, be unto him that sitteth upon the throne, and unto the Lamb for ever and ever.

The tune almost universally used for this hymn is Nativity, which was written by Henry Lahee (1826–1912). For 27 years organist at Holy Trinity Church, Brompton, he composed several cantatas and numerous glees, madrigals and part-songs. This is his only hymn-tune still in regular use.

Christ Jesus, the Lamb of God worshipped by all creation

Come, let us join our cheerful songs
With angels round the throne;
Ten thousand thousand are their tongues,
But all their joys are one.

2 'Worthy the Lamb that died,' they cry,
'To be exalted thus',
'Worthy the Lamb,' our lips reply,
'For he was slain for us.'

3 Jesus is worthy to receive
Honour and power divine;
And blessings, more than we can give,
Be, Lord, for ever thine.

4 Let all that dwell above the sky,
And air and earth and seas,
Conspire to lift thy glories high,
And speak thine endless praise.

5 The whole creation join in one
To bless the sacred name
Of him that sits upon the throne,
And to adore the Lamb.

COME, YE THANKFUL
PEOPLE, COME

This is another favourite hymn which appears in a markedly different version in virtually every major hymnbook. It was written by Henry Alford (1810–1871) for use in services to celebrate the harvest and almost certainly remains the most popular of all harvest festival hymns today.

Two of Christ's parables are echoed in the hymn: the story of the wheat and the tares (Mt. 13.24–30) and that which tells of the seed which springs up without the sower knowing about it (Mk 4.26–29), and which includes the line: 'For the earth bringeth forth of herself; first the blade, then the ear, after that the full corn in the ear.'

Henry Alford was the son of an Anglican clergyman and himself took holy orders, becoming Dean of Canterbury Cathedral in 1857. He was a distinguished scholar and wrote numerous books, including an important critical commentary on the Greek New Testament. A strong evangelical, he wrote several hymns which are still popular today, including 'Ten thousand times ten thousand' (no. 123 in this collection: see notes there for a fuller account of his life).

'Come, ye thankful people, come' was first published in Alford's *Psalms and Hymns* in 1844. He revised it for his *Poetical Works* (1865), and it is this revised version, which also appeared in his *Year of Praise* (1867), that is printed here. It can, I think, reasonably be regarded as the authentic text.

The version of the hymn printed in *Hymns Ancient and Modern* differs considerably from this text. When it was first included in that book in 1861, the compilers made substantial alterations, which were firmly repudiated by the author, but which have persisted to this day and can be found in the New Standard version. For example, the last four lines of the second verse run:

Ripening with a wondrous power
Till the final Harvest hour
Grant, O Lord of life, that we
Holy grain and pure may be.

The third and fourth verses of the *Ancient and Modern* version are also completely different from those printed here. The *New English Hymnal* prints yet a third version of these verses. Its final verse is worthy of quotation:

Then, thou Church triumphant, come,
Raise the song of harvest-home;
All be safely gathered in,
Free from sorrow, free from sin,
There for ever purified
In God's garner to abide:
Come, ten thousand Angels, come,
Raise the glorious harvest-home!

The tune which is universally associated with this hymn, St George, by Sir George Elvey (1816–93), was actually written for another hymn, 'Hark, the song of Jubilee'. It first appeared in a selection of psalm and hymn-tunes published in 1858. Elvey was organist and choirmaster at St George's Chapel, Windsor.

After Harvest

Come, ye thankful people, come,
Raise the song of harvest-home:
All is safely gathered in,
Ere the winter storms begin;
God, our Maker, doth provide
For our wants to be supplied:
Come to God's own temple, come,
Raise the song of harvest-home.

2 All this world is God's own field,
Fruit unto His praise to yield;
Wheat and tares together sown,
Unto joy or sorrow grown;
First the blade, and then the ear,
Then the full corn shall appear:
Lord of harvest, grant that we
Wholesome grain and pure may be.

3 For the Lord our God shall come,
And shall take His harvest home;
From His field shall in that day
All offences purge away;
Give His angels charge at last
In the fire the tares to cast;
But the fruitful ears to store
In His garner evermore.

4 Even so, Lord, quickly come;
Bring Thy final harvest home:
Gather Thou Thy people in,
Free from sorrow, free from sin;
There, for ever purified,
In Thy garner to abide:
Come, with all Thine angels, come,
Raise the glorious harvest-home.

COURAGE, BROTHER!
DO NOT STUMBLE

This is one of several fine Victorian pilgrim hymns which exhort Christians to perseverance when the going gets rough and encourage them to lives of action and social engagement. A stirring example of muscular Christianity at its best, it is the work of Norman Macleod (1812–72), a Church of Scotland minister who spent the best part of his life working in a demanding inner-city Glasgow parish and was Queen Victoria's favourite chaplain and preacher.

Born in Campbeltown, Argyllshire, and the son of a minister, Macleod belonged to a family which produced more Moderators of the General Assembly of the Church of Scotland than any other. After studying arts at Glasgow University and Divinity at Edinburgh, he served in parishes in Loudon, Ayrshire and Dalkeith, near Edinburgh. In 1851 he became minister of the Barony Church in Glasgow where he remained for the next 21 years until his death. He ministered tirelessly to the 87,000 people who lived in the parish, holding services to which only people in working clothes were admitted and setting up loan funds, savings banks, literacy schemes and housing initiatives. He was an ardent campaigner for social reform and economic justice, and fell foul of his more conservative colleagues by opposing the narrow Sabbatarianism which so cramped the leisure pursuits of working-class communities in mid-Victorian Scotland. He was bitterly attacked by fellow members of Glasgow Presbytery when he campaigned to get buses and trams running and parks and museums opened on Sundays so that they could be enjoyed by working people on their one day of rest. He also ran into trouble with more conservative and puritanical colleagues in the Church by refusing to back calls for teetotalism and for championing the virtues of moderate consumption of alcohol. One wonders if he had these attacks in mind when he penned the lines 'some will hate thee, some will love thee'.

Macleod first preached before Queen Victoria at Crathie Church in 1854. She wrote in her diary afterwards, 'the sermon was quite admirable, so simple and yet so eloquent and so beautifully argued and put'. Thereafter, he was frequently a guest at Balmoral, especially after Prince Albert died, when he became one of the Queen's most trusted confidants and consolers. The Prince of Wales once dared to ask Macleod if he might consider preaching slightly shorter sermons, to which the reply came: 'I am a Thomas à Becket and resent the interference of the State.' The next time that he had the Prince in his congregation, Macleod preached for three-quarters of an hour, 'only so well' according to his biographer, 'that His Royal Highness wished it had been longer'.

A prolific author and poet, Macleod edited the *Edinburgh Christian Magazine* and it was in its pages that 'Courage, brother' first appeared in print. It was originally written in four-line verses as an exhortatory poem to conclude a lecture to working men in London. It is printed here in the form that it appears in the first edition of the *Church Hymnary* in 1898. In its original form, it included another four-line verse which has not generally found its way into hymnbooks:

> Clouds and sunshine both await thee,
> Noonday radiance, stormy night,
> Yet through all he'll safely lead thee,
> Trust in God, and do the right.

Commended by George Matheson, author of 'O love that wilt not let me go' (no. 97), as 'a good and practical hymn', Macleod's stirring call to muscular Christianity is still much sung and much loved in the Church of Scotland. It was sung with particular effect at the funeral of the Labour Party leader John Smith, in Edinburgh in May 1994. It deserves to be much better known south of the border. Those allergic to sexist language can always change the second word from 'brother' to 'pilgrim'.

Courage, brother, do not stumble,
Though thy path be dark as night;
There's a star to guide the humble –
Trust in God, and do the right.
Let the road be rough and dreary,
And its end far out of sight,
Foot it bravely, strong or weary,
Trust in God, and do the right.

2   Perish policy and cunning,
Perish all that fears the light!
Whether losing, whether winning,
Trust in God, and do the right.
Trust no party, sect or faction;
Trust no leaders in the fight;
But in every word and action
Trust in God, and do the right.

3   Trust no lovely forms of passion –
Fiends may look like angels bright;
Trust no custom, school or fashion:
Trust in God, and do the right.
Some will hate thee, some will love thee,
Some will flatter, some will slight:
Lift thine eyes and look above thee,
Trust in God, and do the right.

4   Simple rule, and safest guiding,
Inward peace, and inward light,
Star upon our path abiding –
Trust in God, and do the right.
Courage brother! do not stumble,
Though thy path be dark as night;
There's a star to guide the humble –
Trust in God, and do the right.

CROWN HIM WITH
MANY CROWNS

This is yet another hymn that appears in several different versions. The original, printed here, is the work of Matthew Bridges (1800–93), but it was subsequently altered by Godfrey Thring (1823–1903), and several hymnals print composite versions which use verses by both men.

Matthew Bridges (not to be confused with Robert Bridges) was born in Maldon, Essex. He was brought up as an Anglican, but later became a Roman Catholic and spent much of his life in Canada. He died in Sidmouth, Devon.

'Crown him with many crowns' first appeared in Bridges' *Hymns of the Heart* in 1851. The title which he gave it comes from Revelation 19.12. In 1874 Godfrey Thring, a prebendary of Wells Cathedral, wrote a hymn modelled on Bridges' with the title 'Crown him with crowns of gold'. Six years later Thring published a composite version which began with Bridges' first verse and continued with stanzas of his own. Subsequently several versions of the hymn appeared which mixed the verses of the two men. For *Songs of Praise* in 1931 Percy Dearmer made further substantial alterations to produce a version which stressed the social message of the gospel. Its first verse went as follows:

Crown him upon the throne
Of justice and of right,
In him the love of God is shown,
To shine in human light:
He reigns, the Son of Man,
All grace divine is his:
Pierce through the creeds, his features scan,
And see him as he is.

Most hymnbooks have now reverted to printing Bridges'
original version, with the sixth verse omitted, although the
Church Hymnary gives Thring's revision which retains only the
first verse of the original and contains the following second verse:

> Crown him the Lord of Life
> Who triumphed o'er the grave,
> And rose victorious in the strife
> For those he came to save.
> His glories now we sing,
> Who died and rose on high;
> Who died, eternal life to bring,
> And lives that death may die.

Hymns for Church and School contains a different composite
version which includes the above stanza and another of Thring's
verses:

> Crown him the Son of God,
> Before the worlds began;
> And ye, who tread where he hath trod,
> Crown him the Son of Man,
> Who every grief hath known
> That wrings the human breast,
> And takes and bears them for his own,
> That all in him may rest.

The expression 'mystic Rose' which occurs in the fifth line of
Bridges' original second verse is a medieval title for the Virgin
Mary. The next two lines echo Isaiah 11.1–2: 'And there shall
come forth a rod out of the stem of Jesse, and a Branch shall
grow out of his roots: and the spirit of the Lord shall rest upon
him.'

Several tunes are associated with this hymn. The most popular
is almost certainly Diademata by Sir George Elvey, whom we
have just encountered as the composer of the tune used for
'Come, ye thankful people, come'. Diademata was written for

the first appearance of 'Crown him with many crowns' in *Hymns Ancient and Modern* in 1868. Another tune written especially for the hymn is Corona, composed in 1927 by C. Hylton Stewart (1884–1932).

On his head were many crowns

Crown Him with many crowns,
The Lamb upon His throne;
Hark! How the heav'nly anthem drowns
All music but its own:
Awake, my soul, and sing
Of Him Who died for thee,
And hail Him as thy matchless King
Through all eternity.

2   Crown Him the Virgin's Son,
The God Incarnate born,
Whose arm those crimson trophies won
Which now His brow adorn:
Fruit of the mystic Rose,
As of that Rose the Stem;
The Root whence mercy ever flows,
The Babe of Bethlehem.

3   Crown Him the Lord of love:
Behold His hands and side,
Those wounds yet visible above
In beauty glorified:
No Angel in the sky
Can fully bear that sight,
But downward bends his burning eye
At mysteries so bright.

4   Crown Him the Lord of peace,
      Whose power a sceptre sways
      From pole to pole, that wars may cease,
      And all be prayer and praise:
      His reign shall know no end,
      And round His piercèd feet
      Fair flowers of Paradise extend
      Their fragrance ever sweet.

5   Crown Him the Lord of years,
      The Potentate of time,
      Creator of the rolling spheres,
      Ineffably sublime.
      Glassed in a sea of light,
      Where everlasting waves
      Reflect his throne – the Infinite,
      Who lives – and loves – and saves.

6   Crown Him the Lord of heaven,
      One with the Father known,
      And the blest Spirit through him given
      From yonder triune throne:
      All hail, Redeemer, hail!
      For thou hast died for me!
      Thy praise shall never, never fail
      Throughout eternity.

DEAR LORD AND
FATHER OF MANKIND

This is indisputably one of the most popular of all hymns in the English language. It has consistently been among the top three in BBC *Songs of Praise* polls over the last 20 years, and also appears high in North American lists of favourite hymns. Yet its author, John Greenleaf Whittier (1807–92), would have been horrified at the thought of it being sung in church, and particularly by the lusty enthusiasm with which it is often tackled in public school chapels. It comes from a long poem which he wrote comparing the heartiness and excitement of much Christian worship to the stimulation found by followers of certain Eastern religions through the use of hallucinogenic drugs.

Whittier was an American Quaker descended from one of the Pilgrim Fathers who arrived in Massachusetts from England in 1638. Brought up on a New England farm, he was an early campaigner against slavery, and in 1835 was elected to the Massachusetts state legislature. He devoted much of his life to writing. Despite his dislike of singing in worship, more than 50 of his poems have been turned into hymns, including 'Immortal love forever full', 'O Brother man, fold to thy heart thy brother!' and 'O Lord and master of us all'.

'Dear Lord and Father of mankind' is taken from a poem which Whittier wrote in 1872 called 'The Brewing of Soma'. Soma was an intoxicating drink which was almost certainly made from the fungus *Amanita muscaria*, or Fly Magic, and used in Vedic rituals by Hindus in India. A few scraps of the fungus were soaked in milk, and the mixture when digested produced the soma which had a strongly hallucinogenic effect and could induce a state of religious frenzy.

In the latter part of his poem Whittier compared the stirring of the emotions in Christian worship through music, ceremonial and the like to the Indians' use of drugs to achieve religious ecstasy:

> In sensual transports, wild as vain,
> We brew in many a Christian fane
> The heathen Soma still!

It is for these 'foolish ways' that Christians are urged to beg forgiveness from God in the lines that form the beginning of the hymn that we now sing with such gusto. Whittier had a strong dislike of highly emotional religion and of hearty, tub-thumping gospel songs. His particular *bête noire* was 'Hold the fort for I am coming' (no. 51 in this book). The theme of his poem is the Quaker conviction that God is to be found in silence and stillness, through the inward peace of the worshipper rather than outward stimulation and sensual excitement.

The last six verses of 'The Brewing of Soma' were turned into a hymn by an English Congregationalist, William Garrett Horder, who included 'Dear Lord and Father of mankind' in his *Congregational Hymns*, published in 1884. He made several alterations to Whittier's original, substituting 'feverish' for 'foolish' in the second line of the first verse and 'pulses of desire' for 'heats of our desire' in the first line of the last verse. Nearly all modern hymnals print Whittier's original words, however, and they appear in the text opposite.

In the USA the hymn is usually sung to Woodland by Nathaniel Gould. In Britain and the Commonwealth it is generally sung to the haunting melody Repton by Sir Hubert Parry (1848–1918). Parry's tune was originally written in 1887 for the contralto aria 'Long since in Egypt's pleasant land' in his oratorio *Judith*. In 1924 Dr George Gilbert Stocks, director of music at Repton School in Derbyshire, set it to 'Dear Lord and Father of mankind' in a supplement of tunes for use in the school chapel. This inspired matching of words and music caught on and is surely one of the main reasons for the great popularity of the hymn today.

The Brewing of Soma

❧

Dear Lord and Father of mankind,
Forgive our foolish ways!
Reclothe us in our rightful mind,
In purer lives thy service find,
In deeper reverence praise.

2 In simple trust like theirs who heard,
Beside the Syrian sea,
The gracious calling of the Lord,
Let us, like them, without a word
Rise up and follow thee.

3 O Sabbath rest by Galilee!
O calm of hills above,
Where Jesus knelt to share with thee
The silence of eternity,
Interpreted by love!

4 With that deep hush subduing all
Our words and works that drown
The tender whisper of thy call,
As noiseless let thy blessing fall
As fell thy manna down.

5 Drop thy still dews of quietness,
Till all our strivings cease;
Take from our souls the strain and stress,
And let our ordered lives confess
The beauty of thy peace.

6 Breathe through the heats of our desire
Thy coolness and thy balm;
Let sense be dumb, let flesh retire;
Speak through the earthquake, wind, and fire,
O still small voice of calm!

32

ETERNAL FATHER,
STRONG TO SAVE

Known throughout the world as the sailors' hymn, this stirring plea for God's mercy towards all in peril on the sea is regularly sung on board ships great and small. It is also one of the best expressions in hymnody of the central Christian doctrine of the Trinity, with its verses clearly delineating the three persons and the respective functions of God the Father, God the Son and God the Holy Spirit.

It is the work of William Whiting (1825–78), the son of a London grocer. Educated at the Winchester Training Institution, a college for teachers, he stayed on in the city to become the first master of the Quiristers of Winchester College, a group of boys who were supposed to sing in the chapel but were in fact little more than unpaid servants to the young gentlemen attending the college. He continued as the Quiristers' tutor for the next 36 years.

The story goes that Whiting wrote this hymn for one of the Winchester quiristers who was about to sail for America. Whether that was in fact its origin, we do know that in 1860 he submitted it as a possible entry for the new *Hymns Ancient and Modern* in a version which began:

> O Thou Who bidd'st the ocean deep,
> Its own appointed limits keep,
> Thou, Who didst bind the restless wave,
> Eternal father, strong to save.

The compilers of *Hymns Ancient and Modern* revised the hymn for inclusion in the first edition in 1861 and gave it the opening with which we are now familiar. Whiting himself rewrote the entire hymn in 1869, and it is this amended version which may be regarded as the authoritative text and which appears here.

Some of the imagery in the hymn seems to have been taken from John Milton's *Paradise Lost*. The first verse recalls the description in Book 7 of the Almighty bidding 'the deep within appointed bounds [to] be heaven and earth', while the opening of the third verse echoes the line near the beginning of Book 1 which tells of the Holy Spirit 'who Dove-like sat'st brooding on the vast abyss'.

'Eternal Father, strong to save' has been sung on many great naval occasions in the last hundred years. When Winston Churchill and Theodore Roosevelt had their secret meeting in the North Atlantic in the middle of the Second World War, Churchill chose it to be sung at Divisions aboard HMS *Prince of Wales*. It has traditionally been sung in shipboard Sunday services on the liners crossing the Atlantic. Recently a new verse has been added to remember those travelling by air and those serving in the airforce and air–sea rescue work:

> Lord of the heavens, by whose might,
> Mankind has learned the skill of flight,
> To span the world from land to land,
> Released from earth's restraining hand.
> Be with us, Father, as we rise
> To brave the challenge of the skies.

There have been several parodies of this hymn. As well as the one quoted in the introduction to this book, perhaps I may be permitted to quote the somewhat irreverent first verse of 'For those in peril on the Holy See', a set of cautionary warnings for ministers which appeared some years ago in the Church of Scotland *Ministers' Forum*:

> Whene'er you climb the pulpit stair,
> Proceed with caution, and beware,
> Lest tripping o'er your long black gown
> You find you go not up, but down.
> And earthbound falling at full throttle,
> Hear the faithful cry 'He's on the bottle!'

The tune universally associated with the hymn, Melita, was written to accompany its first appearance in *Hymns Ancient and Modern* by the Revd John Bacchus Dykes, minor canon and precentor of Durham Cathedral. Dykes heard of the proposed new hymnbook by chance and wrote to the music editor, Dr Monk, enclosing some tunes. Seven of them, including Melita, were accepted and used in the first edition, and 24 more appeared in subsequent editions. The name 'Melita' is taken from the story of St Paul's journey from Caesarea to Rome. Acts 28.1 records that after a shipwreck Paul and his fellow prisoners were able to swim to the island of Melita, as Malta was then known.

For those at Sea

Eternal Father, strong to save,
Whose arm doth bind the restless wave,
Who bidd'st the mighty ocean deep
Its own appointed limits keep:
   Oh hear us, when we cry to thee,
   For those in peril on the sea.

2   O Saviour, whose almighty word
The winds and waves submissive heard,
Who walkedst on the foaming deep
And calm amidst its rage didst sleep;
   O hear us when we cry to thee
   For those in peril on the sea.

3   O sacred Spirit, who didst brood
Upon the chaos dark and rude,
Who bad'st its angry tumult cease
And gavest light and life and peace:
   O hear us when we cry to thee
   For those in peril on the sea.

4   O Trinity of love and power,
Our brethren shield in danger's hour,
From rock and tempest, fire and foe,
Protect them wheresoe'er they go:
   And ever let there rise to thee
   Glad hymns of praise from land and sea.

FIGHT THE GOOD FIGHT

Despite its first line, 'Fight the good fight' is not a Christian battle-song in the style of 'Onward, Christian soldiers' or 'Soldiers of Christ, arise'. It is rather an injunction to faithfulness and steadfastness. Each of its stanzas is based firmly on lines from the Epistles. The first echoes 1 Timothy 6.12: 'Fight the good fight of faith, lay hold on eternal life'; the second follows Hebrews 12.1. 'Let us run with patience the race that is set before us'; the third, 1 Peter 5.7: 'Casting all your care upon him, for he careth for you'; and the fourth, Colossians 3.11: 'Christ is all, and in all'.

This hymn, which first appeared in 1863, is the work of the Revd John Samuel Bewley Monsell (1811–75). Born in Ireland and educated at Trinity College, Dublin, he was ordained into the Anglican Church in 1834 and became chaplain to Bishop Mant, the author of 'Bright the vision that delighted' (no. 20). Monsell came to England in 1853 as vicar of Egham in Surrey. In 1870 he moved to St Nicholas, Guildford. While there, he supervised a major rebuilding programme of the church. One day he was inspecting the progress of the work on the roof when he slipped and fell, sustaining injuries from which he died shortly afterwards.

Monsell published more than 300 hymns of which this and 'O worship the Lord in the beauty of holiness' (no. 103) are the only ones regularly sung today. He believed that hymns should be fervent and joyous. 'We are too distant and reserved in our praises', he wrote, 'we sing not as we should of him who is Chief among ten thousand, the altogether Lovely.'

'Fight the good fight' is sung to a variety of tunes, the most common of which is almost certainly the bouncy Duke Street, or Honiton, generally attributed to John Hatton (?–1793), a native of St Helens, Lancashire. The tune first appeared anonymously under the heading 'Addison's Nineteenth Psalm' in *A Select Collection of Psalms and Hymn Tunes*, published in Glasgow and Edinburgh in 1793. Other tunes include the English traditional melody, Shepton-Beauchamp, Pentecost by William Boyd (1847–1928), Rushford by Henry G. Lee (1887–1962) and Cannock by Walter Kendall Stanton.

The Fight for Faith

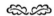

Fight the good fight with all thy might,
Christ is thy strength and Christ thy right;
Lay hold on life, and it shall be
Thy joy and crown eternally.

2   Run the straight race through God's good grace,
Lift up thine eyes and seek his face;
Life with its way before thee lies,
Christ is the path and Christ the prize.

3   Cast care aside; upon thy Guide
Lean, and his mercy will provide;
Lean, and the trusting soul shall prove
Christ is its life, and Christ its love.

4   Faint not nor fear, his arms are near;
He changeth not and thou art dear;
Only believe, and thou shalt see
That Christ is all in all to thee.

FIRMLY I BELIEVE AND
TRULY

Like 'Dear Lord and Father of mankind', this was not originally written to be sung at all. It comes from a long poem, *The Dream of Gerontius*, by John Henry Newman (1801–90). Unlike Whittier, however, I suspect that Newman would be quite happy to know that his verses were being sung by church congregations nearly a century after his death.

Newman is perhaps the best known of the figures associated with the Oxford Movement. The son of a rich London banker of evangelical views, he had a brilliant academic career at Trinity College, Oxford, and was ordained at the age of 23. As a clergyman, he moved from the evangelical wing of the Church of England to the Anglo-Catholic or High Church wing and became one of the leading lights of the Tractarian movement. From 1828 to 1843 he was vicar of St Mary's, Oxford, the University church where John Keble preached his famous service on national apostasy in 1833.

In 1845, after much agonizing, Newman was received into the Roman Catholic Church. He spent a year and a half in Rome, and in 1849 he established an English branch of the brotherhood of St Philip Neri in the Birmingham suburb of Edgbaston. In 1879 he was made a cardinal and there are now moves afoot to canonize him.

Newman wrote *The Dream of Gerontius* in 1865. It is a dramatic monologue recounting the thoughts of an elderly monk facing death and describing the passage of his soul to the afterlife. In 1900 the poem was turned into an oratorio with music by Elgar. Six years later the compilers of the *English Hymnal* extracted the five verses printed here to form the hymn 'Firmly I believe and truly'. They left out the following verse which in the original poem formed the penultimate stanza of this section:

And I take with joy whatever
now besets me, pain or fear,
And with a strong will I sever
All the ties which bind me here.

A Latin verse was also omitted which, with minor variations, is repeated three times in the original poem:

Sanctus fortis, sanctus Deus,
De profundis oro te,
Miserere, Judex meus,
Parce mihi, Domine.

'Firmly I believe and truly' is not the only hymn to have been taken from *The Dream of Gerontius*. In 1868, while Newman was still alive, the editors of *Hymns Ancient and Modern* printed a group of verses from a later section of the poem to form the hymn 'Praise to the holiest in the height' (no. 109).

The most appropriate tune for this hymn is, I think, the sprightly Shipston, another of the English traditional melodies which Vaughan Williams selected for the *English Hymnal*. Alternatives include Halton Holgate by William Boyce (1710–79), which is favoured by *Hymns Ancient and Modern*, and the rather muted melody in the minor key, Ottery St Mary, by Henry G. Lee (1887–1962) which is the preferred choice of both *Hymns for Church and School* and the *Church Hymnary*.

Sanctus fortis

Firmly I believe and truly
God is Three, and God is One;
And I next acknowledge duly
Manhood taken by the Son.

2   And I trust and hope most fully
In that Manhood crucified;
And each thought and deed unruly
Do to death, as he has died.

3   Simply to his grace and wholly
Light and life and strength belong,
And I love supremely, solely,
Him the holy, him the strong.

4   And I hold in veneration,
For the love of him alone,
Holy Church as his creation,
And her teachings as his own.

5   Adoration aye be given,
With and through the angelic host,
To the God of earth and heaven,
Father, Son, and Holy Ghost.

FOR ALL THY SAINTS
WHO FROM THEIR
LABOURS REST

A magnificent processional song of triumph rejoicing in the communion of saints, this hymn is not, thank goodness, sung only on All Saints' Day, to which strictly speaking it belongs.

Its author, William Walsham How (1823–97), was one of the most conscientious and well-loved of all Victorian clergymen. Born and educated in Shrewsbury, where his father was a solicitor, he started writing hymns as a young boy for services which he held with his brother and stepsister. As an undergraduate at Wadham College, Oxford, in the early 1840s he was much influenced by the Tractarian movement and he remained a High Churchman for the rest of his life. He was ordained in 1846 and became a curate first at Kidderminster and then at Shrewsbury. Five years later he became Rector of Whittington in Shropshire, where he remained for 28 years, writing hymns and indulging his passion for ferns and fishing. In 1879 he was appointed suffragan bishop of London with particular responsibility for the East End. His work among the poor in the dockland slums earned him the love of thousands, and he was known as the 'omnibus bishop' because he shunned a private carriage and prefered to travel on public transport.

How turned down several offers of bishoprics, but in 1889 he felt compelled to become the first bishop of the new industrial diocese of Wakefield in west Yorkshire. Shortly after his translation there, he was offered the much more attractive see of Durham, but he declined it to remain with the factory and mill-workers of the West Riding.

Like most of his 54 hymns, 'For all Thy saints' was written while How was Rector of Whittington. It appeared as a processional hymn for All Saints' Day in Earl Nelson's *Hymn for a Saint's Day and other Hymns* in 1864. Seven years later in *Church Hymns*, a collection published by the Society for the Propagation of Christian Knowledge and edited by How and another Shropshire rector, John Ellerton (see notes to no. 126), the first line was changed to 'for all the saints', and so it has remained in most hymnals ever since. The original version, which is printed here, ran to eleven verses. The third, fourth and fifth verses are generally omitted from modern hymnbooks.

For many years the hymn was sung to the tune For All the Saints, written especially for it in 1869 by Sir Joseph Barnby (1838–96), a noted Victorian composer who was director of music at Eton and later principal of the Guildhall School of Music. In 1906 Ralph Vaughan Williams composed a new tune which he called *Sine nomine* for the hymn's appearance in the *English Hymnal*; this is now almost universally used.

The Procession of Faith

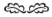

For all Thy saints who from their labours rest,
Who Thee by faith before the world confessed,
Thy Name, O Jesus, be for ever blest. Alleluia!

2   Thou wast their Rock, their Fortress, and their Might;
Thou, Lord, their Captain in the well-fought fight;
Thou, in the darkness drear, their one true Light. Alleluia!

3   For the Apostles' glorious company,
Who bearing forth the Cross o'er land and sea,
Shook all the mighty world, we sing to thee: Alleluia!

4   For the Evangelists, by whose pure word,
Like fourfold stream, the garden of the Lord,
Is fair and fruitful, be Thy name adored. Alleluia!

5   For Martyrs, who with rapture-kindled eye,
      Saw the bright crown descending from the sky,
      And, seeing, grasped it, thee we glorify. Alleluia!

6   O may Thy soldiers, faithful, true, and bold,
      Fight as the saints who nobly fought of old,
      And win, with them, the victor's crown of gold. Alleluia!

7   O blest communion, fellowship divine!
      We feebly struggle, they in glory shine;
      Yet all are one in Thee, for all are Thine. Alleluia!

8   And when the strife is fierce, the warfare long,
      Steals on the ear the distant triumph song,
      And hearts are brave again, and arms are strong. Alleluia!

9   The golden evening brightens in the west;
      Soon, soon to faithful warriors cometh rest;
      Sweet is the calm of Paradise the blest. Alleluia!

10   But, lo! there breaks a yet more glorious day;
      The saints triumphant rise in bright array;
      The King of Glory passes on His way. Alleluia!

11   From earth's wide bounds, from ocean's farthest coast,
      Through gates of pearl streams in the countless host,
      Singing to Father, Son, and Holy Ghost. Alleluia!

FOR THE BEAUTY OF
THE EARTH

This is an interesting example of a hymn that has undergone alterations for doctrinal reasons. In its original form it was regarded by a number of hymnbook compilers as too Catholic in its theology and too inclined to stress the sacrificial element in the communion service; consequently, the language has been watered down in various ways.

Its author, Folliott Sandford Pierpoint (1835–1917), was a devout Tractarian. Born in Bath and educated at the grammar school there and then at Queens' College, Cambridge, he spent most of his life as a classics master at the Somersetshire College. After retiring, he lived in various places in the West Country. He published three collections of poems.

'For the beauty of the earth' was written about 1863 and first published in the Revd Orby Shipley's *Lyra eucharistica* in 1864 in the form printed here. It was designed for use as a communion hymn and took its refrain from the post-communion prayer in the Book of Common Prayer which begins: 'O Lord and heavenly Father, we thy humble servants entirely desire thy fatherly goodness mercifully to accept this our sacrifice of praise and thanksgiving.'

Partly because they were worried about its theological implications, and also to make the hymn suitable for general use and not just restricted to communion services, the compilers of *Hymns Ancient and Modern* changed the refrain to:

> Lord of all, to Thee we raise
> This our grateful hymn of praise.

They also changed the last line of the fourth verse from 'for all gentle thoughts and mild' to 'pleasures pure and undefiled' and dropped the last three verses of the hymn which they regarded as rather too Catholic in their language for an Anglican hymnal. This practice was followed by nonconformist hymnbooks. In the words of the companion to the *Baptist Church Hymnal*: 'It has been shortened and edited, the omitted verses emphasizing a view of the Eucharist we do not share'.

In fact, growing convergence of views on the importance and significance of the Eucharist has meant that there is now much less variation in the way this hymn is presented in different hymnbooks than used to be the case. The New Standard edition of *Hymns Ancient and Modern* has restored the original refrain, and while omitting the third verse, prints the sixth, substituting 'Church' for 'bride' in its first line. This alteration is also made in the *New English Hymnal* which breaks with the High Church traditions of its predecessors and drops the seventh and eighth verses. The *Church Hymnary* also happily prints Pierpoint's original refrain.

No two hymnbooks that I have consulted offer the same tune for this hymn. To my mind the most appropriate is England's Lane, adapted by Geoffrey Shaw from a traditional English melody for the *English Hymnal*. Alternatives are the similar-sounding but slightly boring and predictable Dix by C. Kocher (1786–1872), Incarnation by Henry Smart, St Brannock by E.J. Hopkins, St Ninian by W.H. Monk, Ratisbon by Johann Crüger (1598–1662), Moseley by John Joubert (1927–), *Lucerna laudoniae* by David Evans (1874–1948) and Noricum by F. James (1858–1922). There is also a pleasing choral setting by John Rutter which has become increasingly popular with choirs.

The Sacrifice of Praise

For the beauty of the earth,
For the beauty of the skies,
For the love which from our birth
Over and around us lies:
 Christ our God, to thee we raise
 This our sacrifice of praise.

2 For the beauty of each hour
Of the day and of the night,
Hill and vale, and tree and flower,
Sun and moon and stars of light:

3 For the joy of ear and eye,
For the heart and brain's delight,
For the mystic harmony
Linking sense to sound and sight:

4 For the joy of human love,
Brother, sister, parent, child,
Friends on earth, and friends above,
For all gentle thoughts and mild:

5 For each perfect gift of thine
To our race so freely given,
Graces human and divine,
Flowers of earth and buds of heaven:

6 For thy Bride that evermore
Lifteth holy hands above,
Offering up on every shore
This pure sacrifice of love:

7   For the Martyrs' crown of light,
      For thy Prophets' eagle eye,
      For thy bold Confessors' might,
      For the lips of infancy:

8   For thy Virgins' robes of snow,
      For thy Maiden-mother mild,
      For thyself, with hearts aglow,
      Jesu, Victim undefiled:

FORTH IN THY NAME, O LORD, I GO

Considering the important role that work occupies in most lives, there are surprisingly few hymns about the subject and how the Christian should approach it. John Keble's 'New every morning is the love' (no. 89) has the important message that 'the trivial round, the common task will furnish all I need to ask', and George Herbert's 'Teach me my God and King' reminds us that

> A servant with this clause
> Makes drudgery divine;
> Who sweeps a room, as for thy laws,
> Makes that and the action fine.

But these verses by Charles Wesley (see notes to no. 11 for biographical details) provide the most comprehensive treatment of the subject.

Wesley (1707–88) wrote the hymn in 1749 and it was first published in his *Hymns and Sacred Poems* in the same year. In most hymnbooks it appears in the morning section, but it does not really have to be sung at the beginning of the day – a fact which the *English Hymnal* long acknowledged with a discreet note to the effect that it is 'suitable also for midday services'. All hymnbooks substitute the phrase 'thy good and perfect will' for 'thy acceptable will' in the last line of the second verse, a change which was made partly for musical and partly for theological reasons. It is also quite common practice for the third verse printed here to be omitted. Indeed, John Wesley left it out when he included his brother's hymn in the *Wesleyan Hymn Book* of 1780.

The tune almost always used for this hymn is Angel's Song, or Song 34, by Orlando Gibbons (1583–1625), the famous madrigal composer who was organist of the Chapel Royal and

Westminster Abbey. It was one of a set of tunes which he wrote for George Wither's *Hymns and Songs of the Church*, published in 1623. In that book it was set to the hymn 'Thus Angels sung, and thus sing we', hence its title. Another of Wesley's hymns, 'O for a heart to praise my God', is often sung to Gibbons's Song 67, or St Matthias, which comes from the same collection.

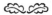

Forth in thy name, O Lord, I go,
My daily labour to pursue;
Thee, only thee, resolved to know,
In all I think or speak or do.

2   The task thy wisdom hath assigned
O let me cheerfully fulfil,
In all my works thy presence find,
And prove thy acceptable will.

3   Preserve me from my calling's snare,
And hide my simple heart above,
Above the thorns of choking care,
The gilded baits of worldly love.

4   Thee may I set at my right hand,
Whose eyes my inmost substance see,
And labour on at thy command,
And offer all my works to thee.

5   Give me to bear thy easy yoke,
And every moment watch and pray,
And still to things eternal look,
And hasten to thy glorious day;

6   For thee delightfully employ
What'er thy bounteous grace hath given,
And run my course with even joy,
And closely walk with thee to heaven.

FROM HEAVEN YOU
CAME, HELPLESS BABE

This is the first of two hymns in this anthology written by the leading contemporary English Christian singer/song-writer Graham Kendrick, who was born in 1950. (Biographical details on him may be found in the notes accompanying no. 81, 'Lord, the light of your love is shining'.) 'The Servant King', to give it its proper title, has rightly become one of the most popular modern hymns and was voted 37th in the 2002 *Songs of Praise* poll.

Kendrick wrote 'The Servant King' in 1984 for the Christian arts festival, Greenbelt. As with virtually all his work, he wrote both the words and the tune which he first picked out on the piano at home. This short and simple hymn has a wonderful theological sweep and breadth. Its starting-point is very clearly the Incarnation. Indeed, its opening line is highly reminiscent of the first line of Martin Luther's Christmas hymn, 'From heaven above to earth I come'. It goes on to cover the agony of Jesus in 'the garden of tears' and his crucifixion, and calls on us to serve him. Like another of Kendrick's best-known songs, 'Meekness and majesty', 'The Servant King' very effectively points up the central paradox that Jesus is both king and servant, priest and victim: the one whose weakness is strength and who conquers through love. It takes us from the helpless babe to the man on the cross, from Incarnation to crucifixion and from creator to sacrificial victim.

Its most powerful and poetic lines are surely 'Hands that flung stars into space / To cruel nails surrendered'. These alone seem to me to make this hymn worthy to stand alongside the great classics of evangelical hymnody by Isaac Watts and Charles Wesley. It can be sung at many different seasons and occasions. I myself have included it in an anthology of Christmas hymns and carols. The editors of *Rejoice and Sing* place it in a section devoted to discipleship, while for *Baptist Praise and Worship* it is above all a hymn of renewed commitment.

There is much debate nowadays about the relative merits of traditional hymns and contemporary worship-songs, and about what distinguishes them. 'The Servant King' could be said to have a foot in both camps, although for me it is ultimately a hymn in the classic tradition rather than a worship-song. It is addressed to Christ, and both its verses and chorus are cast in strophic, metrical form. Kendrick's tune is in an unmistakably modern idiom. The result is a fine contemporary hymn which does not 'dumb down' in terms of theological subtlety and profundity and does not suffer from the excessive individualism of so many contemporary worship-songs.

The Servant King

From heaven you came, helpless babe,
Entered our world, your glory veiled;
Not to be served but to serve,
And give your life that we might live.

This is our God, the Servant King,
He calls us now to follow him,
To bring our lives as a daily offering
Of worship to the Servant King.

2   There in the garden of tears,
My heavy load he chose to bear;
His heart with sorrow was torn,
'Yet not my will but yours,' he said.

3   Come, see his hands and his feet,
The scars that speak of sacrifice,
Hands that flung stars into space
To cruel nails surrendered.

4   So let us learn how to serve,
And in our lives enthrone him;
Each other's needs to prefer,
For it is Christ we're serving.

GLORIOUS THINGS OF
THEE ARE SPOKEN

This is another much-loved hymn written by John Newton (1725–1809), the ne'er-do-well slave-trader turned fervent born-again Christian (see no. 10 for his life-story). Newton attached to this hymn the biblical reference Isaiah 33.20–2:

Look upon Zion, the city of our solemnities: thine eyes shall see Jerusalem a quiet habitation, a tabernacle that shall not be taken down; not one of the stakes thereof shall ever be removed, neither shall any of the cords thereof be broken. But there the glorious Lord will be unto us a place of broad rivers and streams; wherein shall no galley with oars, neither shall any gallant ship pass thereby.

The hymn takes its first line from the third verse of Psalm 87: 'Glorious things are spoken of thee, O city of God.' The seventh line of the first verse is based on Isaiah 26.1: 'We have a strong city; salvation will God appoint for walls and bulwarks' and the first line of the second verse echoes Psalm 46.4: 'There is a river, the streams whereof shall make glad the city of God.' There are other biblical references in the hymn, notably to the book of Revelation.

'Glorious things of thee are spoken' is printed here as it first appeared in the *Olney Hymn Book* which John Newton and his friend William Cowper produced in 1779. The fourth verse has been dropped in all modern hymnbooks and several also omit the third verse which is rarely sung nowadays. Where that verse does appear, the fifth line has almost invariably been changed to 'Thus they march, the pillar leading', and the seventh to 'Daily on the manna feeding'.

Some hymnbooks have altered the first line of the last verse to read 'Saviour, since of Zion's city'. This apparently small change of wording makes a very major difference to the meaning. Newton was a strict Calvinist who believed that no man could be absolutely certain whether he belonged to the elect who had been chosen by God to dwell in the eternal city. Modern theology tends towards a more universal and confident view of mankind's chances of salvation.

The tune still first and foremost associated with this hymn is, I suppose, Austria, which was written by Franz Josef Haydn (1732–1809) as a hymn to the Habsburg Emperor, Francis. The hymn was first performed on the Emperor's birthday in 1797. It is said to have been a particular favourite of Haydn's, and the story goes that it was the last piece of music that the composer ever played on his piano. It was first used as a hymn-tune in England in 1805. Later it was taken up as the tune for the German national anthem, 'Deutschland! Deutschland! über alles'. Kaiser Wilhelm II is said to have been very startled when on a visit to his godmother Queen Victoria at Windsor Castle, he found himself singing it to the words of Newton's hymn.

A more flowing and less bombastic alternative to Austria is Abbot's Leigh by Cyril Taylor (1907–91). His tune spread largely thanks to the medium of the wireless and was printed in leaflet form in 1941, appearing in *Hymns Ancient and Modern* in 1950.

Zion, or the City of God

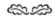

Glorious things of thee are spoken,
Zion, city of our God!
He whose word cannot be broken
Formed thee for his own abode:
On the Rock of Ages founded,
What can shake thy sure repose?
With salvation's walls surrounded,
Thou may'st smile at all thy foes.

2 See, the streams of living waters,
   Springing from eternal love,
   Well supply thy sons and daughters,
   And all fear of want remove:
   Who can faint while such a river
   Ever flows their thirst to assuage?
   Grace, which like the Lord the Giver,
   Never fails from age to age.

3 Round each habitation hov'ring,
   See the cloud and fire appear
   For a glory and a cov'ring,
   Showing that the Lord is near.
   Thus deriving from their banner
   Light by night and shade by day;
   Safe they feed upon the manna
   Which he gives them when they pray.

4 Bless'd inhabitants of Zion,
   Wash'd in the Redeemer's blood!
   Jesus, whom their hopes rely on,
   Makes them kings and priests to God.
   'Tis his love his people raises
   Over self to reign as King,
   And, as priests, his solemn praises
   Each for a thank-offering brings.

5 Saviour, if of Zion's city
   I, through grace, a member am,
   Let the world deride or pity,
   I will glory in thy name:
   Fading is the worldling's pleasure,
   All his boasted pomp and show;
   Solid joys and lasting treasure
   None but Zion's children know.

40

GOD BE WITH YOU TILL
WE MEET AGAIN

This is an unashamedly sentimental hymn and, such things being out of fashion nowadays, it fails to make an appearance in most modern hymnbooks. However, it is still sung at partings and farewells and never fails to bring a lump to the throat. I can think of nothing more appropriate or moving to sing at such occasions. My father recalls it being sung when his father was about to leave home to fight in the trenches of Flanders in the First World War.

The author, Dr Jeremiah Eames Rankin (1828–1904), was a Congregational minister and president of Howard University, Washington DC. He wrote this hymn in 1882, basing it on the etymology of the word 'goodbye' which is a shortened form of 'God be with you'.

The hymn was first sung at the First Congregational Church in Washington, where Rankin was minister. It was immensely popular. He himself attributed its popularity largely to the tune, which had been composed by William Gould Tomer (1832–96). Rankin had sent the first verse of the hymn to two composers, one nationally known and the other the unknown Tomer – a former soldier in the Civil War and clerk in the US treasury department who had taken up school-teaching.

Tomer's tune, God be with you, was for long favoured by British nonconformists but Anglicans have largely rejected it in favour of Ralph Vaughan Williams's Randolph. The latter is undoubtedly more sophisticated, but I have to say that I much prefer Tomer's melody, despite the fact that one critic has dismissed it as 'a tedious maudlin tune'. Its sentimentality goes well with Rankin's words.

As I mentioned above, *Hymns for Church and School*, the successor to the old *Public School Hymn Book*, contains a version of this hymn. It is the very last entry in the book and is headed for singing at a farewell. Several schools use it at end-of-term services. Sung to Randolph, and with new words by Donald Hughes (1911–), it bears little resemblance to the Rankin–Tomer original, although the opening and closing lines of each verse are the same. Its language is less personal and more challenging, but its underlying message equally moving and reassuring. It is probably too much to ask for the resurrection of the original hymn today, but it would be good to see this modern version in more hymnbooks. The first and last verses run as follows:

> God be with you till we meet again,
> May he through the days direct you;
> May he in life's storms protect you;
> God be with you till we meet again.

> God be with you till we meet again;
> May he go through life beside you,
> And through death in safety guide you;
> God be with you till we meet again.

At a Farewell

God be with you till we meet again;
By his counsels guide, uphold you,
With his sheep securely fold you:
God be with you till we meet again.

2   God be with you till we meet again;
'Neath his wings protecting hide you,
Daily manna still provide you:
God be with you till we meet again.

3   God be with you till we meet again;
When life's perils thick confound you,
Put his arms unfailing round you:
God be with you till we meet again.

4   God be with you till we meet again;
Keep love's banner floating o'er you,
Smite death's threatening wave before you:
God be with you till we meet again.

GOD IS WORKING HIS
PURPOSE OUT

Several of the hymns in this collection were first written for schoolboys to sing. We have already encountered Thomas Ken's fine morning hymn for the scholars of Winchester, 'Awake, my soul, and with the sun' (no. 15), and we will later meet 'Lift up your hearts! We lift them, Lord, to thee' (no. 76) which Henry Montagu Butler penned for the pupils of Harrow. This hymn was written for the boys of Britain's most famous public school: Eton.

The author, Arthur Campbell Ainger (1841–1919), was the son of the vicar of Hampstead. Educated at Eton, he returned to teach there after a brief spell as an undergraduate at Cambridge where he gained first-class honours in the classical tripos. He remained at the school as an assistant master for 37 years and was much liked by his pupils. He is reported to have 'preserved admirable and friendly discipline by means of a dry and ready irony, which was never harsh or unamiable. He set no punishments, and his justice, courtesy, and unruffled good humour won the respect and admiration of the boys.'

Ainger wrote a large number of poems and hymns. He was also responsible for a collection of Eton songs, a book of reminiscences about the school, an English–Latin verse dictionary and a learned treatise on the game of fives.

'God is working his purpose out' was written in 1894 and dedicated to Archbishop Benson, a former master at Rugby and headmaster of Wellington College who was Archbishop of Canterbury from 1882 until his death in 1896. The last line of each verse echoes the words of Habakkuk 3.14: 'For the earth shall be filled with the knowledge of the glory of the Lord, as the waters cover the sea.'

When the hymn was first published in leaflet form it was set to the tune Benson which had been specially composed for it by Miss Millicent D. Kingham (1866–1927), organist at St Andrew's, Hertford. That tune is still given in *Hymns for Church and School*, although the *Public School Hymn Book* used its own specially commissioned tune, Alveston. Most other modern hymnbooks set Ainger's hymn to Purpose by Martin Shaw (1875–1958).

God is working his purpose out as year succeeds to year;
God is working his purpose out and the time is drawing near;
Nearer and nearer draws the time, the time that shall surely be,
When the earth shall be filled with the glory of God as the
   waters cover the sea.

2 From utmost east to utmost west where'er man's foot hath trod,
  By the mouth of many messengers goes forth the voice of God,
  'Give ear to me, ye continents, ye isles, give ear to me,
  That the earth may be filled with the glory of God as the
     waters cover the sea.'

3 What can we do to work God's work, to prosper and increase
  The brotherhood of all mankind, the reign of the Prince of
     Peace?
  What can we do to hasten the time, the time that shall surely be,
  When the earth shall be filled with the glory of God as the
     waters cover the sea?

4 March we forth in the strength of God with the banner of
     Christ unfurled.
  That the light of the glorious gospel of truth may shine
     throughout the world;
  Fight we the fight with sorrow and sin, to set their captives free.
  That the earth may be filled with the glory of God as the
     waters cover the sea.

5 All we can do is nothing worth unless God blesses the deed;
  Vainly we hope for the harvest-tide till God gives life to the
     seed;
  Yet nearer and nearer draws the time, the time that shall surely
     be,
  When the earth shall be filled with the glory of God as the
     waters cover the sea.

GOD MOVES IN A
MYSTERIOUS WAY

A hymn of vivid poetic imagery which conveys perhaps better than any other the mystery and impenetrability of God, this is the work of William Cowper (1731–1800), who produced some of the finest religious verse in the English language despite a life spent in acute mental torment.

Cowper came from a distinguished literary and ecclesiastical family. His father was a chaplain to George II and his mother a descendant of John Donne, the Dean of St Paul's and metaphysical poet. He went to Westminster School, where he showed considerable promise as a versifier in both Latin and English, and then read for the Bar. However, from the age of 21 he began to be affected by severe bouts of melancholia (depression). These continued, with increasing severity, for the rest of his life. He was committed to a private lunatic asylum in the early 1760s and never managed to hold down a steady job.

The one anchor in Cowper's stormy and unhappy life was his strong evangelical faith, the result of a conversion while he was a patient in a private lunatic asylum run by a convinced evangelical. In 1767, at the invitation of John Newton (for whom see notes to no. 10), he went to live at Olney, Buckinghamshire, where he was looked after by a clergyman's widow and did what he could to assist in the life of the parish.

Together Cowper and Newton wrote hymns to be sung at the weekly prayer meetings held in Olney Church. They also collaborated on a hymnbook which was published in 1779, with 67 entries by Cowper and 280 by Newton. But what Cowper's contributions lacked in quantity they more than make up for in quality. They include some of the gems of English hymnody, including 'O for a closer walk with God' (no. 92), 'Hark my Soul! It is the Lord' and 'Jesus, where'er thy people meet'.

'God moves in a mysterious way' was written in the early 1770s when Cowper was in an almost permanent state of depression, alleviated only by occasional periods of calm. The biblical text that he attached to it was from Jesus's words to Simon Peter in John 13.7: 'What I do thou knowest not now; but thou shalt know hereafter.' There is a story that he wrote the hymn after being saved from a suicide attempt, but this is apocryphal. Although its language at times suggests a certain anguish, its overall theme is of resounding Christian hope. That is certainly how it has been taken by generations of Christians to whom it has given encouragement. It is reported that when during the 1840s a Lancashire mill-owner told his workers that the depression in trade would cause the closure of the works, they roused their spirits by singing 'Ye fearful Saints fresh courage take', led by a young girl. The last verse has a particularly strong message of assurance for those who are perplexed, as we surely all are at times, by the seeming irrationality and arbitrariness of God's ways.

Cowper's verses printed here first appeared in July 1774, in an appendage to a collection of letters by John Newton on religious subjects. They were also published the same month in the *Gospel Magazine*. When the hymn appeared three years later in that same journal, the second verse was omitted and the following verse was added at the end:

> When midnight shades are all withdrawn
> The opening day shall rise,
> Whose ever calm and cloudless morn
> Shall know no low'ring skies.

The tunes most commonly used for the hymn both come from the *Scottish Psalter*. Dundee comes from the 1615 edition and London New from that of 1635.

Light shining out of darkness

God moves in a mysterious way
His wonders to perform;
He plants his footsteps in the sea,
And rides upon the storm.

2   Deep in unfathomable mines
Of never-failing skill
He treasures up his bright designs,
And works his sovereign will.

3   Ye fearful saints, fresh courage take;
The clouds ye so much dread
Are big with mercy, and will break
In blessings on your head.

4   Judge not the Lord by feeble sense,
But trust him for his grace:
Behind a frowning providence
He hides a smiling face.

5   His purposes will ripen fast,
Unfolding every hour;
The bud may have a bitter taste,
But sweet will be the flower.

6   Blind unbelief is sure to err,
And scan his work in vain;
God is his own interpreter,
And he will make it plain.

GOD SAVE OUR
GRACIOUS QUEEN

Some readers may be surprised to find the national anthem included in this collection. Yet it fulfils at least one of the major definitions of a hymn in being a supplication addressed to the Almighty, and it appears in most major denominational hymn-books.

Its provenance and authorship are obscure. In his fascinating study of the anthem, Percy Scholes traces its origins back to 1688 when 'God save great James our king' was sung by Stuart loyalists on the eve of William of Orange's invasion. The song may conceivably be older and have been sung during the reign of Charles II. Indeed, it may even originally have come from across the Channel − a French song, '*Grand Dieu, sauvez le roi*', uncannily similar in language, structure and metre to the British national anthem, was sung at the Court of Louis XIV in 1686. Jacobite versions appeared on wine glasses in the early eighteenth century.

At what stage this Stuart anthem was appropriated for the Hanoverians is not clear but it was undoubtedly the threat of the Jacobite rebellion in 1745 that brought it into the public demesne. 'God Save great George our King' received its first known public performance at the Theatre Royal Drury Lane on 28 September 1745, following the theatre manager's announcement that he was raising a troop of soldiers to fight for the King with his actors as its nucleus. It was sung there by the men who had been enlisted, and conducted by Thomas Arne, whose tune for 'Rule Britannia' had been heard in the theatre six months earlier. The anthem was taken up by other theatres and sung in public places.

The anthem first appeared in its familiar modern form as printed here (except for the substitution of 'King' for 'Queen' and 'him' for 'her' in appropriate places) in *The Gentleman's Magazine* (October 1745), where it was described as having been sung in several London playhouses. The first two verses had appeared in a slightly modified form two or three years earlier in a publication called *Harmonia anglicana*. The words have often been attributed to Henry Carey (?–1743), the poet who was responsible for both the words and music of the popular song, 'Sally in our Alley', but this attribution cannot be proved. 'God save the King' seems first to have been sung in churches during George III's bouts of illness, when new verses were added to pray for the king's deliverance and thank God for his recovery. The first coronation to include the national anthem was that of George IV in 1821, and by Victoria's reign it had become the inevitable accompaniment to public appearances by the monarch.

The national anthem was a peculiarly British invention, rapidly copied by other countries, twenty of which at one time or another adopted or adapted the tune of 'God save the King' for their own national songs. What distinguished the British version was the fact it was so clearly addressed to God rather than to the Fatherland, the flag or some other symbol, and that it focused directly on the person of the sovereign rather than on the nation or people. While it clearly called on the Almighty to bless and protect the monarch, however, there was no hint of Divine Right theory. Indeed, the third verse introduced a note of conditionality indicative of a contractual view of monarchy.

During Victoria's reign the national anthem was often turned into an anti-Catholic rallying cry. The widespread anti-papal demonstrations which followed Pope Pius IX's creation of a hierarchy of bishops for England and Wales in 1850 were accompanied by the singing of an amended version of the second verse with the line 'Frustrate their Popish tricks, confound their politics'. The following year a new verse provided 'for the use of Her Majesty's loyal subjects in their social circles and public assemblies' invoked divine protection for the anti-Catholic cause:

Let now thine arm be seen,
Guarding our gracious Queen
From papal power.

The British national anthem has spawned numerous offspring and imitators, the best-known being probably the one written by an American Unitarian minister, Charles T. Brooks (1813–83) and first published in 1836. Still much sung in the USA, it begins:

God bless our native land!
Firm may she ever stand
Through storm and night!
When the wild tempests rave,
Ruler of wind and wave,
Father eternal save
Us by thy might!

The distinctly xenophobic and bellicose character of the second verse of the national anthem has long caused unease and it is normally omitted from modern hymnals. The New Standard edition of *Hymns Ancient and Modern* offered as a substitute a verse written in 1836 by William Edward Hickson (1803–70), a London boot-manufacturer turned social reformer, as part of an 'alternative' national anthem of a more pacific and Christian character. The whole of Hickson's version may be found in the second edition of the *Church Hymnary*. The verse by Hickson suggested as a substitute middle verse for the National Anthem, which was also strongly commended by the Church of England's liturgical commission in 1990, runs as follows:

Nor on this land alone –
But be Thy mercies known
From shore to shore.
Lord, make the nations see
All men should brothers be,
One league, one family,
One, the world o'er.

The tune of 'God save the Queen' is sometimes attributed to Dr John Bull (?–1628), organist at Antwerp Cathedral. Thomas Arne has also been credited with writing as well as conducting and arranging it, but the truth is that we do not know who was responsible. What we do know is that it is one of the most recognizable tunes, both in the United Kingdom and throughout the world.

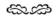

God save our gracious Queen,
Long live our noble Queen,
God save the Queen.
Send her victorious,
Happy and glorious,
Long to reign over us:
God save the Queen.

2   O Lord our God, arise,
Scatter her enemies,
And make them fall;
Confound their politics,
Frustrate their knavish tricks;
On thee our hopes we fix:
God save us all.

3   Thy choicest gifts in store
On her be pleased to pour,
Long may she reign.
May she defend our laws,
And ever give 'us cause
To sing with heart and voice,
God save the Queen.

GREAT IS THY
FAITHFULNESS

This hymn, written in the USA in the early 1920s, really owes its popularity in Britain to its use by Billy Graham in his evangelistic crusade in Haringey, north London, in 1954. Although it has taken some time to find its place in the major denominational hymnbooks here, it now stands high in the UK hymnological hit-parade, ranking fourth in the latest *Songs of Praise* poll. It has much in common with the hymn that currently occupies the top place in the poll, 'How great thou art'. Both hymns hail from the early twentieth century, both display a strong emphasis on creation and nature and both have broad, soaring tunes.

'Great is thy faithfulness' is the work of Thomas Chisholm (1866–1960). A devout Methodist from Kentucky, he worked successively as a journalist, a school teacher and a life-insurance agent before becoming ordained as a Methodist minister. He wrote these verses in 1923, and later reflected that there were no special circumstances surrounding their writing and that he was simply expressing his impressions of God's faithfulness as recounted in the Bible. He sent them, along with several other poems, to his friend and collaborator William Runyan (1870–1957), a fellow Methodist who achieved considerable fame in the USA as a composer of sacred music and gospel songs.

The early popularity of the hymn in the USA was greatly helped by its promotion by Dr Will Houghton, president of the Moody Bible Institute, who frequently used it in his services both at the Institute and on its radio station, WMBI. It was as a singer on that station's daily early morning programme 'Hymns from the Chapel' that George Beverly Shea first encountered 'Great is thy faithfulness'. Later, as the lead singer at Billy Graham's evangelistic rallies, Beverly Shea frequently sang it and helped to popularize it across America.

The opening verse is directly based on scriptural affirmations about God. Lamentations 3.22 and 33 proclaim that 'His compassions fail not. They are new every morning: great is thy faithfulness' and James 1.17 declares that 'Every good gift and every perfect gift is from above, and cometh down from the Father of lights, with whom is no variableness, neither shadow of turning.'

William Runyan's tune Faithfulness has been this hymn's inseparable companion since the author first sent the composer the words.

❧❧

Great is thy faithfulness, O God my Father,
there is no shadow of turning with thee;
thou changest not, thy compassions they fail not,
as thou hast been thou for ever wilt be.

Great is thy faithfulness!
Great is thy faithfulness!
Morning by morning new mercies I see;
all I have needed thy hand hath provided –
great is thy faithfulness, Lord, unto me!

2 Summer and winter, and spring-time and harvest,
sun, moon and stars in their courses above,
join with all nature in manifold witness
to thy great faithfulness, mercy and love.

3 Pardon for sin and a peace that endureth,
thine own dear presence to cheer and to guide;
strength for today and bright hope for tomorrow,
blessings all mine, with ten thousand beside!

GUIDE ME, O THOU
GREAT JEHOVAH

A favourite with football crowds and church congregations alike, this rousing Welsh hymn stands at no. 11 in the 2002 BBC *Songs of Praise* poll.

The Welsh original of which it is a very free translation, '*Arglwydd, arwain trwy'r anialwch*', was written in 1745 by William Williams (1717–91), and ran to five verses. Williams, who came from Llandovery in Carmarthenshire, trained for the medical profession but decided to enter the Church in 1738 after hearing a sermon by Howell Harris, the leader of the Evangelical Revival in Wales. He was ordained a deacon in the established Anglican Church by the Bishop of St Davids, but left three years later to become a preacher in the Welsh Calvinistic Methodist connexion. He started writing hymns at Harris's suggestion. Altogether he wrote some 800 hymns and travelled almost 100,000 miles on foot and horseback during more than 40 years as an itinerant minister. He is often known as 'Pantycelyn', the name of the farm near Llandovery where he lived after his marriage.

In 1771 a very free English translation of the first, third and fifth verses of Williams's hymn was published by Peter Williams (1722–96), a Methodist itinerant preacher and no relation of the author of the Welsh original, in his *Hymns on Various Subjects*. The first verse of this translation was included in a four-verse version of the hymn which William Williams published the following year as a leaflet with the title 'A favourite hymn sung by Lady Huntington's Young Collegians'. This is the version which appears here. It is made up of Peter Williams's translation of the first verse of the original Welsh hymn, William Williams's translation of the third and fourth verses and a new English verse added by him.

Most hymnbooks use this version, with the fourth stanza omitted, but some substitute 'Redeemer' for 'Jehovah' in the first line. The last line of the first verse is sometimes rendered either 'Feed me now and evermore' or 'Feed me till my want is o'er'. The hymn has been rewritten a number of times. John Keble produced a version beginning 'Guide us, Thou whose Name is Saviour' and the disciples of Robert Owen, the Welsh-born industrialist and utopian socialist, came up with a more drastic revision which began:

> Guide us, Truth, thou star refulgent,
> Travellers through a darksome land;
> We are weak, but thou art mighty
> To support our social band;
> Lead us onward,
> Bending to thy high command.

The imagery of the hymn is taken from the biblical story of the Israelites' journey from Egypt to the Promised Land. The 'bread of heaven' comes from Exodus, 16.4: 'Then said the Lord unto Moses, Behold, I will rain bread from heaven for you.' The 'crystal fountain' comes from Exodus 17.6: 'Behold, I will stand before thee upon the rock in Horeb; and thou shalt smite the rock, and there shall come water out of it, that the people may drink.' The 'fiery, cloudy pillar' is found in Exodus 13.21: 'And the Lord went before them by day and night: he took not away the pillar of the cloud by day, nor the pillar of fire by night, from before the people.'

The tune Cwm Rhondda, which must be one of the best-known and certainly one of the most lustily sung of all hymn-tunes, is surprisingly recent in origin. It was composed for the annual Baptist 'Cymanfa Ganu' (singing festival) at Pontypridd in 1905 by John Hughes (1873–1932), an official of the Great Western Railway and precentor of Salem Baptist Church in Pontypridd. Legend has it that he originally wrote it in chalk on a piece of tarpaulin, but more likely is his wife's recollection that he penned it one Sunday morning while in the Salem chapel.

What is certain is that its popularity was greatly boosted by its frequent use in the trenches of Flanders in the First World War, where it was sung so melodiously by Welsh soldiers that German troops took it up. Hughes originally called the tune Rhondda after the great mining valley in South Wales, but had to add the word Cwm, or valley, to its title after discovering that there was already a tune called Rhondda. The Welsh use the tune for a completely different hymn, '*Wele'n sefyll rhwng y myrtwydd*'.

Praying for Strength

Guide me, O thou great Jehovah,
Pilgrim through this barren land;
I am weak, but thou art mighty;
Hold me with thy powerful hand;
Bread of heaven, bread of heaven,
Feed me till I want no more.

2   Open now the crystal fountain,
Whence the healing stream doth flow;
Let the fire and cloudy pillar
Lead me all my journey through;
Strong Deliv'rer, Strong Deliv'rer,
Be thou still my strength and shield.

3   When I tread the verge of Jordan,
Bid my anxious fears subside;
Death of deaths, and hell's destruction,
Land me safe on Canaan's side;
Songs of praises, songs of praises,
I will ever give to thee.

4   Musing on my habitation,
Musing on my heav'nly home,
Fills my soul with holy longings:
Come, my Jesus, quickly come;
Vanity is all I see;
Lord, I long to be with Thee!

HAIL THE DAY THAT SEES
HIM RISE

Another ever-popular hymn by Charles Wesley (1707–88: for biographical note see no. 11), this has been substantially rewritten. Indeed, not one verse of the original survives unscathed in the version that is now so widely sung at Ascension Day services.

The hymn as Wesley wrote it is printed here. It was first published in *Hymns and Sacred Poems* in 1739. It gives a vivid description of the Ascension of Christ and a clear explanation of what Christians believe its significance to be. The view of heaven presented in verses 7, 8 and 9 may seem a little too definitely located 'up there' for modern tastes, but there can be no denying the poetry of the lines, somewhat muted in the version we sing now: 'High above yon azure height' and 'Following thee beyond the skies'.

The second verse quotes almost verbatim from Psalm 24.7:

> Lift up your heads, O ye gates;
> And be lift up, ye everlasting doors;
> the King of glory shall come in.

The curious reference in verse 7 to Christ being 'taken from our head' comes from 2 Kings 2.5: 'Knowest thou that the Lord will take away thy master from thy head today?', while the next verse shows Wesley's strong liturgical sense and echoes the Collect for Ascension Day in the Book of Common Prayer:

Grant, we beseech thee, Almighty God, that like as we do believe thy only begotten Son our Lord Jesus Christ to have ascended into the heavens; so we may also in heart and mind thither ascend; and with him continually dwell.

In 1820 Wesley's hymn was substantially altered by Thomas Cotterill (1779–1823), vicar of Lane End, Staffordshire and later perpetual curate of St Paul's, Sheffield. The general effect of his revision was to tone down the ecstatic and emotional language of the original. This version appears in a number of modern hymnbooks, including the *New English Hymnal*. It begins as follows:

> Hail the day that sees him rise   Alleluya!
> Glorious to his native skies;   Alleluya!
> Christ, awhile to mortals given,   Alleluya!
> Enters now the highest heaven!   Alleluya!

The practice of adding 'Alleluya' to the end of every line dates from 1852. In 1861 the compilers of *Hymns Ancient and Modern* further altered the hymn, and their version appears in a number of contemporary hymnals, including the New Standard edition of *Hymns Ancient and Modern*. It begins:

> Hail the day that sees him rise,   Alleluia.
> To his throne above the skies;   Alleluia.
> Christ, the Lamb for sinners given,   Alleluia.
> Enters now the highest heaven.   Alleluia.

The most commonly used tune for this hymn is the joyful and exuberant Ascension, composed in 1861 by W.H. Monk (1823–89) for *Hymns Ancient and Modern*, of which he was musical editor. Alternatives include Llanfair by Robert Williams (1781–1821) and Chislehurst.

Hymn for Ascension Day

Hail the day that sees him rise,
Ravished from our wishful eyes!
Christ, awhile to mortals given,
Reascends his native heaven.

2   There the pompous triumph waits:
'Lift your heads, eternal gates;
Wide unfold the radiant scene;
Take the King of glory in!'

3   Circled round with angel-powers,
Their triumphant Lord, and ours,
Conqueror over death and sin:
'Take the King of glory in!'

4   Him though highest heaven receives,
Still he loves the earth he leaves;
Though returning to his throne,
Still he calls mankind his own.

5   See! he lifts his hands above.
See! he shows the prints of love.
Hark! his gracious lips bestow
Blessings on his Church below.

6   Still for us his death he pleads;
Prevalent he intercedes;
Near himself prepares our place,
Harbinger of human race.

7   Master, (will we ever say,)
Taken from our head today,
See thy faithful servants, see,
Ever gazing up to Thee.

8   Grant, though parted from our sight,
      High above yon azure height,
      Grant our hearts may thither rise,
      Following thee beyond the skies.

9   Ever upward let us move,
      Wafted on the wings of love,
      Looking when our Lord shall come,
      Longing, gasping after home.

10   There we shall with thee remain,
      Partners of thy endless reign,
      There thy face unclouded see,
      Find our heaven of heavens in thee.

HAIL THEE, FESTIVAL DAY!

There are at least four different versions of this exciting medieval processional hymn, each for use on one of the major festivals in the Christian calendar. The Whit Sunday one, which is printed here, is the most widely sung nowadays, appearing in the hymnbooks of a number of different denominations and not just, as it once did, in those of a High Anglican persuasion.

The original Latin hymn from which it is translated begins:

> *Salve festa dies, toto venerabilis aevo,*
> *Qua Deus de caelo gratia fulsit humo.*

It is first found in the Sarum use in a missal dating from the middle of the thirteenth century and a processional of c. 1360. It also occurs in the York processional of 1530. The first line of the hymn is taken from a poem by Venatius Fortunatus (c. 530–609), an Italian who moved to France and became Bishop of Poitiers. His poem provides the original of the Easter Day version of the hymn,

> Hail thee, Festival Day! blest day that art hallowed for ever;
> Day wherein Christ arose, breaking the kingdom of death

There are other versions: for Ascension Day ('Day when our God ascends high in the heavens to reign') and for a dedication festival ('Day when the Church, Christ's bride, is to her bridegroom espoused'). There is also a version for Corpus Christi, but this is not found in any twentieth-century hymnals.

The fine translation of the Whitsun verses here was made by George Gabriel Scott Gillett (1873–1948) for the *English Hymnal* in 1906. Educated at Westminster School and Keble College,

Oxford, Gillett was ordained in 1898 and served as a curate in London and Brighton before becoming domestic chaplain to Earl Beauchamp and Viscount Halifax. He later worked in South Africa and ended his working life as editorial secretary to the Society for the Propagation of the Gospel.

This hymn takes much of its imagery from the account of the coming of the Holy Spirit to the disciples at Pentecost in Acts 2. But it expands on that account to introduce such richly poetic phrases as the 'sevenfold mystical dowry' – a reference to the seven sacraments of baptism, confirmation, eucharist, penance, matrimony, holy orders and anointing of the sick. The first line of the sixth verse is borrowed from the collect for peace in the Book of Common Prayer which begins: 'O God, who art the author of peace and lover of concord'.

All the Festival Day hymns owe much of their modern popularity to the vigorous unison tune *Salve festa dies* which Ralph Vaughan Williams (1872–1958) composed for their appearance in the *English Hymnal* in 1906.

Salve, festa dies

⚜

Hail thee, Festival Day! blest day that art hallowed for ever;
Day wherein God from heaven shone on the world with his grace.

2 Lo! in the likeness of fire, on them that await his appearing,
   He whom the Lord foretold, suddenly, swiftly, descends.

3 Forth from the Father he comes with his sevenfold mystical
      dowry,
   Pouring on human souls infinite riches of God.

4 Hark! in a hundred tongues Christ's own, his chosen Apostles,
   Preach to a hundred tribes Christ and his wonderful works.

5 Praise to the Spirit of life, all praise to the Fount of our being,
   Light that dost lighten all, Life that in all dost abide.

6 God who art Giver of all good gifts and Lover of concord,
   Pour thy balm on our souls, order our ways in thy peace.

7 God Almighty, who fillest the heaven, the earth and the ocean,
   Guard us from harm without, cleanse us from evil within.

8 Kindle our lips with the live bright coal from the hands of the
      Seraph;
   Shine in our minds with thy light; burn in our hearts with thy
      love.

HAIL TO THE LORD'S
ANOINTED!

There can be few hymn-writers who have suffered imprisonment on account of their radical political views but that was the fate on two occasions of the author of this hymn, James Montgomery (1771–1854).

Montgomery was brought up a Moravian. This relatively small religious sect, which had close links with the Lutheran Church and to which John Wesley owed his conversion, had been founded in 1722 by Count Nicholas Ludwig von Zinzendorf as a revival of the fifteenth-century Bohemian Bretheren. Montgomery's father was an Irish peasant who became a Moravian pastor and settled in Irvine, Ayrshire, Scotland. Shortly after James's birth there his parents went out as missionaries to the slaves on the sugar plantations in the West Indies. They died within a few years and James was sent away to be educated at the Moravian seminary at Fulneck in Yorkshire.

He was originally attracted to the Moravian ministry, but did not pursue the idea, becoming instead a shopkeeper in Mirfield, near Huddersfield. Then in 1792 he moved to Sheffield, and became assistant to Joseph Gales, a well-known printer and bookseller. Gales was the proprietor of the *Sheffield Register*, well known for its extreme political radicalism, and it was this periodical that Montgomery took over when he was just 23, after Gales had been forced to flee the country. Montgomery changed the title to the *Sheffield Iris*, but did not change the paper's forceful political line. Among the controversial causes which he championed was the teaching of writing in the Sunday School syllabus – a practice that many in authority felt would instil dangerous ideas into working-class youth. He was also a strong opponent of slavery and of the use of climbing-boys by chimney sweeps. His strong support for the democratic principles of the

French Revolution led him to be regarded as a dangerous Jacobin, and he was imprisoned in 1795 for writing an enthusiastic account of the release of innocent prisoners during the storming of the Bastille. An equally sympathetic account of a reform riot in Sheffield led to a second spell of imprisonment a few years later.

In 1814 Montgomery became a member of the Wesleyan Society. Later on in life he became a communicant member of the Anglican Church. An important influence on his switch to Anglicanism, and on his career as a hymn-writer, was the Revd Thomas Cotterill, perpetual curate of St Paul's Church in Sheffield (see no. 46). In the absence of any Anglican hymnbooks at this time, Montgomery helped Cotterill to produce a hymnal for use in his church. Some members of the congregation who objected to learning a lot of new hymns, and who felt hymn-singing to be a Dissenting and distinctly un-Anglican practice, dredged up an ancient church law that prohibited the singing in churches of hymns of 'human composure', as opposed to versions of psalms and scriptures. They took their case to the church courts where the ancient law was upheld, and it looked briefly as though the practice of hymn-singing might have to end in the Established Church. However, the Archbishop of York moved to have the law repealed, and from 1821 hymn-singing was officially legitimized in the Church of England.

Altogether Montgomery wrote more than 400 hymns, several of which were written for Cotterill's hymnbook and all of which appeared in a collected volume in 1853. Erik Routley has written that 'His work is good, sound, hard-wearing stuff with a touch of the genuinely inspired here and there that makes us able to regard him as the typical English hymn-writer ... Without any question on the verdict of posterity, Montgomery was the greatest of Christian lay hymn-writers.' One of his great strengths was undoubtedly his association with several different denominations which freed him from the narrowness which afflicts some other early nineteenth-century hymn-writers.

According to John Julian's *Dictionary of Hymnology*, a quarter of Montgomery's vast output was still in regular use at the end of the nineteenth century. Nowadays most hymnals carry at least half a dozen of his hymns. Among those which continue to be sung are 'Stand up and bless the Lord' (no. 116), 'For ever with the Lord', 'Songs of praise the angels sang', 'Lift up your heads, ye gates of brass', 'According to thy gracious word', 'Prayer is the soul's sincere desire' and the ever-popular carol, 'Angels from the realms of glory'. Strangely, this last attracted no attention at all when it appeared in the *Sheffield Iris*, where Montgomery first published several of his hymns, and it was only when it was included in one of his later collections that it began to be sung in churches.

'Hail to the Lord's Anointed!', which is printed here in its full original form, was written for and sung in a Christmas ode at a Moravian settlement in 1821. The following April, Montgomery recited the hymn at the close of an address in the Wesleyan chapel in Liverpool. In the congregation was the distinguished Methodist theologian Dr Adam Clarke, who asked for the manuscript and printed it in his own commentary beside the 72nd Psalm. In June it appeared in the *Evangelical Magazine* and later in Montgomery's *Songs of Zion*.

The hymn is based on Psalm 72 (Give the king thy judgments, O God). The start of the second stanza echoes the fourth verse of the psalm: 'He shall judge the poor of the people, He shall save the children of the needy' and the beginning of the fourth stanza closely parallels verses 6 and 7: 'He shall come down like rain upon the mown grass: As showers that water the earth'. The memorable and evocative phrases 'Arabia's desert ranger' and 'the Ethiopian stranger' in verse 5 are derived rather loosely from lines 10 and 11 of the psalm: 'The kings of Tarshish and of the isles shall bring presents: The kings of Sheba and Seba shall offer gifts.' Modern hymnbooks print a shortened version of the original hymn, often including only the first, fourth, sixth and eighth verses.

The tune almost always used for 'Hail to the Lord's Anointed' is Crüger, an adaptation by W.H. Monk of a tune by Johann Crüger (1598–1662) which was originally published in 1640. Crüger was for 40 years cantor at the Cathedral of St Nicholas in Berlin. (For notes on Monk see no. 2.)

Hail to the Lord's Anointed!
Great David's greater Son;
Hail, in the time appointed,
His reign on earth begun!
He comes to break oppression,
To set the captive free,
To take away transgression,
And rule in equity.

2   He comes in succour speedy
To those who suffer wrong;
To help the poor and needy,
And bid the weak be strong;
To give them songs for sighing,
Their darkness turn to light,
Whose souls, condemned and dying
Were precious in his sight.

3   By such shall he be fearéd
While sun and moon endure;
Beloved, obeyed, reveréd;
For he shall judge the poor
Through changing generations,
With justice, mercy, truth,
While stars maintain their stations,
Or moons renew their youth.

4   He shall come down like showers
Upon the fruitful earth,
And love, joy, hope, like flowers
Spring in his path to birth:
Before him on the mountains,
Shall Peace, the herald, go;
And righteousness, in fountains
From hill to valley flow.

5   Arabia's desert ranger
     To him shall bow the knee,
     The Ethiopian stranger
     His glory come to see:
     With offerings of devotion,
     Ships from the isles shall meet,
     To pour the wealth of ocean
     In tribute at his feet.

6   Kings shall bow down before him,
     And gold and silver bring;
     All nations shall adore him,
     His praise all people sing:
     For he shall have dominion
     O'er river, sea and shore,
     Far as the eagle's pinion
     Or dove's light wing can soar.

7   For him shall prayer unceasing
     And daily vows ascend;
     His kingdom still increasing,
     A kingdom without end:
     The mountain dews shall nourish
     A seed in weakness sown,
     Whose fruit shall spread and flourish,
     And shake like Lebanon.

8   O'er every foe victorious,
     He on his throne shall rest,
     From age to age more glorious,
     All-blessing and all-blest;
     The tide of time shall never
     His covenant remove;
     His name shall stand for ever;
     That name to us is Love.

HARK, THE GLAD SOUND!
THE SAVIOUR COMES

While many of James Montgomery's hymns first saw the light of day in the pages of a radical newspaper, those of Philip Doddridge (1702–51) had a more othodox début, being first heard in the Northampton chapel where he was minister. Doddridge wrote most of his 370 hymns to emphasize the message of his sermons. They were generally sung at the end of the service and based on the biblical text from which he had just preached.

Doddridge was the youngest of the 20 children of an oil merchant. He came of staunch Puritan stock. He was interested in religion from his earliest days, and before he could read he learned Old Testament history from pictures on Dutch tiles in his house. In 1729 he opened a Dissenting academy in Market Harborough on the advice of Isaac Watts. The following year he became pastor of the Congregational chapel at Castle Hill, Northampton. He continued to run the academy, which trained 120 candidates for the ministry.

Doddridge wrote several books including *The Progress of Religion in the Soul*, which was instrumental in the conversion of William Wilberforce to evangelical religion. He suffered from consumption and died in Lisbon where he had gone in the hope of finding some relief in the warm climate. His hymns were not published until after his death.

'Hark, the glad sound!' was written in December 1735 to accompany an Advent sermon on the text of Luke 4.18–19 in which Christ reads from the prophet Isaiah in the synagogue at Nazareth:

The spirit of the Lord is upon me, because he hath anointed me to preach the gospel to the poor; He hath sent me to heal the brokenhearted, to preach deliverance to the captives, and recovering of sight to the blind, to set at liberty them that are bruised, to preach the acceptable year of the Lord.

It is hardly surprising that modern hymnbooks omit the original fourth verse of this Advent hymn with its inelegant references to 'thick films of vice' and 'the eyeballs of the blind'. But it is surely a pity that the second and sixth verses have also disappeared. The latter provides one of the all-too-rare references in hymnody to the year of Jubilee, that wiping of the slate clean which occurred every 50 years in Ancient Israel when slaves were freed, all debts cancelled and the land allowed to lie fallow. Interestingly, a different version of that verse is still sung in Scotland where an amended version of Doddridge's hymn is given in the *Church Hymnary* as paraphrase 39:

> The sacred year has now revolved,
> Accepted of the Lord,
> When heaven's high promise is fulfilled
> And Israel is restored.

Another of Doddridge's hymns, 'O God of Bethel, by whose hand', continues to be very popular in Scotland. In 1854 'Hark the glad sound!' was apparently sung on board the flagship of the American fleet sent to secure Japan's abandonment of neutrality and the opening up of trading and diplomatic relations with the USA. The views of the Japanese as they heard their would-be saviours approach are not recorded.

The hymn is generally sung to the tune Bristol, which is first found in Ravenscroft's Psalter of 1621.

Hark, the glad sound! the Saviour comes,
The Saviour promised long!
Let every heart prepare a throne,
And every voice a song.

2   On him the Spirit largely pour'd
Exerts its sacred fire:
Wisdom and might, and zeal and love
His holy breast inspire.

3   He comes the prisoners to release
In Satan's bondage held;
The gates of brass before him burst,
The iron fetters yield.

4   He comes from the thick films of vice
To purge the mental ray,
And on the eyeballs of the blind
To pour celestial day.

5   He comes the broken heart to bind,
The bleeding soul to cure,
And with the treasures of his grace
To enrich the humble poor.

6   The silver trumpets publish loud
The Jub'lee of the Lord;
Our debts are all remitted now,
Our heritage restored.

7   Our glad hosannas, Prince of peace,
Thy welcome shall proclaim,
And heaven's eternal arches ring
With thy beloved name!

HILLS OF THE NORTH,
REJOICE

This is a Victorian missionary hymn with something of the
flavour of Reginald Heber's 'From Greenland's icy mountains'.
Unlike Heber's effort, it has not been consigned to the scrapheap
and appears in most modern hymnbooks, albeit in a fairly
emasculated form.

It is the work of Charles Edward Oakley (1832–65). Educated
at Oxford, Oakley took holy orders in 1855 and became rector
of Wickwar in Gloucestershire, while at the same time being an
examiner in jurisprudence and civil law at his old university. In
1863 he became rector of St Paul's, Covent Garden, the fine
Inigo Jones church which stands at the western end of the old
vegetable market, now the covered shopping piazza.

This was apparently the only hymn which Oakley wrote in his
short life. It first appeared as an Advent or Epiphany hymn in
Bishop T.V. French's *Hymns Adapted to the Christian Seasons* and
then in the *Hymnal Companion* of 1870.

'Hills of the North' is still in the *Songs of Praise* top hundred
and appears in its original version, as here, in the book *Your
Favourite Songs of Praise* published in 1986. Other hymnbooks all
have watered-down versions, quite understandably in view of the
language of verse 3 in particular with its shades of 'the heathen in
his blindness', although it is counterbalanced with the message of
verse 4 which speaks with a new relevance to our own age when
California might be said to be the temple of materialism and
secularism.

Hymns for Church and School sticks mostly closely to the
original text, only feeling it necessary to provide the following
substitute for verse 3:

Lands of the East arise,
Yours is the first bright dawn:
Open the seeing eyes,
Greet you the world's true morn.
The God of all, whom you would know
And seek on high, seeks you below.

Both the *New English Hymnal* and the new standard edition of *Hymns Ancient and Modern* print the heavily revised version produced by the editors of *English Praise* in 1975. I personally find the surgery that they have performed a bit too drastic. This is how they render the first two verses:

Hills of the North, rejoice,
Echoing songs arise,
Hail with united voice
Him who made earth and skies:
He comes in righteousness and love,
He brings salvation from above.

Isles of the Southern seas,
Sing to the listening earth,
Carry on every breeze
Hope of a world's new birth:
In Christ shall all be made anew,
His word is sure, his promise true.

Whether altered or in its original form, the hymn is almost always sung to Martin Shaw's vigorous tune Little Cornard.

Hills of the North, rejoice:
Rivers and mountain-spring,
Hark to the advent voice!
Valley and lowland, sing!
Though absent long, your Lord is nigh,
He judgment brings, and victory.

2   Isles of the Southern seas,
    Deep in your coral caves
    Pent be each warring breeze,
    Lulled be your restless waves:
    He comes to reign with boundless sway,
    And makes your wastes His great highway.

3   Lands of the East, awake!
    Soon shall your sons be free,
    The sleep of ages break,
    And rise to liberty:
    On your far hills, long cold and grey,
    Has dawned the everlasting day.

4   Shores of the utmost West,
    Ye that have waited long,
    Unvisited, unblest,
    Break forth to swelling song;
    High raise the note, that Jesus died,
    Yet lives and reigns – the Crucified!

5   Shout while ye journey home!
    Songs be in every mouth! –
    Lo, from the North we come,
    From East, and West, and South:
    City of God, the bond are free;
    We come to live and reign in thee.

HO, MY COMRADES! SEE
THE SIGNAL

Despite the fact that it had the honour of being the very first entry in Ira Sankey's classic *Sacred Songs and Solos*, this rousing gospel-song is absent from virtually every modern hymnbook. Many of my readers will no doubt feel that it ought to remain so, and will share John Greenleaf Whittier's strong distaste for its vulgarity and heartiness. It finds a place in this collection not just because it is a supreme example of its genre, with all the faults as well as the strengths to be found in the gospel-songs of nineteenth-century America, but also because I happen to find it a stirring and uplifting expression of an important part of the Christian gospel.

'Hold the fort', as the song is generally known, has its origin in a message waved from mountain to mountain by General Sherman just before his famous march to the sea at the height of the US Civil War in 1864 to relieve the besieged Unionist troops who were holding a supply depot at Altoona Pass in Georgia which was surrounded by Confederate (Southern) troops. As hope was running out, the besieged garrison commander saw far away across a valley the message spelled out in semaphore flags, 'Hold the fort; I am coming, W.T. Sherman'. The story of Sherman's message was related by Major Whittle at a Sunday School meeting in Rockford, Illinois, in May 1870. One of those present at the meeting, Philip Bliss, was inspired to write both the words and music of this song.

Bliss (1838–76) was born in a remote forest area of north Pennsylvania. He had a natural instinct for music and became a close friend and associate of the famous American evangelists Dwight Moody and Ira Sankey. The day after hearing of Sherman's message, Bliss was speaking at a YMCA meeting in Chicago. He walked over to the blackboard and wrote the chorus of this hymn on the blackboard. He had worked out the verses the previous evening and a few days later had the whole song published in sheet form with the biblical text attached: 'That which ye have hold fast till I come' (Rev. 2.25).

'Hold the fort' effectively became the theme song of the evangelistic meetings held in Britain during the 1870s by Moody and Sankey. In his memoirs Sankey recalls the great Baptist preacher C.H. Spurgeon asking him to sing it in his tabernacle in 1879 to accompany a sermon on the army. The chorus could be heard in adjacent streets. At a meeting to mark the end of an earlier Moody and Sankey crusade in London the great philanthropist and evangelical statesman Lord Shaftesbury said, 'If Mr Sankey has done no more than teach the people to sing "Hold the Fort" he has conferred an inestimable blessing on the British Empire.'

Bliss had a particular talent for writing hymns based on topical events. After a shipwreck in Cleveland Harbor, caused by the extinguishing of the lower lights in the lighthouse during a storm, he wrote some verses, long found in the Methodist hymnbook, which begin:

> Brightly beams our Father's mercy
> From his lighthouse evermore;
> But to us He gives the keeping
> Of the lights along the shore.
> Let the lower lights be burning,
> Send a gleam across the wave;
> Some poor fainting, struggling seaman
> You may rescue, you may save.

Among his other hymns which achieved strong popularity in Britain were 'Man of Sorrows! what a name' and 'Whosoever heareth! Shout, shout the sound'. He died tragically at the age of 38 when the train in which he and his wife were returning from spending Christmas in Pennsylvania caught fire. Although he escaped, his wife was trapped in the carriage and in his efforts to save her he was burned to death.

The parodies of this song include a wonderful one for singing if the Sunday lunch is rather late on the table:

> Hold the forks, the knives are coming,
> Plates and dishes, too,
> All the people here are waiting
> For the Irish stew.

Hold the Fort

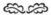

Ho, my comrades! see the signal
Waving in the sky!
Reinforcements now appearing,
Victory is nigh!

> *'Hold the fort, for I am coming',*
> *Jesus signals still,*
> *Wave the answer back to heaven,*
> *'By thy grace we will.'*

2 See the mighty host advancing,
   Satan leading on:
   Mighty men around us falling,
   Courage almost gone!

3 See the glorious banner waving!
   Hear the trumpet blow!
   In our Leader's name we'll triumph
   Over every foe.

4 Fierce and long the battle rages,
   But our help is near:
   Onwards comes our great Commander,
   Cheer, my comrades, cheer!

HOLY, HOLY, HOLY!
LORD GOD ALMIGHTY

The great Victorian Poet Laureate Alfred, Lord Tennyson regarded this as the finest hymn in the English language. It is not difficult to see why. With a fine economy of words, while yet containing an abundance of memorable images and pleasing poetic phrases, it expresses clearly and in adoration the complex Christian doctrine of the Trinity.

It is one of the hymns written by Reginald Heber (1783–1826: see no. 21 for notes on his life) while he was vicar of Hodnet in Staffordshire, for the solemn days, feast-days and ordinary Sundays in the Church of England calendar. 'Holy, Holy, Holy' was written to be sung at Hodnet on Trinity Sunday. It was first published shortly after Heber's death in *A Selection of Psalms and Hymns for the Parish Church of Banbury*.

The hymn is based in part on the passage from Revelation 4.8–11 which forms the Epistle for Trinity Sunday in the Book of Common Prayer and which begins: 'Holy, holy, Lord Almighty, which was, and is, and is to come.' Nowadays, its use is no longer restricted to Trinity Sunday, nor is it always treated as a morning hymn despite the second line of the first verse. In an effort to adapt it to any time of the day, various alterations have been made to that line, among them 'Gratefully adoring, our song shall rise to thee' and 'Morning, noon and night, our song shall rise to thee', but most hymnbooks are happy to stick to the original.

Heber was fastidious in his approach to hymn-writing. He once said, 'I avoid all fulsome, indecorous or erotic language to HIM whom no unclean lips dare approach.' Given this care and sensitivity, it is ironic that, as we have seen, one of his best-known hymns, 'Brightest and best of the sons of the morning' (no. 21) should have caused offence to different generations of hymn-book compilers and been banished from their collections. For very different reasons, his missionary hymn 'From Greenland's icy mountains' has also been dropped from all modern hymnbooks. This, perhaps the most widely used of all his hymns, has happily never faced the possibility of being silenced, although it has suffered the indignity of being parodied. Soldiers in the First World War sang:

> Raining, raining, raining,
> Always bloody well raining.
> Raining in the morning,
> And raining in the night.

> Marching, marching, marching,
> Always bloody well marching;
> Marching all the morning
> And marching all the night.

> Grousing, grousing, grousing
> Always bloody well grousing
> Grousing at the rations,
> And grousing at the pay.

> Marching, marching, marching
> Always bloody well marching,
> When the war is over,
> We'll damn well march no more.

The tune for 'Holy, Holy, Holy', which is singularly well suited to a marching song, was written by the Revd John Bacchus Dykes (1823–76) for the original edition of *Hymns Ancient and Modern* in 1861. It has similarities to the German tune *Wachet auf*, but was probably inspired by the tune Trinity by John Hopkins, to which Heber's hymn was set in 1850. Dykes called his tune Nicaea – it was at the Council of Nicaea in 325 that the doctrine of the Trinity was clearly defined in the face of the Arian heresy.

Holy, Holy, Holy! Lord God Almighty!
Early in the morning our song shall rise to thee:
Holy, Holy, Holy! merciful and mighty!
God in Three Persons, blessèd Trinity!

2 Holy, Holy, Holy! all the saints adore thee,
Casting down their golden crowns around the glassy sea,
Cherubim and Seraphim falling down before thee,
Which wert, and art, and evermore shalt be.

3 Holy, Holy, Holy! though the darkness hide thee,
Though the eye of sinful man thy glory may not see,
Only thou art holy; there is none beside thee,
Perfect in power, in love, and purity.

4 Holy, Holy, Holy! Lord God Almighty!
All thy works shall praise thy name in earth and sky and sea;
Holy, Holy, Holy! merciful and mighty!
God in Three Persons, blessèd Trinity!

HOW SWEET THE NAME
OF JESUS SOUNDS

This is another ever-popular hymn by John Newton (1725–1807: see notes to no. 10). It was first published in the *Olney Hymnbook* of 1779 and is based on the Song of Solomon 1.3: 'Thy name is as ointment poured forth.'

Several changes have been made for doctrinal reasons to the original version printed here. The fourth verse is generally, and surely rightly, omitted. It harps a little too much on sin, reflecting Newton's own strict Calvinistic position. Towards the end of his life he wrote: 'My memory is nearly gone, but I remember two things, that I am a great sinner and Jesus is a great Saviour.' Many hymnbook compilers have also been unhappy about the reference in the first line of verse 5 to Christ as 'husband'. They have felt, quite reasonably, that Christ's bride is the Church as a whole rather than an individual, and that the expression 'husband' is unsuited to congregational use even though it fits with the mood of the Song of Solomon. Various substitutions have been made, the most common being 'brother' which occurs in *Hymns Ancient and Modern*, the *New English Hymnal* and *Hymns for Church and School*.

Thomas Cotterill (on whom see note to no. 46) was unhappy about the somewhat cloying flavour of the hymn's opening line and substituted 'blest' for 'sweet' when he included it in the eighth edition of his *Selection of Psalms and Hymns* in 1819. This alteration has not, however, been followed in any subsequent hymnbooks.

There is another well known evangelical hymn which pursues very much the same theme as Newton's. It is by Frederick Whitfield (1829–1904), vicar of St Mary's, Hastings:

There is a name I love to hear,
I love to sing its worth;
It sounds like music in mine ear,
The sweetest name on earth.
Oh, how I love Jesus,
Oh, how I love Jesus,
Oh, how I love Jesus,
Because he first loved me!

The tune universally used for Newton's hymn is by Alexander Robert Reinagle (1799–1877), organist of St Peter's in the East in Oxford. It first appeared in 1836 in a publication entitled *Psalm Tunes for the Voice and Pianoforte* where it was set to Psalm 118. It is variously called St Peter and Christchurch.

The Name of Jesus

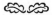

How sweet the name of Jesus sounds
In a believer's ear!
It soothes his sorrows, heals his wounds,
And drives away his fear.

2   It makes the wounded spirit whole,
And calms the troubled breast;
'Tis manna to the hungry soul,
And to the weary rest.

3   Dear name! the rock on which I build,
My shield and hiding-place,
My never-failing treasury filled
With boundless stores of grace.

4   By thee my prayers acceptance gain,
Although with sin defiled;
Satan accuses me in vain,
And I am owned a child.

5   Jesus! my Shepherd, Husband, Friend,
My Prophet, Priest, and King,
My Lord, my Life, my Way, my End,
Accept the praise I bring.

6   Weak is the effort of my heart,
And cold my warmest thought;
But when I see thee as thou art,
I'll praise thee as I ought.

7   Till then I would thy love proclaim
With every fleeting breath;
And may the music of thy name
Refresh my soul in death.

I BIND UNTO MYSELF
TODAY

This beautiful hymn, which is traditionally attributed to St Patrick (372–466), shows very clearly the blending of pagan mythology with Christian teaching in the Celtic Church. It combines the function of incantation, war-song and credal statement. Against 'Satan's spells and wiles' and 'the wizard's evil craft' are invoked not just the power of Christ, the wisdom of God and the 'strong name of the Trinity' but also the forces of nature, such as 'the virtues of the star-lit heaven' and 'the whiteness of the moon at even'. The whole poem is given a tremendous force and unity by the notion of binding, which is so characteristic in Celtic art with its intricate knots and never-ending interlacing patterns.

The original Gaelic poem on which the hymn is based is known as St Patrick's Lorica, or Breastplate. A lorica was a spiritual coat or breastplate which not only charmed away disease or danger but secured a place in heaven for those who wore it day and night. The word came to be applied to spiritual poems such as this one which characteristically had three distinct parts: the invocation of the Trinity and the angels; the enumeration of various parts of the body to be safeguarded; and a list of dangers from which immunity was being sought. The second of these elements is not as clearly marked in this poem as it is, for example, in that other lorica which has been turned into a popular hymn:

> God be in my head and in my understanding:
> God be in my eyes, and in my looking;
> God be in my mouth, and in my speaking;
> God be in my heart, and in my thinking;
> God be at my end, and at my departing.

But it is there in verse 8, where Christ's presence in every part of the body is carefully invoked.

Legend has it that St Patrick composed his lorica shortly after landing in Ireland in 432 to spread the Christian faith there. He is said to have sung it as he made his way to Tara to confront Leogaire, or Leary, the pagan high king of Ireland who was in the midst of one of his regular triennial conventions with his vassal-kings. Patrick and his followers halted at the Hill of Slane near the River Boyne, ten miles from Tara, and lit a great fire to celebrate the eve of the Christian festival of Easter. The high king, who was celebrating a pagan festival, was furious when he saw the Christians' fire in the distance and sent men out to destroy it. However, his soldiers drew back when they got near the flames, fearing that Patrick might cast a spell on them. Seeing the chariots of the king's forces drawn up before him, Patrick recited Psalm 20, with its seventh verse, 'Some trust in chariots, and some in horses, but we will remember the name of the Lord our God', and then launched into his lorica. It is sometimes also known as 'The Deer's Cry' because King Leogaire's men are said to have mistaken Patrick and his followers for deer in the darkness surrounding the fire and to have spared them from the massacre which had been ordered.

Whether or not St Patrick himself wrote the lorica, it is a supreme expression of that sense of the holiness and the wholeness of nature that marks Celtic Christianity, and which is summed up in another statement attributed to him: 'Our God is the God of Heaven and Earth, of sea and river, sun and moon and stars, of the lofty mountain and lowly valley.' The fourth verse has a new relevance for us, in our belatedly ecologically conscious age.

The translation printed here, the best known of several that have been made of St Patrick's Breastplate, is the work of Mrs Cecil Frances Alexander (1818–95, see no. 8 for biographical notes). Erik Routley has described it in his *Panorama of Christian Hymnody*★ as: 'easily her finest piece of hymnic literature... [She] makes of it a credal recitation, entirely appropriate to the ancient rites of baptism, and supremely appropriate to the celebrations of

Holy Saturday, or Easter eve, which was associated in the early church with baptism and confirmation.'

Mrs Alexander made her translation for use on St Patrick's Day in 1889 at the request of Dean H.H. Dickinson of the Chapel Royal at Dublin Castle who was preparing a new and enlarged edition of the *Irish Church Hymnal*. He later recalled:

I wrote to her suggesting that she should fill a gap in our *Irish Church Hymnal* by giving us a metrical version of St Patrick's 'Lorica' and I sent her a carefully collated copy of the best prose translations of it. Within a week she sent me that exquisitely beautiful as well as faithful version which appears in the appendix to our *Church Hymnal*.

The hymn soon found its way into hymnbooks, where it was set to an arrangement of the traditional Irish melody, St Patrick, by Sir Charles Villiers Stanford (1852–1924). This is now universally used for the main part of the hymn, which is often now shortened with the third, sixth and seventh verses here being generally omitted. The eighth verse 'Christ be with me' is sung to one of three traditional Irish melodies: an unnamed tune from Donegal, which Stanford adapted for *Songs of Praise*; Deirdre, which was preferred by the compilers of the *English Hymnal*; or Clonmacnoise, which is found in the *Church Hymnary*.

A translation of St Patrick's Breastplate which is closer to the original in form and words, though less well known than Mrs Alexander's version, was made by Robert Alexander Stewart Macalister (1870–1950) for the revised edition of the *Church Hymnary* in 1927. Macalister came from Dublin, where he held the chair in Celtic Archaeology at University College. His version begins:

> Today I arise
> Invoking the Blessed Trinity,
> Confessing the Blessed Unity,
> Creator of all the things that be.

* Erik Routley, *A Panorama of Christian Hymnody* (Collegeville, MW: The Liturgical Press, 1979).

Another excellent recent translation by Noel O'Donoghue, who taught theology for many years at New College, Edinburgh, begins:

> For my shield this day I call:
> A mighty power:
> The Holy Trinity!
> Affirming threeness,
> Confessing oneness,
> In the making of all
> Through love . . .

This version, which can be found in James Mackey's *An Introduction to Celtic Christianity*,★ has been set to music and recorded by the Scottish harpist and singer, Ellen Wycherley

★ James Mackey, *An Introduction to Celtic Christianity* (Edinburgh: T & T Clark, 1989).

St Patrick's Breastplate

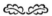

> I bind unto myself today
> The strong name of the Trinity,
> By invocation of the same
> The Three in One and One in Three.

> 2   I bind this day to me for ever
> By power of faith, Christ's incarnation;
> His baptism in Jordan river,
> His death on Cross for my salvation;
> His bursting from the spicèd tomb,
> His riding up the heavenly way,
> His coming at the day of doom
> I bind unto myself today.

3   I bind unto myself the power
Of the great love of Cherubim;
The sweet 'Well done' in judgment hour,
The service of the Seraphim,
Confessors' faith, Apostles' word,
The Patriarchs' prayers, the prophets' scrolls,
All good deeds done unto the Lord
And purity of virgin souls.

4   I bind unto myself today
The virtues of the star-lit heaven,
The glorious sun's life-giving ray,
The whiteness of the moon at even,
The flashing of the lightning free,
The whirling wind's tempestuous shocks,
The stable earth, the deep salt sea
Around the old eternal rocks.

5   I bind unto myself today
The power of God to hold and lead,
His eye to watch, his might to stay,
His ear to hearken to my need.
The wisdom of my God to teach,
His hand to guide, his shield to ward;
The word of God to give me speech,
His heavenly host to be my guard.

6   Against the demon snares of sin,
The vice that gives temptation force,
The natural lusts that war within,
The hostile men that mar my course;
Or few or many, far or nigh,
In every place and in all hours,
Against their fierce hostility
I bind to me those holy powers.

7   Against all Satan's spells and wiles,
Against false words of heresy,
Against the knowledge that defiles,
Against the heart's idolatry,
Against the wizard's evil craft,
Against the death-wound and the burning,
The choking wave, the poisoned shaft,
Protect me, Christ, till thy returning.

8   Christ be with me, Christ within me,
Christ behind me, Christ before me,
Christ beside me, Christ to win me,
Christ to comfort and restore me.
Christ beneath me, Christ above me,
Christ in quiet, Christ in danger,
Christ in hearts of all that love me,
Christ in mouth of friend and stranger.

9   I bind unto myself the name,
The strong name of the Trinity,
By invocation of the same,
The Three in One and One in Three.
Of whom all nature hath creation,
Eternal Father, Spirit, Word:
Praise to the Lord of my salvation,
Salvation is of Christ the Lord.

I DANCED IN THE
MORNING

Of the thousands of spiritual songs and choruses which have been written in the last 50 years few have been as widely taken up and sung in churches and schools as this infectiously joyful and catchy hymn by Sydney Carter. I call it a hymn, for so it has effectively become through its use in services of worship by many different denominations. The author himself more properly describes it as a carol, 'a dancing kind of song, the life of which is in the dance as much as in the verbal statement'.

Sydney Carter (1915–2004) was born in Camden Town, London, and educated at Christ's Hospital and Balliol College, Oxford. He became, briefly, a schoolmaster, and during the Second World War served in the Friends' Ambulance Unit. (He attributed his later career as a folksong writer and performer, which he combined with teaching and lecturing, to the two years that he spent in Greece with the unit during the war.) A great hymn-lover, he once told me that his own favourites included 'Morning has broken', 'Be thou my vision' and 'Jerusalem'. He also recalled singing Peter Abelard's 'O quanta qualia' in Latin in Balliol College chapel, 'the most uncomfortable place to kneel in that I know'.

'Lord of the Dance' was written in 1963, in the early days of the folk-song revival in Britain. Many of the other songs which Carter wrote at this time had a radical social and political message, and to some extent this song is a protest against the immobility and stuffiness of traditional church services. But this one has a much more positive message as well. In his book *Green Print for Song*★ he wrote:

★ Sydney Carter, *Green Print for Song* (London: Stainer & Bell, 1974).

Scriptures and creeds may come to seem incredible, but faith will still go dancing on. I see Christ as the incarnation of that piper who is calling us. He dances that shape and pattern which is at the heart of our reality. By Christ I mean not only Jesus: in other times and places, other planets, there may be other Lords of the Dance. But Jesus is the one I know first and best. I sing of the dancing pattern in the life and words of Jesus.

In portraying Christ as the 'Lord of the Dance', Carter was, in fact, returning to a strong theme in popular medieval theology, expressed in the carol 'Tomorrow shall be my dancing day', in which Christ is represented as coming into the world 'to call my true love to my dance'. More directly, he was influenced by the Shaker movement of the eighteenth century. The Shakers, who began as a Quaker group in north-west England and then moved to America in 1774, expressed their joyful assurance of salvation and belief in the imminence of Christ's second coming by singing and dancing. Carter used the tune of this Shaker song, 'Simple Gifts', for his own carol:

> 'Tis the gift to be simple, 'tis the gift to be free,
> 'tis the gift to come down where we ought to be,
> And when we find ourselves in the place just right
> 'Twill be in the valley of love and delight.

> When true simplicity is gained
> To bow and to bend we shan't be ashamed;
> To turn, turn, will be our delight
> Till by turning, turning we come round right.

Although they have not achieved the same popularity as 'Lord of the Dance', some of Sydney Carter's other spiritual songs appear in contemporary hymnbooks. Perhaps the best known are 'When I needed a neighbour', 'The Devil wore a crucifix', 'It was on a Friday morning' and one of my own personal favourites, 'One more step along the world I go.'

Lord of the Dance

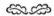

I danced in the morning
When the world was begun,
And I danced in the moon
And the stars and the sun,
And I came down from heaven
And I danced on the earth;
At Bethlehem
I had my birth:

Dance, then, wherever you may be;
I am the Lord of the Dance, said he,
And I'll lead you all, wherever you may be,
And I'll lead you all in the dance, said he.

2   I danced for the scribe
And the pharisee,
But they would not dance
And they wouldn't follow me;
I danced for the fishermen,
For James and John;
They came with me
And the dance went on:

3   I danced on the Sabbath
And I cured the lame:
The holy people
Said it was a shame.
They whipped and they stripped
And they hung me high,
And they left me there
On a cross to die:

4   I danced on a Friday
When the sky turned black;
It's hard to dance
With the devil on your back.
They buried my body
And they thought I'd gone;
But I am the dance
And I still go on:

5   They cut me down
And I leapt up high;
I am the life
That'll never, never die;
I'll live in you
If you'll live in me:
I am the Lord
Of the Dance, said he:

Sydney Carter. Copyright © 1963 Stainer & Bell Ltd., London, England.

I HEARD THE VOICE OF
JESUS SAY

This hymn was written by Horatius Bonar (1808–89), often described as the prince of Scottish hymn-writers, during his ministry in Kelso in the Scottish Borders. It has become easily the most popular of Bonar's many hymns and is found in numerous hymnals of all denominations.

Bonar was born in Edinburgh, where his father was a solicitor of excise. Educated at the Edinburgh High School and Edinburgh University, he served as a missionary assistant at St James's Church, Leith, and in 1837 was ordained and inducted as minister of the North Parish, Kelso. He left the Church of Scotland in the Disruption of 1843 and remained in Kelso as a minister of the Free Church of Scotland. In 1866 he was called to Chalmers Memorial Free Church in Edinburgh, and in 1883 he served as moderator of the Free Church General Assembly.

Altogether, Bonar wrote more than 600 hymns. They include 'Light of the world, for ever, ever shining', 'Fill thou, my life, O Lord my God' and the communion hymn, 'Here, O my Lord, I see thee face to face'. His work is characterized by a strong devotional warmth, a tendency towards pre-millenarianism (he was strongly influenced by Edward Irving) and a characteristically Victorian emphasis on the brevity of human life and the need for work and activism, evident in such hymns as 'Go labour on', 'Work, for the time is flying' and 'Make haste, O man, to live'. Although his hymns were widely taken up during his lifetime, he does not seem to have attached great importance to them and did not seek to polish or improve them.

Bonar gave significant endorsement to the Moody and Sankey crusades in Scotland and helped the reception of gospel songs and organs into Scottish churches. The first gospel song tune that Ira Sankey ever wrote was for Bonar's 'Yet there is room'.

Ironically, Bonar's hymns were not sung in the Edinburgh church in which he ministered. Within the Free Church of Scotland the question of whether to permit hymn-singing was left to the discretion of individual kirk sessions. In Chalmers Memorial, only metrical psalms were allowed in worship.

'I heard the voice of Jesus say' was first published in Bonar's *Hymns, Original and Selected* in 1846, and subsequently appeared in the first series of his *Hymns of Faith and Hope* in 1857, where it was given the title 'The Voice from Galilee'. The first verse is based on Jesus's words as recorded in Matthew 11.28–31, the second on his encounter with the Samaritan woman by the well as described in John 4.10–14 and the third on his famous saying 'I am the light of the world' (Jn 8.12). The hymn is very direct and personal, and offers a great sense of consolation and assurance to the weary soul. Bonar originally wrote 'the living water freely take' for the third line of the second verse, which he subsequently changed to 'the living water; thirsty one' and 'Look unto me, thy day shall break, / And all thy path be bright' for the third and fourth lines of the third verse, which later became 'Look unto me, thy morn shall rise, / And all thy day be bright'.

This hymn is sung to two very different tunes. John Bacchus Dykes's *Vox dilecti* was written specifically for it and first appeared in the 1868 appendix to *Hymns Ancient and Modern*. It has the great merit of changing key and mode half-way through each verse, so accentuating the contrast between Jesus's words and the human response to them. For the 1906 *English Hymnal* Vaughan Williams replaced Dykes's tune with his own arrangement of an old English folk-tune which he called Kingsfold. It is more flowing and perhaps also more consoling in its overall effect, but maybe a little too easy on the ear than the more angular *Vox dilecti* which, like so many of the best Victorian hymn tunes, is superbly crafted to fit the mood of the words for which it was written.

I heard the voice of Jesus say:
'Come unto me and rest;
Lay down, thou weary one, lay down
Thy head upon my breast.'
I came to Jesus as I was,
Weary and worn and sad,
I found in him a resting-place,
And he has made me glad.

2   I heard the voice of Jesus say:
'Behold, I freely give
 The living water; thirsty one,
Stoop down and drink and live.'
I came to Jesus, and I drank
Of that life-giving stream;
My thirst was quenched, my soul revived,
And now I live in him.

3   I heard the voice of Jesus say:
'I am this dark world's Light;
Look unto me, thy morn shall rise,
And all thy day be bright.'
I looked to Jesus, and I found
In him my star, my sun;
And in that light of life I'll walk,
Till travelling days are done.

I, THE LORD OF SEA AND
SKY

This relatively recent North American composition has understandably become one of the most popular hymns and worship-
songs in Britain. It came top of a poll of favourite hymns
conducted in 2004 among readers of the Catholic journal *The
Tablet* and seventeenth in the 2002 *Songs of Praise* Top Twenty.
Its author, Daniel Schutte, intended it to be sung as a dialogue
between a solo voice posing God's question 'Whom shall I send'
and a congregation responding with 'Here I am, Lord', but the
whole thing is now generally treated as a congregational hymn.

Dan Schutte was born in 1947. His grandparents were both
accomplished musicians, and as a boy he often sat at the piano
making up melodies. It was while studying for the Roman
Catholic priesthood at a Jesuit seminary that he discovered the
connection between music and worship and began his prolific
career as a composer of liturgical music, worship songs and
hymns. He has said that he began writing music for worship
because 'it stirs my soul and speaks to my faith'. He is now
Composer in Residence at the University of San Francisco and
Director of Music for the Office of University Ministries.

Schutte wrote 'I, the Lord of sea and sky' during a fifteen-year
collaboration with four fellow musicians: Bob Dufford, John
Foley, Tim Manion and Roc O'Connor, who became
collectively known as the St Louis Jesuits. Their output,
deliberately designed to be played by contemporary instrumen-
talists and sung by untrained voices in the context of the
celebration of the Mass, was prolific and widely taken up by
Roman Catholic churches in both North America and the
United Kingdom. Schutte's other most popular songs include
'Though the mountains may fall', 'Lord, you are near' and 'City
of God'.

Like many contemporary Christian song-writers, Schutte writes both words and music, and it is to his own tune that 'I, the Lord of sea and sky' is sung.

Here I Am, Lord

I, the Lord of sea and sky,
I have heard my people cry.
All who dwell in dark and sin
My hand will save.
I, who made the stars of night,
I will make their darkness bright.
Who will bear my light to them?
Whom shall I send?
> *Here I am, Lord. Is it I, Lord?*
> *I have heard you calling in the night.*
> *I will go, Lord, if you lead me.*
> *I will hold your people in my heart.*

2   I, the Lord of snow and rain,
I have borne my people's pain.
I have wept for love of them.
They turn away.
I will break their hearts of stone,
Give them hearts for love alone.
I will speak my word to them.
Whom shall I send?

3   I, the Lord of wind and flame,
I will tend the poor and lame.
I will set a feast for them.
My hand will save.
Finest bread I will provide
Till their hearts be satisfied.
I will give my life to them.
Whom shall I send?

58

I VOW TO THEE, MY COUNTRY

This is the hymn which film directors invariably turn to when they want to evoke the atmosphere of a vanished England ruled by patriotic public school values. It tends to be heard in the distance over shots of playing fields on which flannelled fools 'play up, play up and play the game'. It also tends to cause considerable controversy in the contemporary church. When Stephen Lowe, the suffragan bishop of Hulme, described it as 'un-Christian' in 2004, he received a deluge of hate mail.

The circumstances in which it was written could have come straight out of the pages of the *Boys' Own Paper*. Its author, Cecil Spring-Rice (1859–1918), was a distinguished member of the British diplomatic corps. After beginning his career as a clerk in the Foreign Office, he served in Teheran, Cairo and Petrograd. In 1908 he went to Stockholm as Minister to Sweden. While there he wrote a poem '*Urbs Dei*' which explored the theme that a Christian is a citizen of two countries, his own and the heavenly kingdom.

In 1912 Spring-Rice was sent as ambassador to Washington. While there he did much to coax the USA out of its neutrality in the First World War. He was naturally somewhat peeved when, following President Woodrow Wilson's decision to enter the war against Germany, he was recalled from Washington at the end of 1917 and replaced by a member of the war cabinet. On the eve of his departure, on 12 January 1918, he recast the poem that he had written in Stockholm. The second verse about the heavenly kingdom he kept much as it was, but the first he altered significantly. In his original poem it had been belligerently patriotic, glorifying war. The experience of the past four years had much altered Spring-Rice's attitudes. He sent the verses to an American friend with an accompanying note that read, 'The greatest object of all – at the most terrific cost and the most tremendous sacrifice – will, I hope, at last be permanently established, Peace.'

The phrase 'The love that asks no question' has often been criticized for advocating a blind, uncritical, 'my country, right or wrong' patriotism. But that is not how Spring-Rice meant it. He was thinking rather in terms of the Christian notion of sacrifice as he pointed out in a speech in Ottawa a few days after completing the revision of his poem: 'The Cross is a sign of patience under suffering, but not patience under wrong. The Cross is the banner under which we fight – the Cross of St George, the Cross of St Andrew, the Cross of St Patrick; different in form, in colour, in history, yes, but the same spirit, the spirit of sacrifice.'

Cecil Spring Rice died suddenly, just a month after rewriting his hymn and while he was still in Ottawa on the first leg of his journey home to Britain. He was 58. His daughter had earlier been sent to St Paul's Girls' School in London, where she was in the same class as Imogen Holst, daughter of the director of music at the school, Gustav Holst (1874–1934). It was almost certainly through this connection that Holst learned of Spring-Rice's poem and came to set it to the melody which he had written early in 1917 for the 'Jupiter' movement of his orchestral suite *The Planets*. He named the hymn-tune Thaxted after the Essex village where he had a cottage and where he had written much of the suite.

'I vow to thee, my country' first appeared in a hymnbook, *Songs of Praise*, in 1925. In July 1981 it was chosen by Lady Diana Spencer for her marriage to the Prince of Wales at St Paul's Cathedral, and it was also sung at her funeral service in Westminster Abbey in September 1997. More recently, the socialist singer-songwriter Billy Bragg and the Labour MP for Battersea, Martin Linton, have collaborated on a new socialist version. Its first verse runs as follows:

We vow to build a country
Where all can live in health,
Where no child need live in poverty,
Where we will share our wealth;
Where we fill the true potential
Of each and every one
And we achieve more together
Than we achieve alone.

The Two Fatherlands

I vow to thee, my country – all earthly things above –
Entire and whole and perfect, the service of my love:
The love that asks no question, the love that stands the test,
That lays upon the altar the dearest and the best;
The love that never falters, the love that pays the price,
The love that makes undaunted the final sacrifice.

2 And there's another country, I've heard of long ago,
Most dear to them that love her, most great to them that know;
We may not count her armies, we may not see her King;
Her fortress is a faithful heart, her pride is suffering;
And soul by soul and silently her shining bounds increase,
And her ways are ways of gentleness and all her paths are Peace.

IMMORTAL, INVISIBLE,
GOD ONLY WISE

A particular favourite of the Queen, this hymn was sung, together with 'Praise my soul the King of Heaven' and 'Now thank we all our God', at the service at the Chapel Royal, Windsor Castle, on 21 April 1986 to mark Her Majesty's 60th birthday. Surprisingly, it is only comparatively recently that it has gained wide popularity. It did not, for example, appear in *Hymns Ancient and Modern* until 1950.

Its author, Walter Chalmers Smith (1824–1908), was born in Aberdeen and educated at the grammar school and university in that city and at New College, Edinburgh. He was ordained in 1850 to the charge of the Scottish Church in Chadwell Street, Islington, north London, and was subsequently minister of Free Church congregations in Milnathort, Glasgow and Edinburgh. The culmination of his career was the moderatorship of the Free Church of Scotland in 1893.

Smith wrote several hymns which appeared in his *Hymns of Christ and the Christian Life* in 1876. It was in that collection that 'Immortal, invisible' first appeared. The hymn is based on 1 Timothy 1.17: 'Now unto the King eternal, immortal, invisible, the only wise God, be honour and glory for ever and ever.' The reference to 'the Ancient of Days' in the third line of the first verse comes from Daniel 7.9, while the third line of verse 2 echoes Psalm 36.6: 'Thy righteousness is like the great mountains.' The last line of the penultimate verse is based on 2 Corinthians 3.15–16: 'Even unto this day, when Moses is read, the veil is upon their heart. Nevertheless when it shall turn to the Lord, the veil shall be taken away.'

In 1884 Garrett Horder included Smith's hymn in his *Congregational Hymns*, omitting the last two lines of verses 4 and 5 to give a new hybrid final verse:

Great Father of Glory, pure Father of Light,
Thine angels adore thee, all veiling their sight;
All laud we would render: O help us to see
'Tis only the splendour of light hideth thee.

It is Horder's version of the hymn which is found in all modern hymnbooks.

The majestic tune, St Denio or Joanna, is based on a Welsh folk-song, *Can Mlynedd i'nawr*. It first appeared as a hymn-tune in a Welsh collection published in 1839.

God, All in All

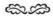

Immortal, invisible, God only wise,
In light inaccessible hid from our eyes,
Most blessèd, most glorious, the Ancient of Days,
Almighty, victorious, thy great name we praise.

2 Unresting, unhasting, and silent as light,
Nor wanting, nor wasting, thou rulest in might –
Thy justice like mountains high-soaring above
Thy clouds which are fountains of goodness and love.

3 To all life thou givest, to both great and small;
In all life thou livest, the true life of all;
We blossom and flourish as leaves on the tree,
And wither and perish; but naught changeth thee.

4 Great Father of Glory, pure Father of Light,
Thine angels adore thee, all veiling their sight;
But of all thy rich graces this grace, Lord, impart –
Take the veil from our faces, the vile from our heart.

5 All laud we would render; O help us to see
'Tis only the splendour of light hideth thee,
And so let thy glory, almighty, impart,
Through Christ in his story, thy Christ to the heart.

JERUSALEM THE GOLDEN

This sweet, perhaps too sweet, evocation of the joys of the heavenly city of Zion comes somewhat unexpectedly from a satirical medieval poem which was largely concerned with lampooning the corrupt state of the Church, and Christendom in general in the twelfth century.

'*De contemptu mundi*', or '*Hora novissima*' as it is also sometimes known from its opening line, '*Hora novissima, tempora pessima sunt: vigilemus!*', was the work of St Bernard of Cluny (born c. 1100). Although both his parents were English, Bernard was born and grew up in Morlaix in Brittany and spent most of his life as a monk in the great abbey at Cluny. He dedicated his poem, which was written around 1140, to the abbot, Peter the Venerable.

Like so many other medieval lyrics which have found their way into the hymnbooks, we owe 'Jerusalem the golden' to J.M. Neale (1818–66: see no. 22 for biographical details). After reading all 2,966 lines of St Bernard's poem in the original Latin, Neale wrote: 'The greater part is a bitter satire on the fearful corruptions of the age. But as a contrast to the misery and pollution of the earth, the poem opens with a description of the peace and glory of heaven, of such rare beauty as not easily to be matched by any medieval composition on the same theme.'

Neale first translated some of the verses of St Bernard's poem in 1849. Nine years later he published *The Rhythm of Bernard de Morlaix, Monk of Cluny, on the Celestial Country*, a translation of 218 lines from the *Hora novissima*. His translation of sixteen verses from near the beginning of the poem, which portray the glories of heaven as a contrast to the evils of the world, has yielded four separate hymns, 'Jerusalem the golden', 'Brief life is here our portion', 'The world is very evil' and 'For thee, O dear, dear country'. 'Jerusalem the golden', translated from verses which began '*Urbs Sion aurea*' has been by far the most popular.

The fourth verse was substantially altered in 1860 by the compilers of *Hymns Ancient and Modern*. Their revision has been adopted in many modern hymnbooks, though not in the *New English Hymnal*. It is certainly easier to sing than Neale's original, but loses much of its force and assurance. It reads:

> O sweet and blessed country,
> The home of God's elect!
> O sweet and blessed country
> That eager hearts expect!
> Jesu, in mercy bring us
> To that dear land of rest;
> Who art, with God the Father
> And spirit ever blest.

The majestic melody Aurelia which Samuel Sebastian Wesley wrote for this hymn is seldom, if ever, used for it now (see note to no. 124). The preferred tune, known variously as Ewing, Argyle, Bernard or St Bede's, was written in 1853 by Lieutenant-Colonel Alexander Ewing (1830–95). for another of Neale's hymns derived from *De contemptu mundi*, 'For thee, O dear, dear country'. Ewing, who seems never to have written a note of music apart from this tune, read law at Aberdeen University and subsequently went into the army, serving with distinction in the Crimean War and in China with General Gordon. His cousin, who bore the same name, and was Bishop of Argyll and the Isles in the Scottish Episcopal Church, was left to negotiate with hymnal editors about the tune's use during the composer's absence on active service abroad. He objected strongly when it was assigned to 'Jerusalem the Golden' in the 1861 edition of *Hymns Ancient and Modern*, and complained to the editor, Sir Henry Baker, that the tune did not suit the words, being 'pathetic, not triumphant'. Despite these protests, however, Ewing's melody has remained firmly wedded to Neale's hymn ever since.

Urbs Sion aurea

Jerusalem the golden,
With milk and honey blessed,
Beneath thy contemplation
Sink heart and voice oppressed.
I know not, O I know not
What joys await us there,
What radiancy of glory,
What light beyond compare.

2   They stand, those halls of Zion,
Conjubilant with song,
And bright with many an angel,
And all the martyr throng;
The Prince is ever in them,
The daylight is serene:
The pastures of the blessèd
Are decked in glorious sheen.

3   There is the throne of David,
And there, from care released,
The shout of them that triumph,
The song of them that feast;
And they who, with their Leader,
Have conquered in the fight,
For ever and for ever
Are clad in robes of white.

4   O sweet and blessed country,
Shall I ever see thy face?
O sweet and blessed country,
Shall I ever win thy grace?
Exult, O dust and ashes,
The Lord shall be thy part:
His only his for ever
Thou shalt be, and thou art.

JESU, LOVER OF MY SOUL

There are several different accounts of the circumstances which prompted Charles Wesley (1707–88) to write this powerful appeal for the Saviour's protection. One story has it that he was moved by a narrow escape from death during a storm while crossing the Atlantic, another that he was sitting at his desk when a small bird, which was being pursued by a hawk, flew in through the open window. The safety of the bird in his study supposedly inspired him to write of the safety to be found in Christ's haven.

In his book *Sacred Songs and Solos*, Ira Sankey maintains that Wesley wrote the hymn while on an open-air preaching tour in County Down, Ireland. After being attacked by a gang who disliked his doctrines he sought refuge in a farmhouse. When the mob arrived at the door he escaped through a rear window and hid under a hedge. According to Sankey, it was in that hiding-place, with the cries of his pursuers in his ears, that he wrote the hymn.

All three stories are probably apocryphal, but whatever the events that inspired it, 'Jesu, lover of my soul', which was written around 1740, is undoubtedly one of Wesley's greatest hymns. Curiously, his brother John omitted it from the Methodist collection of 1780. It has not been without its critics. The great Liberal statesman W.E. Gladstone commented: 'It has no unity, no cohesion, no procession and no special force.' He took particular exception to the second line, maintaining that the familiarity of a hymn ought not to go beyond that of Scripture. 'St John undoubtedly lay on the bosom of his Lord. But he alone; and we are not all St Johns.' Others have objected to the notion of grace conveyed by the second line of the last verse. *Hymns Ancient and Modern* substitutes 'Grace to cleanse from every sin' and also changes 'nearer' to 'gathering' in the third line of the first verse. The third verse is omitted in all modern hymnbooks.

But if the hymn has had its detractors, it has also had many admirers. Henry Ward Beecher, the great nineteenth-century American theologian, said:

I would rather have written that hymn than to have the fame of all the kings that ever sat upon the earth ... It will go on singing until the trump brings forth the angel band; and then I think it will mount up on some lip to the very presence of God.

Dr George Duffield, the author of 'Stand up, stand up for Jesus' (no. 117), described it as 'the hymn of the ages'. Ira Sankey, who recalls that it was sung as the body of his fellow-evangelist Dwight Moody was lowered into the grave, tells a moving story about an incident in the American Civil War. A Confederate soldier had aimed his rifle and was about to shoot through the heart a Unionist sentry when he was stopped short by hearing his intended victim singing the lines 'Cover my defenceless head, with the shadow of thy wing.' Nearly 30 years later the Confederate veteran recognized the voice of the man whose life he had spared singing the same hymn on an excursion steamer on the Potomac River. He went up and told him how and why his life had been spared.

At first Wesley's hymn was sung to Hotham by M. Madan, and later to Hollingside by J.B. Dykes (1828–76) to which it is still set in some hymnals. But now it is almost invariably sung to the haunting melody in the minor key by Joseph Parry (1841–1903) entitled Aberystwyth. Parry, who came from Merthyr Tydfil was an ironmaster turned professional musician. He wrote one hymn tune every Sunday for a number of years, Aberystwyth being composed in the seaside town of that name in 1879.

In Temptation

Jesu, lover of my soul,
Let me to thy bosom fly,
While the nearer waters roll,
While the tempest still is high;
Hide me, O my Saviour, hide,
Till the storm of life is past;
Safe into the haven guide,
O receive my soul at last.

2 Other refuge have I none,
Hangs my helpless soul on thee;
Leave, ah! leave me not alone,
Still support and comfort me:
All my trust on thee is stayed,
All my help from thee I bring;
Cover my defenceless head
With the shadow of thy wing.

3 Wilt thou not regard my call?
Wilt thou not accept my prayer?
Lo! I sink, I faint, I fall!
Lo, on thee I cast my care!
Reach me out thy gracious hand!
While I of thy strength receive,
Hoping against hope I stand,
Dying, and behold I live.

4 Thou, O Christ, art all I want;
More than all in thee I find;
Raise the fallen, cheer the faint,
Heal the sick, and lead the blind.
Just and holy is thy name;
I am all unrighteousness:
False and full of sin I am;
Thou art full of truth and grace.

5   Plenteous grace with thee is found,
    Grace to cover all my sin;
    Let the healing streams abound,
    Make and keep me pure within:
    Thou of life the fountain art;
    Freely let me take of thee;
    Spring thou up within my heart,
    Rise to all eternity.

JESUS BIDS US SHINE

This classic Victorian children's hymn still finds a place in several modern hymn-books despite being dismissed by some as a dated piece of sentimental piety.

It is the work of Miss Susan Warner (1819–85), who was born and grew up in New York. Her father was, in the words of the *Companion to the Church Hymnary*, 'a lawyer of high character who fell into underserved misfortune'. In order to help the meagre family fortunes, Susan and her younger sister Anna, who were both deeply religious, sought to earn money by story-writing and became the chief family breadwinners. Susan's first book, *The Wide, Wide World*, published in 1850 under the pseudonym of Elizabeth Wetherell, was second only to *Uncle Tom's Cabin* in popularity among mid-nineteenth-century American novels. She wrote numerous other novels, all with an improving flavour, and a large number of books based on stories in the Bible.

Despite the apparent crash in their father's fortunes, Susan and Anna Warner lived for most of their lives in a large mansion on Constitution Island in the Hudson River. Every Sunday afternoon cadets from the nearby West Point Military Academy were rowed over to the island by a servant to take part in Bible classes run by the Warner sisters which were followed by tea and gingerbread. Susan was subsequently buried at West Point.

'Jesus bids us shine' first appeared anonymously in a book called *The Little Corporal* published in Chicago in 1868, and went on to achieve enormous popularity on both sides of the Atlantic. Like her sister Anna's equally popular 'Jesus loves me! this I know' (no. 66), Susan Warner's hymn has tended to come under attack in recent years for its simplistic piety and sentimentalism. But it still seems to me to be a valid restatement in language that all can understand of Christ's enormously challenging and difficult command to the crowd who had flocked to hear the Sermon on the Mount: 'Let your light so shine before men that they may see your good works and give glory to your Father who is in Heaven' (Mt. 5.16). The idea of 'you in your small corner and I in mine' is admittedly potentially misleading in its individualistic implications – as the third verse of the hymn reminds us, shining our lights should be a corporate rather than just an individual activity. But overall I find little with which to quarrel in the message of this hymn. Indeed, it strikes me that the comparison of the light which Christ asks us to shine to a candle is singularly apt. Unlike the predictable beam of an electric light, a candle can falter and flicker – just as we do in our attempts to follow the Christian way. It casts shadows and is not of a uniform brightness. But its light is warm and comforting, not harsh and glaring like that of a fluorescent tube.

The tune Lumetto to which this hymn is always sung was written specially for it by David Evans (1874–1948). Born in Resolven in Wales, and also known as Edward Arthur, he wrote a number of hymn-tunes, of which at least one other, *Lucerna laudoniae*, is still used today (see note to no. 36).

Jesus bids us shine
With a pure, clear light,
Like a little candle
Burning in the night.
In this world is darkness;
So let us shine.
You in your small corner,
And I in mine.

2   Jesus bids us shine,
First of all for Him;
Well He sees and knows it,
If our light grows dim:
He looks down from heaven
To see us shine,
You in your small corner,
And I in mine.

3   Jesus bids us shine,
Then, for all around;
Many kinds of darkness
In the world are found –
Sin, and want, and sorrow;
So we must shine,
You in your small corner,
And I in mine.

63

JESUS CALLS US: O'ER
THE TUMULT

This is another hymn from the prolific pen of Mrs Cecil Frances Alexander (1823–95). It was written for St Andrew's Day (30 November) and is based on the story of Christ's calling of his first disciples in Matthew 4.18–20:

As Jesus walked by the Sea of Galilee, he saw two brothers, Simon who is called Peter and Andrew his brother, casting a net into the sea, for they were fishermen. And he said to them, 'Follow me and I will make you fishers of men.' Immediately they left their nets and followed him.

The message of this simple and moving hymn is essentially the same as that of the second verse of 'Dear Lord and Father of mankind' (no. 31) which tells of the same episode in the Gospels:

> In simple trust like theirs who heard,
> Beside the Syrian sea,
> The gracious calling of the Lord,
> Let us, like them, without a word
> Rise up and follow thee.

'Jesus calls us: o'er the tumult' first appeared in 1852 in *Hymns for Public Worship*, published by the Society for the Propagation of Christian Knowledge. Mrs Alexander revised the hymn slightly in 1881, changing the third line of the first verse to 'Day by day his voice is sounding' and the third line of the fifth verse to 'Give our hearts to thy obedience'. Most modern hymnbooks print this revised version and some have other minor variations in the text.

The first line of the second verse is sometimes changed to 'As of old apostles heard it' to make the hymn suitable for singing at all times of the year, and not just on St Andrew's Day. But this seems to me an unnecessary alteration. Although 'Jesus calls us' has a special association with St Andrew's Day, and therefore a special significance for Scots, it is really quite suitable as it stands for use at any time of the year. Its theme of the universality and insistence of Christ's call is certainly not restricted in its applicability to 30 November.

The most appropriate tune for this hymn is surely St Andrew, which was composed by Edward Henry Thorne (1834–1916) for *Hymns Ancient and Modern* in 1875. Thorne was educated at St George's Chapel, Windsor, under Sir George Elvey, the composer of *Diademata* (see no. 30). He became assistant organist to Elvey at the remarkably early age of 12, and went on to serve as organist at a number of parish churches in London and the south of England and also at Chichester Cathedral. He wrote a large amount of music for the organ as well as anthems and part-songs. Other tunes to which 'Jesus calls us' is sometimes set are Wraysbury by Edward John Hopkins (1818–1901), organist of the Temple Church, and *Omni die* from Corner's *Gesangbuch* of 1631.

Jesus calls us: o'er the tumult
Of our life's wild restless sea
Day by day his sweet voice soundeth,
Saying, 'Christian, follow me':

2   As of old Saint Andrew heard it
    By the Galilean lake,
    Turned from home and toil and kindred,
    Leaving all for his dear sake.

3   Jesus calls us from the worship
    Of the vain world's golden store,
    From each idol that would keep us,
    Saying, 'Christian, love me more.'

4   In our joys and in our sorrows,
    Days of toil and hours of ease,
    Still he calls, in cares and pleasures,
    'Christian, love me more than these.'

5   Jesus calls us: by thy mercies,
    Saviour, may we hear thy call,
    Give our hearts to thine obedience,
    Serve and love thee best of all.

JESUS CHRIST IS RISEN
TODAY

This, perhaps the most popular and commonly sung of all Easter hymns, has undergone a number of very radical changes. The version which is sung today bears little resemblance to the original English text printed here which dates from the early eighteenth century.

The hymn is based on a fourteenth-century Latin hymn, '*Surrexit Christus hodie*', by an unknown Bohemian author. It first appeared in English in a fairly literal translation in a collection of divine songs and hymns published in 1708 under the title *Lyra Davidica*.

The modern form of the hymn dates from 1749 when the following version appeared in Arnold's *Compleat Psalmodist*:

> Jesus Christ is risen today. Hallelujah.
> Our triumphal holy day;
> Who did once, upon the Cross,
> Suffer to redeem our loss.

> Hymns of praise then let us sing
> Unto Christ our heavenly King,
> Who endured the Cross and grave,
> Sinners to redeem and save.

> But the pain that he endured
> Our salvation has procured;
> Now above the sky he's King,
> While the Angels ever sing.

As can be seen, only the first verse of the above bears any relation to the original. The second and third verses in fact depart completely from the Latin text. A supplement to Tate and Brady's *New Version of the Psalms* published in 1816 included the hymn in virtually the same form that it had appeared in 1749. Three small changes were made – 'then' was inserted into the middle of the first line of the second verse to make it scan better, the first line of the third verse was changed to 'But the pains which he endured', and the first word of the last line was changed to 'where'.

Most modern hymnbooks use the 1816 version of the hymn. Some change 'pain' to 'anguish' in the first line of the third verse and the third line of this verse is usually rendered nowadays as 'Now beyond our sight he's king', presumably to avoid the suggestion that heaven is 'up there' in the sky. Charles Wesley added a doxology which is found in some hymnbooks:

> Sing we to our God above
> Praise eternal as His love;
> Praise Him, all ye heavenly host,
> Father, Son, and Holy Ghost.

Amidst all this change, it is at least reassuring to know that the tune (Salisbury or Easter hymn) to which the hymn is always sung has been the same since its first appearance in the *Lyra Davidica*. Its authorship is unknown.

Surrexit Christus hodie

 Jesus Christ is risen today, Halle-Halle-lujah.
Our triumphant holy day!
Who so lately on the cross
Suffer'd to redeem our loss;

2   Haste ye females from your fright,
Take to Galilee your flight.
To His sad disciples say
Jesus Christ is risen today.

3   In our Paschal joy and feast
Let our Lord of Life be blest
Let the Holy Trine be praised
And thankful hearts to Heaven be raised.

JESUS LIVES!

❧❧❧ ✤ ❧❧❧

This joyful and confident Easter hymn is based on Jesus's words in John 14.19: 'Because I live, you shall live also.' It comes from a German original by Christian Furchtegott Gellert (1715–69).

The son of a country clergymen, Gellert was born in Saxony and studied at Meissen and Leipzig with the intention of going into the Lutheran ministry. But feeling too shy to be a preacher, he instead became a lecturer in poetry and eloquence at Leipzig University and later Professor of Philosophy there. He numbered among his pupils Goethe and Lessing and was a much-loved tutor and lecturer. He wrote and published 54 hymns as well as volumes of poems, essays, tales and fables. His remains were buried in a vault in St John's Church, Leipzig, alongside the tomb of J.S. Bach.

Gellert's hymn, '*Jesus lebt, mit Ihm auch ich*', first appeared in a collection of spiritual odes and songs published in Leipzig in 1757. It was translated into English by Frances Elizabeth Cox (1812–97) and first appeared in the form printed here in her *Sacred Hymns from the German* (1841), headed by the text: 'He that raised up Christ from the dead shall also quicken your mortal bodies' (Rom. 8.11). Frances Cox, who came from Oxford, translated a total of 56 hymns from German into English which were published in two volumes.

In 1851 the hymn was recast, with the author's approval, in a shorter, more corporate and less individualistic form for inclusion in Rorison's *Hymns and Anthems*. It is this revised version which is sung now. It is usually sung to the tune St Albinus which was written by Henry John Gauntlett (1805–76) in 1852 for another Easter hymn, 'Angels to our Jubilee', and goes as follows:

Jesus lives! thy terrors now
Can, O death, no more appal us;
Jesus lives! by this we know
Thou, O grave, canst not enthrall us. *Allelulia!*

2   Jesus lives! henceforth is death
But the gate of life immortal;
This shall calm our trembling breath,
When we pass its gloomy portal.

3   Jesus lives! for us He died;
Then, alone to Jesus living,
Pure in heart may we abide,
Glory to our Saviour giving.

4   Jesus lives! my heart knows well
Naught from us His Love shall sever;
Life, nor death, nor powers of hell,
Tear us from his keeping ever.

5   Jesus lives! to Him the Throne
Over all the world is given;
May we go where He is gone,
Rest and reign with Him in heaven.

Easter Hymn

Jesus lives! no longer now
Can thy terrors, Death, appal me;
Jesus lives! by this I know
From the grave He will recall me;
Brighter scenes at death commence;
This shall be my confidence.

2   Jesus lives! to Him the Throne
High o'er heaven and earth is given;
I may go where He is gone,
Live and reign with Him in heaven:
God through Christ forgives offence;
This shall be my confidence.

3   Jesus lives! Who now despairs,
Spurns the Word which God hath spoken
Grace to all that Word declares,
Grace whereby sin's yoke is broken:
Christ rejects not penitence;
This shall be my confidence.

4   Jesus lives! for me He died;
Hence will I, to Jesus living,
Pure in heart and act abide,
Praise to Him and glory giving:
Freely God doth aid dispense;
This shall be my confidence.

5   Jesus lives! my heart knows well
Nought from me His Love shall sever;
Life, nor death, nor powers of hell,
Part me now from Christ for ever:
God will be a sure Defence;
This shall be my confidence.

6   Jesus lives! henceforth is death
     Entrance-gate of life immortal;
     This shall calm my trembling breath,
     When I pass its gloomy portal:
     Faith shall cry, as fails each sense,
     Lord, Thou art my Confidence.

JESUS LOVES ME! THIS I
KNOW

This children's hymn has recently been the subject of considerable controversy, not, as one might expect, because of its words,
but rather as a result of it having been given a new tune which is
not to everyone's taste.

It was written by Anna Bartlett Warner (1820–1915), whose
elder sister, Susan, we have already come across as the author of
'Jesus bids us shine' (no. 62). Anna wrote a number of novels
under the pseudonym of Amy Lothrop, and under her own
name she edited *Hymns of the Church Militant* (1858) and
Wayfaring Hymns, Original and Translated (1869). Another of her
hymns, 'The world looks very beautiful', was until recently
found in a number of British and American hymnbooks.

'Jesus loves me! this I know' first appeared in *Say and Seal*
(1859), a novel on which both the Warner sisters collaborated. It
rapidly achieved immense popularity as a Sunday School and
missionary hymn. Ira Sankey tells of a missionary in India who
heard a young Hindu boy singing it in the street. He soon
gathered an audience who asked him who Jesus was and what
was the Bible. The boy, who had picked up the song at
missionary school, told them, 'the Bible is the book from God,
they say, to teach us how to get to heaven; and Jesus is the name
of the Divine Redeemer that came into the world to save us from
our sins: that is what the missionaries say.' His hearers were
uncertain about this explanation but they liked the song and
asked him to sing some more. 'And so the little boy went on',
the missionary recalled,

a heathen himself, and singing to the heathen – about Jesus and his love.
'That is preaching the Gospel by proxy', I said to myself, as I turned my
pony and went away, well satisfied to leave my little proxy to tell his

interested audience all he himself knew, and sing them over and over that sweet song of salvation.

Such a simplistic and sentimental hymn as this one undoubtedly is might well be expected to be out of favour now, and it certainly is with some hymnologists. In his book *Solid Joys and Lasting Treasures*, published in 1985, Tyler Whittle describes it as 'a mawkish, infinitely popular hymn of the era'. But it still does duty in Sunday Schools and children's assemblies up and down the land and is to be found in a number of contemporary hymnbooks.

Increasingly, and especially in Scotland, 'Jesus loves me! this I know' is now sung to the tune of an old Gaelic lullaby, *Mo Churachan*, which tells of a woman who left her baby lying in a field. There have been many protests about the imposition of this tune, particularly from older church members who remember from their youth the original rather sugary tune, written by William Batchelder Bradbury (1816–68). A native of Maine, Bradbury turned out a large number of Sunday School tunes including Woodworth which is still used for Charlotte Elliott's hymn 'Just as I am' (no. 69). He also wrote a very popular sacred cantata, *Esther*.

Jesus loves me! this I know,
For the Bible tells me so;
Little ones to Him belong;
They are weak, but He is strong.
 Yes! Jesus loves me!
 The Bible tells me so.

2 Jesus loves me! He who died
  Heaven's gate to open wide;
  He will wash away my sin,
  Let His little child come in.

3 Jesus loves me! He will stay
  Close beside me all the way;
  Then His little child will take
  Up to heaven, for His dear sake.

JESUS SHALL REIGN
WHERE'ER THE SUN

This majestic paraphrase of Psalm 72 is by Isaac Watts (1674–1748: see no. 27 for biographical details). Like James Montgomery's 'Hail to the Lord's Anointed' (no. 48) it transforms the Hebrew psalm into a Christian hymn by applying to Christ words which were almost certainly originally intended to apply to King Solomon. The first verse of 'Jesus shall reign' takes up the theme of the fifth, seventh and eighth verses of the psalm which proclaimed of the Israelite king:

> They shall fear thee as long as the sun and moon endure,
> throughout all generations.
> In his days shall the righteous flourish; and abundance of peace so
> long as the moon endureth.
> He shall have dominion also from sea to sea, and from the river
> unto the ends of the earth.

Not only did Watts Christianize the great sacred poems of the Jews but he also anglicized them. In some of his other paraphrases he changed the names of Judah and Israel to England and Scotland and the names of Old Testament kings to those of British monarchs. His paraphrase of Psalm 147, 'Praise ye the Lord: for it is good to sing praises unto our God', began:

> O Britain, praise thy mighty God,
> And make his honours known abroad;
> He bid the ocean round thee flow;
> Not bars of brass could guard thee so.

'Jesus shall reign' first appeared in Watts's *Psalms of David Imitated in the Language of the New Testament and applied to the*

Christian State and Worship, which was published in 1719 and contained paraphrases of 138 of the 150 psalms in the Bible. Verses 2, 3, 4 and 7 are now generally omitted, although a few hymnals still print verse 4 with the first line changed to 'To him shall endless pray'r be made'.

This hymn is often regarded as the first proper missionary hymn, and it has been sung in many far-off lands. On Whit Sunday 1862, for example, it was sung by thousands of South Sea Islanders at a service to mark the adoption of a Christian form of government. An observer noted: 'Who so much as they could realise the full meaning of the poet's words? They had been rescued from heathenism and cannibalism and they were that day met for the first time under a Christian constitution, under a Christian king, and with Christ Himself reigning in the hearts of most of those present.'

Several tunes are associated with the hymn, including Galilee, which was written for it in the revised edition of *Hymns Ancient and Modern* by Philip Armes (1836–1908), cathedral organist at Chichester and Durham; Warrington by Ralph Harrison (1748–1810), a Presbyterian minister from Lancashire; Rimington by F. Duckworth (1862–1941); Duke Street by John Hatton (d. 1793); and Truro which comes from *Psalmodia Evangelica* published in 1789. My own preferences lie between the warm and easily flowing Warrington and the affirmative Truro.

Christ's Kingdom among the Gentiles

Jesus shall reign where'er the sun
Does his successive journeys run;
His kingdom stretch from shore to shore,
Till moons shall wax and wane no more.

2   Behold the Islands with their Kings,
And Europe her best tribute brings;
From North to South the Princes meet
To pay their homage at his feet.

3   There Persia glorious to behold,
There India stands in Eastern Gold;
And barbarous nations at his word
Submit and bow and own their Lord.

4   For him shall endless pray'r be made,
And praises throng to crown his head;
His name like sweet perfume shall rise
With every morning sacrifice;

5   People and realms of every tongue
Dwell on his love with sweetest song;
And infant voices shall proclaim
Their early blessings on his name.

6   Blessings abound where'er he reigns,
The prisoner leaps to lose his chains,
The weary find eternal rest,
And all the sons of want are blest.

7   Where he displays his healing power
Death and the curse are known no more;
In him the tribes of Adam boast
More blessings than their father lost.

8   Let every creature rise and bring
Peculiar honours to our king;
Angels descend with songs again,
And earth repeat the long *Amen*.

68

JUDGE ETERNAL,
THRONED IN
SPLENDOUR

With the welcome reassertion of the social teachings of the Gospel that has taken place in recent years, it is surprising that this robust hymn by Henry Scott Holland (1847–1918), the Christian socialist, is not heard more often nowadays. Admittedly the language of its third verse is rather dated with its references to 'heathen' and 'Empire', but the hymn as a whole breathes a spirit of justice and social concern. It is a powerful call for God's judgement on our sinful and divided society, reminiscent in some ways of the Chartist hymn by Ebenezer Elliott (1781–1849):

> When wilt Thou save the people?
> O God of mercy, when?
> The people, Lord, the people,
> Not thrones and crowns, but men!
> Flowers of Thy heart, O God, are they;
> Let them not pass like weeds away,
> Their heritage a sunless day.
> God save the people!

Of aristocratic background, Henry Scott Holland was educated at Eton and Balliol College, Oxford, ordained in 1872 and after a series of academic and church appointments became precentor of St Paul's Cathedral in 1886. From 1910 until his death he was Regius Professor of Divinity at Oxford.

Henry Scott Holland had a passionate attachment to social reform. He was one of the founders of the Christian Social Union, which was set up in 1889 and was an important influence in making the Church of England more socially and politically conscious. For 22 years he edited the *Commonwealth*, a journal concerned with the social application of the Christian faith, and it was there in 1902 that 'Judge Eternal' first appeared. So far as is known, it was his only hymn. He was, in fact, a great lover of music and greatly raised the musical standards at St Paul's during his time there. He was part-editor of the *New Cathedral Psalter* and of the *English Hymnal*, the first edition of which carried his hymn.

Those modern hymnals which still include 'Judge Eternal, throned in splendour' have generally altered the third verse to erase its offending references to the heathen and the Empire, and it now reads as follows:

> Crown, O God, thine own endeavour;
> Cleave our darkness with thy sword;
> Feed the faithless and the hungry
> With the richness of thy word;
> Cleanse the body of this Nation
> Through the glory of the Lord.

When this hymn is sung it is invariably to the astringent traditional Welsh melody Rhuddlan.

Judge Eternal, throned in splendour,
Lord of lords and King of kings.
With Thy living fire of judgement
Purge this land of bitter things;
Solace all its wide dominion
With the healing of Thy wings.

2   Still the weary folk are pining
For the hour that brings release;
And the city's crowded clangour
Cries aloud for sin to cease;
And the homesteads and the woodlands
Plead in silence for their peace.

3   Crown, O God, Thine own endeavour;
Cleave our darkness with Thy sword;
Feed the faint and hungry heathen
With the richness of Thy word;
Cleanse the body of this Empire
Through the glory of the Lord.

JUST AS I AM, WITHOUT ONE PLEA

This ever-popular evangelical hymn, which has both a great simplicity and considerable emotional power, was the work of a remarkable woman who spent 50 years of her life as an invalid.

Charlotte Elliott (1789–1871) was the grand-daughter of the Reverend Henry Venn, one of the members of the famous Clapham Sect which gathered around William Wilberforce. Her father, Henry Venn Elliott, was an evangelical clergyman who moved from Clapham to Brighton which, like many seaside resorts, was something of a stronghold of 'vital religion' in Victorian times.

At the age of 32 Charlotte was stricken by an illness which continued to afflict her for the rest of her life. Although largely confined to bed, she lived to the grand old age of 82 and wrote several hundred hymns which appeared in volumes with titles like *The Invalids' Hymn Book* and *Hours of Sorrow Cheered and Comforted*. Among her contemporaries she was probably best known for 'My God and Father while I stray' and 'Christian, seek ye not repose'.

'Just as I am' was written in 1834 at a time when Charlotte's brother, Harry, was raising money to build a college in Brighton to educate the daughters of poor clergymen. The whole Elliott household was busily engaged in organizing a bazaar to raise money for the proposed school and Charlotte, sitting in her sickroom, felt particularly useless and helpless. As she sat alone a sense of peace and contentment came over her, and in that spirit she wrote the verses which have brought comfort and strength to so many. For the opening phrase of each verse she drew on words which had been addressed to her twelve years earlier by a visting Swiss evangelist, Dr Cesar Malan. In response to a protestation of her unworthiness to come to Christ, he had told her to come to the Saviour 'just as you are'.

'Just as I am' first appeared in leaflet form in 1835 and was published the following year in *The Invalids' Hymn Book*, headed with the text 'Him that cometh unto Me, I will in no wise cast out' (Jn 6.37). It ran to just six verses, the seventh being added by the author later that year. One of the first to derive spiritual benefit from the hymn was William Wordsworth's daughter Dora, who asked for it to be read to her every morning as she lay dying in the Lake District village of Grasmere.

Two other very similar hymns were directly inspired by Charlotte Elliott's verses. In 1850 Russell Sturgis Cook, an American Congregational minister, penned some verses which found their way into *American Hymns Old and New*. The first stanza ran:

> Just as thou art, without one trace
> Of love or joy, or inward grace,
> Or meetness for the heavenly place,
> O wretched sinner, come.

In 1887 Marianne Hearn (1834–1909), a prolific religious lyricist, contributed a six-verse hymn to a Sunday School collection under her pen-name of Marianne Farningham. Her hymn, which was designed for healthy young people and achieved considerable popularity, began:

> Just as I am, Thine own to be,
> Friend of the young, who lovest me,
> To consecrate myself to Thee,
> O Jesus Christ, I come.

Of the several tunes to which Charlotte Elliott's hymn is set, the best known is almost certainly Saffron Walden by Arthur Henry Brown (1830–1926). Strongly influenced by the Oxford Movement, Brown was a pioneer in the restoration of Plain Chant and did much to revive the use of Gregorian chant in Anglican worship.

The Lamb of God

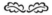

Just as I am, without one plea
But that Thy blood was shed for me,
And that Thou bidd'st me come to Thee,
    O Lamb of God, I come.

2   Just as I am, and waiting not
To rid my soul of one dark blot,
To Thee, whose blood can cleanse each spot,
    O Lamb of God, I come.

3   Just as I am, though tossed about
With many a conflict, many a doubt,
Fightings and fears within, without,
    O Lamb of God, I come.

4   Just as I am, poor, wretched, blind;
Sight, riches, healing of the mind,
Yea, all I need, in Thee to find,
    O Lamb of God, I come.

5   Just as I am, Thou wilt receive,
Wilt welcome, pardon, cleanse, relieve;
Because Thy promise I believe,
    O Lamb of God, I come.

6   Just as I am – Thy love unknown
Has broken every barrier down –
Now to be Thine, yea, Thine alone,
    O Lamb of God, I come.

7   Just as I am, of that free love
The breadth, length, depth, and height to prove,
Here for a season, then above, –
    O Lamb of God, I come.

KING OF GLORY, KING
OF PEACE

The poems of George Herbert (1593–1633) rightly have a prominent place in nearly all modern hymnbooks. Yet although they were written some 350 years ago it is only in the last hundred years that they have come to be sung in churches.

Herbert was a man who might have risen to high political office but instead chose the life of a country clergyman. Of aristocratic family, and educated at Westminster School and Trinity College, Cambridge, he was a close friend of John Donne and Sir Francis Bacon, and attracted the notice of King James I. In 1624 he became MP for Montgomery and a glittering public career seemed to beckon. However, the death of his royal patron the following year, coupled with the onset of tuberculosis, led Herbert to reject the career on which he had embarked and take holy orders. He was also strongly influenced by Nicholas Ferrar, the saintly quietist of Little Gidding in Oxfordshire.

After serving as prebendary of Leighton Broomswold in Huntingdonshire he became in 1630 rector of Bemerton in Wiltshire, where he combined his priestly duties with the writing of some of the finest poetry in the English metaphysical tradition. Greatly loved for his simplicity and saintliness, Herbert only enjoyed three years at Bemerton before he succumbed to his illness.

A few weeks before his death Herbert gave the manuscript of a book of verse to his executor, Edmond Duncon, with the instruction:

Sir, I pray deliver this little book to my brother Ferrar, and tell him that he shall find in it a picture of the many spiritual conflicts that have passed betwixt God and my soul, before I could subject mine to the will of Jesus my master; in whose service I have now found perfect freedom; desire him to read it, and then, if he can think it may turn to the advantage of any dejected poor soul, let it be made public; if not let him burn it; for I and it are less than the least of God's mercies.

Ferrar edited Herbert's poems and they were published in a book entitled *The Tempest* in 1633. It was there that the verses printed here first appeared under the title 'Praise II'. They were first turned into a hymn in the *Wellington College Hymn Book* of 1902. Four years later they were chosen along with several other seventeenth-century devotional poems for inclusion in the first edition of the *English Hymnal*. To make the hymn the sixth verse printed here was dropped and the other verses were combined to form three eight-line stanzas.

The last verse of Herbert's poem has striking similarities with the final stanza of the hymn 'When all thy mercies, O my God, my rising soul surveys', written by Joseph Addison (1672–1719) and first published as the conclusion of an essay on gratitude in the *Spectator* in August 1712:

> Through all eternity to thee
> A joyful song I'll raise;
> For O! eternity's too short
> To utter all thy praise.

'King of Glory, King of Peace' is generally sung to the tune *Gwalchmai* by Joseph David Jones (1827–70). Born at Bryner-ygog in Montgomery, Jones taught singing at Ruthin and published a small collection of psalm-tunes.

Praise

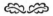

King of Glory, King of Peace,
I will love thee;
And, that love may never cease,
I will move thee.

2   Thou hast granted my request,
Thou hast heard me;
Thou didst note my working breast,
Thou hast spared me.

3   Wherefore with my utmost art
I will sing thee,
And the cream of all my heart
I will bring thee.

4   Though my sins against me cried,
Thou didst clear me,
And alone, when they replied,
Thou didst hear me.

5   Sev'n whole days, not one in sev'n,
I will praise thee;
In my heart, though not in heav'n,
I can raise thee.

6   Thou grew'st soft and moist with tears,
Thou relentedst:
And when Justice call'd for fears,
Thou dissentedst.

7   Small it is, in this poor sort
To enrol thee;
E'en eternity's too short
To extol thee.

LEAD, KINDLY LIGHT, AMID THE ENCIRCLING GLOOM

This is the second great poem by John Henry Newman (1801–90) which was not originally written to be sung. Unlike 'Firmly I believe and truly' (no. 34), 'Lead, kindly Light' was turned into a hymn during the author's lifetime, and although he himself insisted that his verses were 'not a hymn, nor are they suitable for singing', he accepted their appearance in numerous hymnbooks despite the fact that his words were often changed by editors who felt that they did not sufficiently focus on Christ and were filled with too much doubt and ambiguity. It was partly this very quality that made 'Lead, kindly light' one of the two or three best-loved Victorian hymns, equally popular with Catholics, Anglicans and nonconformists. It was a particular favourite of Queen Victoria and was read out to her as she lay dying at Osborne House on the Isle of Wight in January 1901.

Newman wrote this outstanding piece of devotional poetry at a time when he was feeling physically exhausted and intellectually bewildered by the first stirrings of those doubts and convictions which were to take him, fifteen years later, into the Roman Catholic Church. While travelling in southern Italy in the spring of 1833 he was struck down by a viral infection of such severity that there were fears for his life. Greatly weakened, he resolved to hasten home and reached the port of Palermo in Sicily at the end of May. However, he had to wait there three weeks for a boat. When at last he got away it was on board an orange boat bound for Marseilles. The vessel was becalmed for a week in the Straits of Bonifacio between Corsica and Sicily, and it was during this period, on 16 June, as he sat on the deck in the stifling heat of midsummer waiting for a breeze to spring up and carry him on his way home, that he wrote the verses as printed here. Newman eventually reached his mother's home on 9 July 1833. The following Sunday he heard in his own University Church in Oxford his friend John Keble preach the famous sermon on National Apostasy which effectively began the Oxford Movement.

'Lead, kindly Light' was published in the *British Magazine* in 1834 and subsequently in *Lyra apostolica* two years later. In 1845, without consulting Newman, Horatius Bonar put the verses into a hymnbook, altering the first line to 'Lead, Saviour, lead amid the encircling gloom', to add a more distinctively Christological focus, and changing the phrase 'I loved the garish day' to 'I loved the glare of day'. These two lines were further altered in subsequent hymnbooks. A volume produced for use in the American Episcopal Church in 1860, for example, began the hymn: 'Send, Lord, thy light amid the encircling gloom', and continued: 'I loved day's dazzling light.' Newman's verses were rather less mutilated in Unitarian hymnbooks, although even they could not cope with the 'moor and fen' in the third verse which they turned into 'dreary doubts'. It was, of course, the fact that Unitarians could sing Newman's verses so easily that made many hymnbook editors feel that they needed changing and given a more clearly Christocentric focus. When Edward Bickersteth included 'Lead, kindly light' in his *Hymnal Companion to the Book of Common Prayer* in 1870 it was with an extra verse of his own tagged on the end to dispel the mood of doubt that prevailed in the original:

> Meantime along the narrow rugged path
> Thyself hast trod
> Lead, Saviour, lead me home in childlike faith,
> Home to my God,
> To rest for ever after earthly strife
> In the calm light of everlasting life.

Newman was not alerted to this additional verse, which so substantially altered both the tone and meaning of his poem, until four years after Bickersteth's book appeared. His protest was remarkably restrained: 'It is not that the verse is not both in sentiment and in language graceful and good, but I think you will see at once how unwilling an author must be to subject himself to the inconvenience of that being ascribed to him which is not his own.' Bickersteth responded by promising that in the next edition of the *Hymnal* he would make clear that the fourth stanza was not by Newman, but he vigorously defended his editorial initiative, pointing out that the original verses did not make a hymn and required the addition if they were to be sung in church. Once again, Newman's response was a model of forbearance: 'I agree with you that these verses are not a hymn, nor are they suitable for singing, and it is this which at once surprises and gratifies me, and makes me thankful that, in spite of their having no claim to be used as a hymn, they have made their way into so many collections.'

There has been much speculation about the exact meaning of the two closing lines of Newman's original poem. Despite frequent requests, the author refused to elucidate the meaning of the enigmatic closing reference to the angel faces 'which I have loved long since and lost awhile'. Variously conjectured to refer to his Anglican friends or the souls of the departed, the angel faces came for many to symbolize the faith that had once shone more brightly in their hearts and now seemed to have dimmed. Like that great couplet in William Cowper's 'O, for a closer walk with God' which asks 'Where is the blessedness I knew when first I saw the Lord?', the closing lines of 'Lead, kindly Light' struck a deep chord with the Victorians because, in the words of Owen Chadwick, 'hesitant faith was what many souls felt themselves to possess'. Newman himself described his verses as 'the voice of one in darkness asking for help from our Lord'. They continue to perform that function today.

When 'Lead, kindly Light' was included in the appendix to the original edition of *Hymns Ancient and Modern* in 1868, it was set to a tune composed for it three years earlier by Dr J.B. Dykes. *Lux benigna* came to Dykes as he was walking along the Strand past Charing Cross station. Newman typically and modestly attributed the hymn's subsequent great popularity to Dykes's tune rather than his own words. Other tunes specifically composed for the hymn include Sandon by C.H. Purdy; Bonifacio by David Emlyn Evans; Alberta, written by Sir W.H. Harris in 1924 while travelling by train through Canada; and *Lux in tenebris* by Sir Arthur Sullivan. For me, this last is infinitely the most sensitive and appropriate musical setting of Newman's poem. Although primarily written for choirs, it can be managed by most congregations.

Faith – Heavenly Leadings

Lead, kindly Light, amid the encircling gloom,
Lead thou me on;
The night is dark, and I am far from home,
Lead thou me on.
Keep thou my feet; I do not ask to see
The distant scene; one step enough for me.

2   I was not ever thus, nor prayed that thou
Should'st lead me on;
I loved to choose and see my path; but now
Lead thou me on.
I loved the garish day, and, spite of fears,
Pride ruled my will: remember not past years.

3   So long thy power hath blessed me, sure it still
Will lead me on,
O'er moor and fen, o'er crag and torrent, till
The night is gone;
And with the morn those angel faces smile,
Which I have loved long since, and lost awhile.

LEAD US, HEAVENLY
FATHER, LEAD US

Despite the fact that it refers to Our Lord as 'dreary', this hymn has been a firm favourite with congregations ever since it was first written more than 150 years ago for the inmates of an orphanage.

It is the work of James Edmeston (1791–1867) who wrote a grand total of 2,000 hymns for the children of the London Orphan Asylum which he visited regularly. Born and brought up in Stepney in east London and coming of Congregational stock, Edmeston became a successful architect and forsook both the environment and denomination of his childhood, moving to Surrey and espousing Anglicanism. Among his architectural pupils was Sir George Gilbert Scott, the man responsible for the Albert Memorial, the government buildings in Whitehall, St Pancras Station and a host of churches throughout Britain.

It was Edmeston's practice to write a hymn every Sunday and read it at family worship. His first published collection of verses, *The Cottage Minstrel*, was written in response to an advertisement offering £20 for 50 simple hymns suitable for cottage meetings. Subsequent collections included *Infant Breathings* and *Sacred Lyrics*. It was in the latter volume, published in 1821, that 'Lead us, Heavenly Father, lead us' first appeared. It was included in *Baptist Hymns and Psalms* in 1858 and from there passed into most hymnals.

This is the only one of Edmeston's hymns to be still sung regularly today. Others found in hymnals from the early twentieth century include 'Saviour, breathe an evening blessing' and 'God entrusts to all'.

The tune Mannheim normally used for this hymn was adapted from a tune by the German composer Friedrich Filitz (1804–76) in his *Viertimmiges Choralbuch* (1847). Filitz lived in Berlin and Munich and brought out a collection of the chorales of the most distinguished masters of the sixteenth and seventeenth centuries. This particular tune was originally set by Filitz to words by Frelinghausen beginning '*Auf, auf, weil der Tag erschienen*'. It was adapted for Edmeston's hymn by Thomas Binney in his *Congregational Church Music* of 1853.

Hymn written for the children of the
London Orphan Asylum

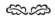

Lead us, heavenly Father, lead us
O'er the world's tempestuous sea;
Guard us, guide us, keep us, feed us,
For we have no help but thee;
Yet possessing every blessing,
If our God our Father be.

2   Saviour, breathe forgiveness o'er us:
All our weakness thou dost know;
Thou didst tread this earth before us,
Thou didst feel its keenest woe;
Lone and dreary, faint and weary,
Through the desert thou didst go.

3   Spirit of our God, descending,
Fill our hearts with heavenly joy,
Love with every passion blending,
Pleasure that can never cloy;
Thus provided, pardoned, guided,
Nothing can our peace destroy.

LET ALL MORTAL FLESH
KEEP SILENCE

This powerful eucharistic hymn, so full of awe and mystery, is taken from one of the early liturgies of the Greek Orthodox Church. Like 'For the beauty of the earth' (no. 36), it appears in two distinct versions expressing different doctrinal viewpoints. In its original and more common form, as printed here, it is a communion hymn and very popular with Roman Catholics – it came in fifth place in the 2004 *Tablet* poll of readers' favourite hymns. The alternative version tones down its sacramental character and suggestion of the real physical presence of Christ in the elements of bread and wine in the Eucharist.

The verses are based on a part of the Liturgy of St James, which dates from the fourth century and is found in both Greek and Syriac. The whole liturgy was first translated into English by J.M. Neale and R.F. Littledale and published in their *Primitive Liturgies* (1868–69). Shortly afterwards Gerard Moultrie (1829–85) versified a section entitled 'Prayer of the Cherubic Hymn' to form this hymn. Moultrie was successively chaplain of Shrewsbury School, vicar of South Leigh and Warden of St James's College, also in South Leigh. He was responsible for several translations of hymns as well as a number of his own composition.

It is Moultrie's translation which appears here and which is found in most Roman Catholic, Anglican and Presbyterian hymnals. However, there are those for whom the second verse smacks too much of the doctrine of the Real Presence. To accommodate their views Percy Dearmer (1867–1936), the leading early twentieth-century Anglican hymnologist and liturgist, produced an alternative version for inclusion in *Songs of Praise* in 1931. It appears in several nonconformist hymnals, including the *Baptist Hymn Book* of 1962. The first two verses of Dearmer's version go as follows:

Let all mortal flesh keep silence,
And with awe and welcome stand;
Harbour nothing earthly-minded;
For, with blessing in his hand,
Christ our Lord with us abideth,
Loving homage to demand.

King is he, yet born a servant,
Lord of all in human guise,
Truly man, yet God revealing,
God as love, to mortal eyes;
God with man, he leads and feeds us,
He the power and he the prize.

The third and fourth verses of Dearmer's hymn differ less radically from Moultrie's original. Both versions are generally sung to the tune Picardy, a French carol melody which probably dates from the seventeenth century.

Let all mortal flesh keep silence,
And with fear and trembling stand;
Ponder nothing earthly-minded,
For with blessing in his hand
Christ our God to earth descendeth
Our full homage to demand.

2   King of kings, yet born of Mary,
As of old on earth he stood,
Lord of Lords, in human vesture –
In the Body and the Blood –
He will give to all the faithful
His own self for heavenly Food.

3   Rank on rank the host of heaven
Spreads its vanguard on the way,
As the Light of light descendeth
From the realms of endless day,
That the powers of hell may vanish
As the darkness clears away.

4   At his feet the six-winged Seraph:
Cherubim with sleepless eye,
Veil their faces to the Presence,
As with ceaseless voice they cry,
'Alleluia! Alleluia!
Alleluia! Lord most high.'

LET ALL THE WORLD IN
EVERY CORNER SING

This is another of the poems of George Herbert (1593–1632) which was only turned into a hymn after the author's death. But unlike 'King of glory, king of peace' (no. 70: see notes there for biographical details of Herbert) and 'Teach me, my God and King' (no. 120), this one seems to have been written specifically for singing in church. Not surprisingly, it was the first of Herbert's poems to be turned into a hymn, unlike others which were not enjoyed by congregations until the twentieth century.

The verses here first appeared in the collection of Herbert's work which was published shortly after his death in 1633 under the title of *The Temple*. They are clearly designed to be sung antiphonally either by two choirs, or by choir and congregation. In 1760 in his *New Book of Psalmody*, John Hill of Lydd set the words to music as Herbert had written them, assigning the first verse to alto and tenor and the second to treble and bass with a four-part chorus. The rearrangement into a conventional congregational hymn of two verses, with the refrain being repeated at the end of the first as well as the second, seems first to have been made in the volume of *Church Hymns* published by the Society for the Propagation of Christian Knowledge in 1871. It was taken up in the revised edition of *Hymns Ancient and Modern* in 1889 and is the version that now appears in all hymnbooks.

Four of the greatest church musicians of the last 150 years have written tunes for 'Let all the world in every corner sing'. The first was William Henry Monk (1823–89) who composed Herbert for the supplement to *Hymns Ancient and Modern*, of which he was music editor. It was one of the last tunes that he wrote before his death. In his remarkably full life he had been organist of four major London churches, Professor of Vocal Music at King's College, London, and the composer of numerous hymn tunes, including such perennial favourites as Eventide (for 'Abide with me'), Ascension (for 'Hail the day that sees him rise') and St Ethelwald (for 'Soldiers of Christ, arise').

In the twentieth century Monk's tune has been largely supplanted by Luckington by Basil Harwood (1859–1925), which was first used in the *Oxford Hymnary* of 1908. Born in Gloucestershire and educated at Charterhouse and Trinity College, Oxford, Harwood was successively organist at St Barnabas, Pimlico, Ely Cathedral and Christ Church Cathedral, Oxford. His other hymn-tunes include Thornbury (for 'Thy hand, O God, has guided').

In 1915 Martin Shaw (1875–1958) supplied High Road which was taken up by the *English Hymnal*. A pupil of Sir Charles Stanford, Charles Parry and Walford Davies at the Royal College of Music, he was organist at St Mary's, Primrose Hill, and St Martin-in-the-Fields before becoming director of music for the Anglican diocese of Chelmsford. We have already come across him as the composer of Little Cornard (for 'Hills of the North rejoice') and as the adaptor of the folk melody Royal Oak for 'All things bright and beautiful'.

Most recently, Erik Routley (1917–1982) wrote Augustine which appears in the third edition of the *Church Hymnary*. Any writer on the subject of hymns owes an enormous debt of gratitude to the work of Routley and I am happy to express my own considerable indebtedness to him here. Almost certainly the leading twentieth-century authority on Christian hymnody, he published ten books on the subject and edited the *Bulletin* of the Hymn Society of Great Britain and Ireland, as well as being an active Congregational minister. His last position was as director of Westminster Choir College, Princeton, New Jersey.

Antiphon

Let all the world in every corner sing,
   My God and King!
The heavens are not too high,
His praise may thither fly;
The earth is not too low,
His praises there may grow.

2   Let all the world in every corner sing,
       My God and King!
    The Church with psalms must shout,
    No door can keep them out;
    But above all, the heart
    Must bear the longest part.

Let all the world in every corner sing,
   My God and King!

LET US WITH A
GLADSOME MIND

This paraphrase of Psalm 136 which forms the basis of an ever-popular hymn was written at the age of 15 by John Milton (1608–74), the man who is generally regarded as second only to Shakespeare in the roll-call of great English poets. I must admit that I find it coming close to doggerel in parts, but it has an originality and freshness that lifts it high above the level of most adolescent verse and so rescues it from triteness.

John Milton was born in Cheapside, London, the son of a scrivener and composer of music. He was educated at St Paul's School and Christ's College, Cambridge, and his father intended that he should pursue a career in the Church. However, his views made it impossible for him to take Anglican orders, and instead he settled into his career of poet, pamphleteer and writer. He came to public attention with powerful tracts against episcopacy, in favour of divorce and, most notably, with his passionate and eloquent defence of freedom of speech and liberty of the press in his *Areopagitica* (1643). During the period of the Commonwealth, Milton was Latin Secretary to the Council of State. It was at this time that he was afflicted with total blindness. At the restoration of the monarchy in 1660 he was arrested and fined, but later released. It was in the years following the Restoration that he completed his greatest work, *Paradise Lost*. He also wrote a treatise on Christian doctrines in which he showed his indifference to all rites and ceremonies and came close to espousing Arianism. He died of gout and was buried next to his father in St Giles', Cripplegate.

Together with a paraphrase of Psalm 114, the verses printed here constitute the earliest example of Milton's work which is still extant. They were written while he was still a pupil at St Paul's and studying French, Italian, Hebrew, Latin and Greek with the aid of a private tutor. The following year he went up to Cambridge. The other youthful paraphrase, which begins 'When the blest seed of Terah's faithfull Son', is strongly reminiscent of the style of Joshua Sylvester (1563–1618), but Milton's approach to Psalm 136 ('O give thanks unto the Lord; for he is good') is much more original and less derivative. Such imagery as that contained in verse 13 ('The floods stood still like Walls of Glass'), for example, seems to be entirely of his own creation.

The paraphrase first appeared in *Poems of Mr John Milton, both English and Latin*, published in 1645. It was not turned into a hymn until more than 200 years later. The *Congregationalist Hymn Book* of 1855 included verses 1, 2, 7, 8, 15, 20, 22 and 23, suitably polished up and made to scan properly. Subsequently verse 9 was also added. Most modern hymnbooks include only six or seven verses in all, including a repeat of the first verse at the end. Only this and the chorus are as Milton originally wrote them. The verses in use today (though not all found together in any one hymnbook) are

Let us, with a gladsome mind,
Praise the Lord, for he is kind:

For his mercies aye endure,
Ever faithful, ever sure.

2   Let us blaze his name abroad,
For of gods he is the God:

7   He with all-commanding might,
Filled the new-made world with light:

8   He the golden-tressèd sun
Caused all day his course to run.

9   Th' hornèd moon to shine by night,
Mid her spangled sisters bright:

15   He his chosen race did bless
In the wasteful wilderness:

22   All things living he doth feed;
His full hand supplies their need:

There are a number of other hymns based on Milton's paraphrase. They include 'Praise, O praise our God and King' by Sir Henry Baker (1821–77), 'Praise, O praise our heavenly King' by H. Trend and 'Come, and let us praises sing' by Thomas Darling (1816–93). In 1873 Arthur Penrhyn Stanley (1815–81), Dean of Westminster Abbey, produced a version of Milton's paraphrase suitable for singing on royal and national occasions. It includes the lines:

Long our island throne has stood,
Planted on the ocean flood;

'Let us with a gladsome mind' is generally sung to the tune Monkland, which is based on the melody of a German song 'Fahre fort, fahre fort', first published in 1704. It first appeared as a hymn-tune in Britain in a collection published by the United Brethren in 1790. In 1824 a modified version, similar to that used now, was included in a collection of hymn-tunes put together by John Lees, organist at the United Brethren chapel at Leominster. Some years later J.B. Wilkes (1785–1869), organist at Monkland where Sir Henry Baker was vicar, set it to Baker's hymn mentioned above. It first gained national currency set to 'O praise our God and King' in *Hymns Ancient and Modern*. I have to say that I find it rather feeble and boring.

In an effort to produce something more lively, the editors of the third edition of the *Church Hymnary* came up with Harts, a simplified form of a melody by Benjamin Milgrove (1731–1810). I commend its use to those who have had their fill of Monkland.

23 Let us therefore warble forth
His mighty Majesty and worth.

24 That his mansion hath on high
Above the reach of mortall eye.

'LIFT UP YOUR HEARTS!'
WE LIFT THEM, LORD,
TO THEE

The worship of the public school chapel may be an imperfect expression of Christianity in many respects (and what earthly and institutional form of worship isn't?) but it has certainly produced an important and distinctive corpus of hymns. 'Lift up your hearts' is perhaps the supreme example of the genre – it is exhilarating, uplifting and uncomplicated, and cries out to be sung by a packed congregation anxious to give their vocal chords a good airing. It was written for the boys of Harrow School in 1881 by their headmaster Henry Montagu Butler (1833–1918) who drew his inspiration from the words of the *Sursum corda* in the Communion service: 'Lift up your hearts', followed by the congregation's response: 'We lift them up unto the Lord.'

Butler was a leading member of a formidable family which has in the last three generations produced twelve fellows of Oxbridge colleges, three public school headmasters, a leading Tory politician and sundry professors. He himself became headmaster of Harrow at the age of 26 and remained there for a further 26 years until he was appointed Dean of Gloucester. In 1886 he became Master of Trinity College, Cambridge. *The Times* described him as 'the most patriarchal figure in English academic life'.

At Harrow, he was a powerful reforming headmaster in the tradition of Dr Arnold of Rugby. He insisted that his classics masters should have first-class degrees and took a strong interest in the development of team games in the school. A keen cricketer, he frequently impressed on pupils the importance throughout life of the maxim 'Play the game'. In his first year as Master of Trinity College, Cambridge, at the age of 53, he caused a sensation among the fellows by marrying a young girl who had just come top of the Classical Tripos. 'It is her goodness, not her Greek and Latin, which have stolen my heart,' he assured them. His devotion to his college knew no bounds. He is said to have commented at the end of a sermon on the Day of Judgement, after praising Christ's action in separating the sheep and the goats, 'We would expect no less of him, since he was, after all, in some sense a Trinity man himself.'

The tune Woodlands is also a fine example of public school Christianity at its best – bold, vigorous and eminently singable. It was written for Butler's hymn by Walter Greatorex (1877–1949) when director of music at Gresham's School, Holt, Norfolk. Greatorex was the son of a bank manager and was born in Southwell, Nottinghamshire. Educated at Derby School and St John's College, Cambridge, he was a music master at Uppingham before going to Gresham's in 1906. He remained there for nearly 30 years and was much loved by those boys who got to know him and shared his love of music and literature. One of the school's most distinguished old boys, the poet W.H. Auden said that it was to Greatorex that he owed all the knowledge of music that he possessed. Another old boy has written to me that 'He was a fine man; looked rather like a stern Pickwick in appearance and really rather shy. I couldn't read a note of music and yet all he taught me by heart I still remember.' The tune was named after the headmaster's boarding house at Gresham's. To generations of boys there, however, it was simply known as 'Gog's tune', that being Greatorex's nickname. It is also used for 'Tell out, my soul, the greatness of the Lord' (no. 122).

'Lift up your hearts!' We lift them, Lord, to thee;
Here at thy feet none other may we see.
'Lift up your hearts!' E'en so, with one accord,
We lift them up, we lift them to the Lord.

2 Above the level of the former years,
The mire of sin, the slough of guilty fears,
The mist of doubt, the blight of love's decay,
O Lord of Light, lift all our hearts today!

3 Above the swamps of subterfuge and shame,
The deeds, the thoughts, that honour may not name,
The halting tongue that dares not tell the whole,
O Lord of Truth, lift every Christian soul!

4 Above the storms that vex this lower state,
Pride, jealousy, and envy, rage, and hate,
And cold mistrust that holds e'en friends apart,
O Lord of Love, lift every brother's heart!

5 Lift every gift that thou thyself has given;
Low lies the best till lifted up to heaven;
Low lie the bounding heart, the teeming brain,
Till, sent from God, they mount to God again.

6 Then, as the trumpet-call in after years,
'Lift up your hearts!', rings pealing in our ears,
Still shall those hearts respond with full accord,
'We lift them up, we lift them to the Lord!'

LO! HE COMES WITH
CLOUDS DESCENDING

This is both a theological and a literary oddity. Although most hymnbooks put it in the Advent section, it is in reality one of the very few popular hymns which treats of the difficult doctrine of the Second Coming of Christ. It also has a complex literary pedigree, being the work of three different writers. It started life in 1752 when John Cennick (1718–55), an Anglican of Quaker parents who became the first Methodist lay preacher and ended up a Moravian, published a hymn which began:

> Lo! he cometh, endless trumpets
> Blow before his bloody sign!
> Midst ten thousand saints and angels
> See the Crucified shine.
> Alleluia!
> Welcome, welcome, bleeding Lamb!

With such an opening, it is perhaps hardly surprising that in 1758 Cennick's hymn was almost completely rewritten by Charles Wesley (1707–88). Two years later Martin Madan (1726–90), founder and chaplain of the Lock Hospital, Hyde Park Corner, and coauthor with Wesley and George Whitefield of 'Hark, the herald Angels sing', made a further rearrangement of the hymn, reintroducing some of Cennick's original verses and producing the version which is printed here. The first, second and fifth verses are by Wesley, the third and fourth substantially by Cennick and the sixth an amalgam of the two men's work.

As sung now, the hymn largely follows Madan's version but with several lines altered. The fifth verse, which he actually took from another hymn by Wesley, 'Rise, ye dearly purchased sinners', has been universally dropped in favour of the third verse of Wesley's rewriting of Cennick's original:

Those dear tokens of His Passion
Still His dazzling Body bears,
Cause of endless exultation
To his ransom'd worshippers:
With what rapture
Gaze we on those glorious scars.

The hymn is always sung to the magnificent tune Helmsley, which Madan recast from a melody written for Wesley's version by Thomas Olivers (1725–99: for biographical details see no. 128). There are several stories, all of them probably apocryphal, about its origins. One has it that Olivers heard the tune being whistled in the street, another that it was based on a Scottish melody, and a third that it derived from a popular hornpipe. More likely is the theory that he based it in part at least on a concert-room song, 'Guardian angels, now protect me'. It also bears a passing resemblance to a melody from Thomas Arne's opera, *Thomas and Sally*. The well-known eighteenth-century actress Miss Catley danced a hornpipe to the tune in a burlesque, but this was in 1776, eleven years after Olivers had composed Helmsley, and it seems that the hornpipe was based on the hymn-tune rather than the other way round. Whatever its origins, it has been extremely popular. It was a particular favourite of Queen Victoria's. When a new organist at her private chapel inadvertently played another tune which had been set to 'Lo! He comes' in *Hymns Ancient and Modern*, a royal request came that in future only Helmsley should be used.

Lo! He comes with clouds descending,
Once for favour'd sinners slain;
Thousand thousand Saints attending
Swell the triumph of His train:
Alleluia!
God appears on earth to reign.

2   Every eye shall now behold Him,
Robed in dreadful majesty;
Those who set at nought and sold Him,
Pierced and nail'd Him to the Tree,
Deeply wailing,
Shall the true Messiah see.

3   Every island, sea, and mountain,
Heav'n and earth, shall flee away;
All who hate Him must, confounded,
Hear the trump proclaim the Day;
Come to judgment!
Come to judgment! come away!

4   Now redemption, long expected,
See in solemn pomp appear!
All His saints, by man rejected,
Now shall meet Him in the air:
Alleluia!
See the Day of God appear!

5   Answer thine own Bride and Spirit,
Hasten, Lord, the gen'ral Doom!
The New Heav'n and Earth t'inherit,
Take thy pining exiles home:
All creation
Travails! groans! and bids Thee come!

6   Yea, Amen, let all adore Thee,
     High on Thine eternal throne;
     Saviour, take the power and glory:
     Claim the Kingdom for Thine own:
     O come quickly!
     Alleluia! Come, Lord, come!

LORD, ENTHRONED IN
HEAVENLY SPLENDOUR

Another public school hymn, this is the work of George Hugh Bourne (1840–1925), headmaster of St Andrew's School, Chardstock, Devon, and later of St Edmund's College, Salisbury. It comes from a series of seven post-communion hymns which he wrote for the use of the latter college and which were privately printed in 1874. It made its first public appearance in the supplement to the revised edition of *Hymns Ancient and Modern* in 1889, when it appeared as printed here. In most modern hymnals the fifth verse is generally omitted.

Bourne was the son of an Anglican clergyman and was educated at Eton and Corpus Christi College, Oxford. He himself was ordained and in addition to his headmasterly duties held the positions of chaplain to the Bishop of Bloemfontein, and sub-dean, treasurer and prebendary of Salisbury Cathedral.

The bright and memorable tune St Helen was composed for the 1889 *Hymns Ancient and Modern* supplement by Sir George Martin (1844–1916). Born at Lambourn in Berkshire, his interest in music was first aroused by hearing Sir Herbert Oakeley play Bach on the organ of the parish church there. He studied under Sir John Stainer, whom he succeeded as organist and master of the choristers at St Paul's Cathedral, having earlier served as organist to the Duke of Buccleuch at Dalkeith.

This hymn was very nearly prefaced in this collection with another from the same general stable. Indeed, it was only after considerable heart-searching and with great reluctance that I decided to drop what in many ways is the most distinctive and atmospheric of all public school hymns, 'Lord, dismiss us with thy blessing', which was written for the boys of Rugby by Henry James Buckoll (1803–71). My own memories of singing it in school chapel in the mid-1960s nearly got the better of me, but when I discovered that it is not now to be found even within the covers of *Hymns for Church and School*, as the old Public School Hymn Book is known, let alone in any other modern hymnal, I realized that its inclusion in this book would have been a piece of self-indulgence hard to justify. So out I am afraid it has had to come.

Lord, enthroned in heavenly splendour,
First-begotten from the dead,
Thou alone, our strong defender,
Liftest up they people's head,
    Alleluia!
Jesu, true and living Bread.

2   Here our humblest homage pay we;
Here in loving reverence bow;
Here for faith's discernment pray we,
Lest we fail to know thee now.
    Alleluia!
Thou art here, we ask not how.

3   Though the lowliest form doth veil thee
As of old in Bethlehem,
Here as there thine angels hail thee,
Branch and Flower of Jesse's stem.
    Alleluia!
We in worship join with them.

4   Paschal Lamb, thine offering, finished
Once for all when thou wast slain,
In its fullness undiminished
Shall for evermore remain,
    Alleluia!
Cleansing souls from every stain.

5   Great High Priest of our profession,
Through the veil Thou wentest in,
By Thy mighty intercession
Grace and peace for us to win;
    Alleluia!
Only sacrifice for sin.

6   Life-imparting heav'nly Manna,
    Stricken Rock with streaming side,
    Heaven and earth with loud hosanna
    Worship thee, the Lamb who died,
        Alleluia!
    Risen, ascended, glorified!

LORD, FOR THE YEARS
YOUR LOVE HAS KEPT
AND GUIDED

This great modern hymn by Timothy Dudley-Smith (see no. 122 for biographical notes) has established itself as a firm favourite for New Year services, anniversaries and national occasions. It came eighteenth in the 2002 *Songs of Praise* poll. Like much of the author's work, it stands in the classic tradition of English hymnody, foursquare, robust and eminently singable.

Dudley-Smith wrote this hymn in 1967 for the centenary of the Scripture Union, the evangelistic organization which works to promote knowledge and understanding of the Christian faith especially among young people. A special centenary service was being held, and it was suggested that he might like to write a hymn for the occasion, with Sibelius's *Finlandia* suggested as a possible tune. In the author's own words:

Owing much to the Scripture Union in my own spiritual pilgrimage, I agreed to try; and I recall writing this text on a train, travelling home from Nottingham to London in the early evening. It was sung at the service, and included in *Youth Praise 2* a couple of years later. Dr George Carey chose it for his Enthronement Service as Archbishop of Canterbury in 1991. It proved popular at services to mark fifty years from the end of the Second World War, and a few years later to celebrate the millennium. It is also requested surprisingly often for weddings, and indeed was sung at the weddings of both our daughters.

The hymn abounds in scriptural references. The second verse draws on Philippians 2.16, Luke 24.32 and 2 Timothy 3.16; the third verse on Luke 8.14; and the fifth verse on Galatians 5.24 and Colossians 3.3. There is a wonderful sweep, both from thanksgiving to intercession and from the nation to the world to ourselves.

At the end of 2001 Dudley-Smith was asked by Churches Together in England to write an extra verse for this hymn to be sung at services celebrating the Golden Jubilee of the Queen's accession the following year. He actually wrote a whole new hymn for the Jubilee, 'To God we come in prayer and praise', but also provided the extra verse requested for 'Lord, for the years', stipulating that it should not become a permanent part of the hymn:

> Lord, for our hopes, the dreams of all our living,
> Christ and his kingdom one united aim;
> Rulers and peoples bound in high thanksgiving,
> Lord of our hopes, our trust is in your Name.

The strength and power of this hymn are hugely enhanced by the majestic tune Lord of the Years, written especially for it by Michael Baughen (1930–). Baughen was the driving spirit behind the two volumes of *Youth Praise* which were to revolutionize hymnody in the Church of England, and it was in the second volume of that book, published in 1969, that his tune first appeared in print married to Dudley-Smith's words. The two men had worked together in the Church Pastoral Aid Society in the early 1960s. By the time he wrote Lord of the Years Baughen was, in the words of the *Church of England Newspaper*, 'a mild-mannered, balding Manchester vicar'. He went on to become a leading light in the Jubilate Hymns movement, which was responsible, among many other things, for *Hymns for Today's Church*. This collection (published in 1982) offended some people for updating traditional words. Baughen, who was Bishop of Chester from 1982 to 1986, has a large number of hymn texts and tunes to his credit. On the whole, his tunes have proved more enduring than his texts. They include Go forth for James Seddon's 'Go forth and tell', Christ Triumphant for Michael Saward's 'Christ triumphant, ever reigning' and two other tunes for Dudley-Smith hymns, Davos for 'I lift my eyes to the quiet hills' and *Majestas* for 'Name of all majesty'.

Lord, for the years your love has kept and guided,
urged and inspired us, cheered us on our way,
sought us and saved us, pardoned and provided,
Lord of the years, we bring our thanks today.

2   Lord, for that word, the word of life which fires us,
speaks to our hearts and sets our souls ablaze,
teaches and trains, rebukes us and inspires us,
Lord of the word, receive your people's praise.

3   Lord, for our land, in this our generation,
spirits oppressed by pleasure, wealth and care;
for young and old, for commonwealth and nation,
Lord of our land, be pleased to hear our prayer.

4   Lord, for our world; when we disown and doubt him,
loveless in strength, and comfortless in pain;
hungry and helpless, lost indeed without him,
Lord of the world, we pray that Christ may reign.

5   Lord, for ourselves; in living power remake us,
self on the cross and Christ upon the throne;
past put behind us, for the future take us,
Lord of our lives, to live for Christ alone.

LORD OF ALL HOPEFULNESS, LORD OF ALL JOY

Two extremely fine twentieth-century hymns are associated with the traditional Irish melody Slane, which we have already come across as the tune for 'Be thou my vision, O Lord of my heart' (no. 17). One is 'Lord of creation, to thee be all praise' and the other is this work by Mrs Joyce Placzek (1901–1953) an English-born emigré to the United States of America who wrote under the pen-name of Jan Struther, derived from her maiden name Anstruther.

Born in London, Mrs Placzek pursued a literary career, contributing articles and poetry to a number of periodicals. She was effectively 'discovered' as a hymn-writer by Percy Dearmer, who asked her to contribute to *Songs of Praise* in 1931. He wanted a hymn to fit the tune Slane and she came up with 'Lord of all hopefulness, Lord of all joy', which, in Dearmer's words, was 'a lovely example of the fitting together of thought, words and music'. Other hymns by Mrs Placzek which are still occasionally sung include 'Round the earth a message runs', the children's hymn 'When a knight won his spurs' and the wedding hymn 'God, whose eternal mind'. She was twice married – first to Anthony Maxtone-Graham in 1923 and secondly to Adolf Placzek in 1948. She spent her last years mostly in the USA.

In an effort to keep Slane for 'Be thou my vision', Cyril Taylor (1907–91) wrote the tune Miniver for this hymn. Taylor, who was educated at Magdalen College School and Christ Church, Oxford, was Precentor of Bristol Cathedral and assistant to the head of religious broadcasting at the BBC before becoming warden and chaplain to the Royal School of Church Music. In 1958 he became perpetual curate of Cerne Abbas, Dorset. Miniver first appeared in 1951 in the *BBC Hymn Book* which Taylor edited. He took the title of his tune from the novel *Mrs Miniver*, which was written by Mrs Placzek and published in 1939, and which was made into a very popular film during the Second World War.

The other modern hymn associated with Slane, 'Lord of creation, to thee be all praise', was written by Jack Copley Winslow (1882–1974). Educated at Eton and Balliol College, Oxford, Winslow was successively a missionary in India, chaplain to Bryanston School in Dorset and chaplain to the Lee Abbey community in North Devon. His hymn, which first appeared in 1961 in *A Garland of Verse*, begins:

> Lord of creation, to thee be all praise!
> Most mighty thy working, most wondrous thy ways!
> Who reignest in glory no tongue can e'er tell,
> Yet deign'st in the heart of the humble to dwell.
>
> Lord of all power, I give thee my will,
> In joyful obedience thy tasks to fulfil.
> Thy bondage is freedom; thy service is song;
> And, held in thy keeping, my weakness is strong.

All Day Hymn

Lord of all hopefulness, Lord of all joy,
Whose trust, ever childlike, no cares could destroy,
Be there at our waking, and give us, we pray,
Your bliss in our hearts, Lord,
    at the break of day.

2 Lord of all eagerness, Lord of all faith,
Whose strong hands were skilled at the plane and the lathe,
Be there at our labours, and give us, we pray,
Your strength in our hearts, Lord,
    at the noon of the day.

3 Lord of all kindliness, Lord of all grace,
Your hands swift to welcome, your arms to embrace.
Be there at our homing, and give us, we pray,
Your love in our hearts, Lord,
    at the eve of the day.

4 Lord of all gentleness, Lord of all calm,
Whose voice is contentment, whose presence is balm,
Be there at our sleeping, and give us, we pray,
Your peace in our hearts, Lord,
    at the end of the day.

LORD, THE LIGHT OF
YOUR LOVE IS SHINING

This contemporary worship song by Graham Kendrick has established itself over the last twenty years as one of the most popular hymns in the British Isles. It came 20th in the 2002 *Songs of Praise* poll and remains the most widely known and sung of the many works by Kendrick which have found their way into the hymnbooks of most denominations.

Born in 1950, the son of a Baptist minister, Graham Kendrick grew up in a succession of Baptist manses in Blisworth, Laindon and Putney. While at teacher-training college, he underwent a profound religious experience in which he felt filled with the Holy Spirit. This set him off on his ministry as an itinerant musician, hymn-writer and worship leader. After working in full-time evangelism, first with the touring team In the Name of Jesus and then for four years with Youth for Christ, he decided in 1984 to focus all his energies on congregational worship music.

Closely involved with the Ichthus Fellowship, one of the largest and most dynamic of the new house churches which have come out of the charismatic revival, Kendrick has been particularly associated with the March for Jesus for which he has written such songs as 'Make way, make way for the king of kings'. He has also written songs for the annual Spring Harvest gatherings. Among his other best-known hymns are 'From heaven you came, helpless babe' (The Servant King) (no. 38), 'Meekness and majesty', 'Restore, O Lord, the honour of your name', 'All I once held dear' (Knowing You), 'Rejoice, Rejoice, Christ is in you' and 'Jesus put this song into our hearts'.

Like much of his work, this song emerged by trial and error as Kendrick experimented with different chords on his guitar. Initially there was no chorus, but the refrain 'Shine, Jesus, shine' came to him as he was singing through the verses. The whole work – words and music – was completed in just 30 minutes and had its first performance at the Spring Harvest gathering in 1987. It rapidly achieved considerable popularity and was used at the service in Westminster Abbey in 1988 to launch the Church of England's Church Urban Fund.

Lord, the light of your love is shining,
In the midst of the darkness, shining:
Jesus, Light of the world, shine upon us;
Set us free by the truth you now bring us –
Shine on me, shine on me.

Shine, Jesus, shine,
Fill this land with the Father's glory;
Blaze, Spirit, blaze,
Set our hearts on fire.
Flow, river, flow,
Flood the nations with grace and mercy;
Send forth your word,
Lord, and let there be light!

Lord, I come to your awesome presence,
From the shadows into your radiance;
By the blood I may enter your brightness:
Search me, try me, consume all my darkness –
Shine on me, shine on me.

As we gaze on your kingly brightness
So our faces display your likeness,
Ever changing from glory to glory:
Mirrored here, may our lives tell your story –
Shine on me, shine on me.

Graham Kendrick
Copyright © 1987 Make Way Music,
P.O. Box 263, Croydon, Surrey. CR9 5AP, UK.
Used by permission.

LOVE DIVINE, ALL LOVES
EXCELLING

This great hymn, which came eighth in the 2002 *Songs of Praise* poll, clearly expresses Charles Wesley's doctrine of perfectionism. It suggests that Christ can transform us into children of God and that in this life it is possible to be cleansed completely from sin and made pure. Many Christians, including the author's own brother John, have balked at this idea, and have toned down the words to suggest a slightly less sweeping doctrine of sanctification.

It is said that Charles Wesley (1707–88; see no. 11 for biographical notes) got the idea for the hymn from a popular song of the day, 'The Song of Venus', which came from John Dryden's play, *King Arthur*, and had been set to music by Henry Purcell. It began:

> Fairest isle, all isles excelling,
> Seat of pleasure and of loves,
> Venus here will choose her dwelling,
> And forsake the Cyprian groves.

The hymn printed here is as it first appeared in Charles Wesley's *Hymns for those that seek, and those that have Redemption* (1747). In his *Wesleyan Hymn Book* of 1780 John Wesley altered the second line of the fourth verse to 'Pure and spotless let us be' to avoid suggesting that Christians could achieve a sinless perfection in this world. He also omitted the second verse of the hymn, which again clearly expresses the notion of a move towards perfection following conversion to Christianity during which the soul is further cleansed and gradually comes closer to God. The 'second rest', referred to in the fourth line, is the relief from the struggle against sin in the life of the true Christian which comes as a further stage after his initial conversion experience. All subsequent hymnbooks have followed John Wesley's changes and some have also altered the second line of the third verse to 'Let us all thy grace receive'. But they have been happy to keep the last verse with its message that individuals will in this life, and before they take their place in heaven, be 'changed from glory into glory' by gradually absorbing and reflecting more and more of the power and influence of Jesus.

The first line of this hymn is recalled in another of Wesley's hymns, written a few years later, which begins:

> O Love divine, how sweet thou art!
> When shall I find my willing heart
> All taken up by thee?
> I thirst, I faint, I die to prove
> The greatness of redeeming love,
> The love of Christ to me.

The closing line, 'Lost in wonder, love, and praise', was almost certainly lifted from the hymn 'When all thy mercies, O my God' by Joseph Addison (see notes to no. 132 for biographical details), which ends with exactly the same phrase.

There is a rich choice of tunes for this hymn. Purcell's tune, which Wesley had in mind when he wrote it, appeared in the Wesleys' hymnbooks of 1761 and 1780 under the name Westminster, but was then dropped and did not reappear until it crept into the *School Hymnal* of the Methodist Church in 1950. Sir John Stainer wrote the tune Love Divine for the 1889 supplement to *Hymns Ancient and Modern*, and Sir Charles Stanford supplied Airedale for the 1904 edition. Nowadays the hymn is generally sung to one of two equally majestic Welsh tunes: Hyfrydol by Rowland Huw Prichard (1811–57), a loom-tender's assistant in the Welsh Flannel Manufacturing Company's mills at Holywell; and Blaenwern by William Penfro Rowlands (1860–1937).

Love divine, all loves excelling,
Joy of heav'n, to earth come down,
Fix in us thy humble dwelling,
All thy faithful mercies crown.
Jesu, thou art all compassion,
Pure unbounded love thou art;
Visit us with thy salvation,
Enter every trembling heart.

2   Breathe, O breathe thy loving spirit
Into every troubled breast!
Let us all in thee inherit,
Let us find that second rest.
Take away our bent to sinning,
Alpha and Omega be;
End of faith, as its beginning.
Set our hearts at liberty.

3   Come, almighty to deliver,
Let us all thy life receive;
Suddenly return, and never,
Never more thy temples leave.
Thee we would be always blessing,
Serve thee as thy hosts above,
Pray, and praise thee, without ceasing,
Glory in thy perfect love.

4   Finish then thy new creation,
Pure and sinless let us be;
Let us see thy great salvation,
Perfectly restored in thee:
Changed from glory into glory,
Till in heav'n we take our place,
Till we cast our crowns before thee,
Lost in wonder, love, and praise!

MAKE ME A CHANNEL OF
YOUR PEACE

Most of the modern hymns which have achieved widespread popularity in recent years have come from the evangelical wing of Protestantism. This simple but highly effective adaptation of the prayer traditionally attributed to St Francis of Assisi comes from the pen of a South African-born Catholic and has been popularized throughout the English-speaking world by the Franciscan Communications Center in Los Angeles, California. It stands seventh in the 2002 *Songs of Praise* poll.

The author, Johann Sebastian von Tempelhoff, who writes under the name Sebastian Temple, was born in Pretoria in 1928. He started writing books at the age of 19 and lived in England for seven years before taking up residence in the USA. He now lives in California and has twelve albums of songs and hymns to his credit.

Sebastian Temple wrote the verses here in response to a request for a collection of songs for the Franciscan Third Order's church in downtown Los Angeles. In a letter to me he says:

I wrote so easily and so prolifically that I took for granted that I could write music to the peace prayer of St Francis. The album's other 12 songs fell out of my lips and on to a tape recorder very easily and I wrote them in two days. The third day was left for the peace prayer. Though inspirations for all came easily to me, its strange form drove me crazy. I could not come up with anything that sounded like music to my ears. I tried for a whole morning but nothing came. Finally, I was disgusted, looked at the little statue of St Francis on my shelf and said angrily, 'Well, if you want to write it, YOU do it. I can't.' I got up, went to the kitchen, made a cup of tea and drank it. When I returned to the guitar, I picked it up, had the tape running, and the song fell out of my mouth as it was recorded a few days later.

Modern scholarship tends to cast doubt on the traditional view that the well-known prayer on which this hymn is based was in fact written by St Francis (on whom see note to no. 3). It is now thought rather to have been the work of a later Franciscan, Jacopone da Todi (c. 1230–1306); but whoever the author was, it is a fine prayer. The traditional English version on which Temple based his hymn goes as follows:

Lord, make me an instrument of your peace. Where there is hatred, let me sow love. Where there is injury, pardon. Where there is doubt, faith. Where there is despair, hope. Where there is darkness, light. Where there is sadness, joy.

O Divine Master, grant that I may not so much seek to be consoled, as to console; to be understood as to understand; to be loved, as to love; for it is in giving that we receive, it is in pardoning that we are pardoned and it is in dying that we are born to eternal life.

It is interesting that in the opening line of his hymn Sebastian Temple makes use of an image which was particularly popular with Martin Luther, who often spoke of humans as channels passing on the love that we get from God to our neighbours. This kind of imagery finds its fullest expression in the writings of the early twentieth-century Swedish Lutheran Anders Nygren who says in his book *Agape and Eros*: 'All that a Christian possesses he has received from God, and all that he possesses he passes on in love to his neighbour. He has nothing of his own to give. He is merely the tube, the channel, through which God's love flows.'★

Temple is responsible for the tune as well as the words of this hymn.

★ Anders Nygren, *Agape and Eros* (London: SPCK, 1982).

Make me a channel of your peace.
Where there is hatred, let me bring you love.
Where there is injury, your pardon, Lord.
And where there's doubt, true faith in you.

2   Make me a channel of your peace.
Where there's despair in life, let me bring hope.
Where there is darkness, only light.
And where there's sadness, ever joy.

3   Oh, Master grant that I may never seek
So much to be consoled as to console,
To be understood as to understand,
To be loved, as to love with all my soul.

4   Make me a channel of your peace.
It is in pardoning that we are pardoned,
In giving of ourselves that we receive,
And in dying that we're born to eternal life.

Prayer of St Francis by Sebastian Temple. Dedicated to Mrs. Frances Tracey. © 1967, OCP Publications, 5536 NE Haosalo, Portland OR 97213, USA. All rights reserved. Used with permission. Administered in the UK by Calamus Music.

MINE EYES HAVE SEEN
THE GLORY OF THE
COMING OF THE LORD

General William Booth of the Salvation Army was not the only person determined that the Devil should not have all the best tunes. This hymn was written by an American lady who heard some soldiers singing 'John Brown's body lies a-mould'ring in the grave' and felt that such a good tune deserved rather more uplifting words. Written at the height of the American Civil War, it has become a virtually indispensable feature of national parades and presidential inaugurations in the USA.

The author, Julia Ward Howe (1819–1910), came of an upper-class New York family and was a Unitarian lay preacher. Her husband, a Bostonian doctor who worked principally with the mentally handicapped, was an ardent advocate of the abolition of slavery. He helped the negro by the name of John Brown on whom the popular song was based: a madman who massacred five whites and led a kingdom of liberated slaves in the mountains before being hanged for treason at Harper's Ferry, Virginia.

One afternoon in November 1861 the Howes went out to visit the Unionist army of Potomac in action near Washington. They spent the night under canvas with the troops who were singing their song about John Brown. A friend, James Freeman Clarke, who had left the Unitarians to found his own Church of the Disciples in Boston, suggested to Julia that she write new words for the tune. That evening she thought about it and the following morning she got up early from her camp bed and lit a candle. 'In the dimness with the old stump of a pen which I remembered to have used the day before, I scrawled the verses almost without looking at the paper.' An early draft of the hymn, still extant, was written out on the notepaper of the Sanitary

Commission in Washington of which her husband was a member.

In turning 'John Brown's Body' into a hymn Julia Howe was in fact restoring the tune's original purpose, as it seems to have started life in Charleston, South Carolina, in the mid-1850s as the melody of a Methodist hymn, 'Say, brother, will you meet us?' For her own hymn she drew on several powerful biblical images. The trampling of the grapes of wrath comes from Isaiah 63.3; the crushing of the serpent from Genesis 3.15; and the idea of Christ being born in the beauty of the lilies, from the Song of Solomon.

'Mine eyes have seen the glory of the coming of the Lord' was first published in the *Atlantic Monthly* (February 1862), where it was entitled 'The Battle Hymn of the Republic'. For all rights in the piece, Julia Howe was paid just four dollars. Her hymn became one of the major marching songs of the North in the American Civil War. When it is sung nowadays, the third line of the fifth verse is often changed to 'As he died to make men holy, let us live to make men free'.

Although it is almost unthinkable to sing 'Mine eyes have seen the glory' to anything other than the tune of John Brown's Body, two other melodies have been composed especially for it by leading British church musicians. Vision by Sir Walford Davies (1869–1941) and Battle Song by Martin Shaw (1875–1958) both first appeared in 1915.

The Battle Hymn of the Republic

Mine eyes have seen the glory of the coming of the Lord;
He is trampling out the vintage where the grapes of wrath are
    stored;
He hath loosed the fateful lightning of his terrible swift sword:
    His truth is marching on

2 I have seen him in the watchfires of a hundred circling camps;
They have builded him an altar in the evening dews and damps;
I have read his righteous sentence in the dim and flaring lamps;
    His day is marching on.

3 I have read a fiery gospel, writ in burnished rows of steel;
As ye deal with my contemners, so with you my grace shall deal:
Let the hero born of woman crush the serpent with his heel;
    Our God is marching on.

4 He has sounded forth the trumpet that shall never call retreat;
He is sifting out the hearts of men before his judgment seat;
O be swift, my soul, to answer him, be jubilant, my feet:
    Our God is marching on.

5 In the beauty of the lilies Christ was born across the sea
With a glory in his bosom that transfigures you and me;
As he died to make men holy, let us die to make men free:
    Our God is marching on.

6 He is coming like the glory of the morning on the wave,
He is wisdom to the mighty, he is succour to the brave;
So the world shall be his footstool, and the soul of time his slave:
    Our God is marching on.

MORNING HAS BROKEN

Like John Newton's 'Amazing grace' (no. 10), this hymn achieved considerable fame as a pop song in the early 1970s. Recorded by Cat Stevens, it was in the Top Ten in both Britain and the USA for several weeks. Now, thankfully, it has been restored to the use for which it was originally written and is a popular hymn both in church services and school assemblies.

'Morning has broken' was written by Eleanor Farjeon (1881–1965) in the early 1920s at the request of Percy Dearmer, the editor of *Songs of Praise*. He wanted a hymn for the new book to fit the Gaelic melody Bunessan and approached her, suggesting the theme of thanksgiving for each new day. I have been told on good authority that the words came to her early one morning when she was camping in woods on the Sussex estate of the Roman Catholic poet, Alice Meynell. Altogether Eleanor Farjeon wrote four hymns for *Songs of Praise*, which came out in 1931, the others being 'More lovely than the noonday rest', 'Lord, thou who gav'st me all I have' and the harvest hymn 'Fields of corn, give up your eyes'. She was paid three guineas for each of them.

Eleanor Farjeon, chiefly remembered today as a children's writer, was, in fact, an author and poet of wide range and considerable accomplishment. Born in London, her father was a novelist, playwright and journalist of Jewish descent and her mother came from an American theatrical family. Eleanor led a somewhat Bohemian life and had a romantic attachment to the poet Edward Thomas before settling down with George Earle. She had a strong interest in religion throughout her life and flirted with both spiritualism and theories of reincarnation. She finally found her spiritual home in the Roman Catholic Church, into which she was received on her 70th birthday. She underwent instruction at Farm Street and was much influenced by the thirteenth-century mystical work, *The Cloud of Unknowing*, as well as by the writings of St Augustine and the spiritual exercises of St Ignatius Loyola.

In her biography of Eleanor Farjeon, which takes its title from the first line of this hymn,* her daughter Annabel writes that 'Catholicism satisfied the ideal longings of this enthusiastic convert, satisfied her innocence and her ripeness with the promise of bliss in a perfect hereafter.' Eleanor herself wrote that her coming to Catholicism was less a conversion

than a progression to a form of faith towards which my own sense of a spiritual life has been moving for the last thirty or forty years. One has to be 'converted' from one faith to another – and I've never had another to be converted from. I have had an always increasing sense of the immortal spirit from a source I could only think of as God.**

The tune Bunessan (or Bùn Easain to give it its original Gaelic name), for which 'Morning is broken' was written and to which it is invariably sung, seems to have been first noted down in the 1880s from the singing of a wandering Highland singer and first published in 1888 in Lachlann MacBean's *Songs and Hymns of the Scottish Highlands*, where it was set to a Gaelic poem, '*Leanabh an Aigh*' (Baby of Good Fortune) written by Mary Macdonald, a noted Gaelic poet who spent all her life in the vicinity of Bunessan in the south-west corner of the Isle of Mull, in 1888. It is still used for the English version of the carol, 'Child in the manger'.

* Annabel Farjeon, *Morning has Broken: A Biography of Eleanor Farjeon* (London: Julia Macrae Books, 1986).
** Ibid.

Thanks for a Day

Morning has broken
Like the first morning.
Blackbird has spoken
Like the first bird.
Praise for the singing!
Praise for the morning!
Praise for them, springing
Fresh from the word!

2   Sweet the rain's new fall
Sunlit from heaven,
Like the first dewfall
On the first grass.
Praise for the sweetness
Of the wet garden,
Sprung in completeness
Where his feet pass.

3   Mine is the sunlight!
Mine is the morning
Born of the one light
Eden saw play!
Praise with elation,
Praise every morning,
God's re-creation
Of the new day!

From *The Children's Bells* by Eleanor Farjeon, published by Oxford University Press. Reproduced by permission of David Higham Associates Ltd.

MY GOD! HOW
WONDERFUL THOU ART

Until a very late stage in the preparation of this book, this slot was occupied by Edward Caswall's hymn, 'My God, I love thee not because I hope for Heaven thereby'. But the more I contemplated its words and overall tone, the less I liked them and I decided to include instead this simple yet profound hymn by Frederick William Faber (1814–63).

It is, indeed, right and proper that Faber should figure in an anthology of the best-loved hymns in the English language. His 'Faith of our fathers! living still' is immensely popular in the USA and among Roman Catholics in Britain. It begins:

> Faith of our fathers! living still
> In spite of dungeon, fire and sword:
> Oh how our hearts beat high with joy
> Whene'er we hear that glorious word.
> Faith of our fathers! Holy Faith!
> We will be true to thee till death.

Most modern hymnbooks on both sides of the Atlantic include Faber's magnificent 'Souls of men, why will ye scatter', with its well-known third verse which is often taken as the opening of the hymn, 'There's a wideness in God's mercy' (no. 134).

Faber was born at Calverley, Yorkshire, where his grandfather was vicar. Educated at Shrewsbury and Harrow schools and Balliol College, Oxford, he moved from extreme evangelicalism to High Anglicanism under the influence of the Oxford Movement. He was ordained into the Church of England in 1837 and became Rector of Elton in Huntingdonshire. In 1845 he followed his great friend and mentor John Henry Newman into the Roman Catholic Church, and set up a small religious community in Birmingham with the name 'Brothers of the Will of God', later shortened to the 'Wilfridians' because Faber took for himself the name Brother Wilfrid. In 1848 he joined Newman's Oratory in Birmingham and the following year he established a branch of the Oratory in London. Faber remained as Superior of the Brompton Oratory, as it came to be known, for the rest of his life.

Faber's considerable literary output included a 42-volume *Lives of the Saints*, books on meditation and theology and 150 hymns. He was keen to encourage the practice of hymn-singing in the Roman Catholic Church in Britain and hoped that his work might have the same effect that the *Olney Hymns* had had on evangelical Anglicanism. Some of his hymns come close to doggerel, but there are others which though they no longer appear in hymnals, deserve to be brought back. Perhaps the best are 'Hark! hark! my soul! angelic songs are swelling', 'O Saviour, bless us as we go' and the Good Friday hymn, 'O come and mourn with me awhile'.

'My God, how wonderful Thou art' first appeared in Faber's collection, *Jesus and Mary*, which was published in 1849. In modern hymnals the first line of the third verse is generally changed to 'How wonderful, how beautiful' and verses 6 and 8 are omitted.

The hymn is invariably sung to Westminster by James Turle (1802–82) which first appeared in Novello's *The Psalmist* in 1836. Turle was organist and master of the choristers at Westminster Abbey from 1831 to 1875.

Our Heavenly Father

My God! how wonderful thou art,
Thy Majesty how bright,
How beautiful thy mercy-seat
In depths of burning light!

How dread are thine eternal years,
O everlasting Lord!
By prostrate spirits day and night
Incessantly adored!

How beautiful, how beautiful
The sight of thee must be,
Thine endless wisdom, boundless power
And aweful purity!

Oh how I fear thee, living God!
With deepest, tenderest fears,
And worship thee with trembling hope
And penitential tears.

Yet I may love thee, living God!
Almighty as thou art,
For thou hast stooped to ask of me
The love of my poor heart.

O then this worse than worthless heart
In pity deign to take
And make it love thee, for thyself
And for thy glory's sake.

No earthly father loves like thee,
No mother half so mild
Bears and forbears, as thou hast done,
With me, thy sinful child.

Only to sit and think of God,
Oh, what a joy it is!
To think the thought, to breathe the Name,
Earth has no higher bliss!

Father of Jesus, love's reward,
What rapture will it be,
Prostrate before thy throne to lie,
And gaze, and gaze on thee!

MY SONG IS LOVE UNKNOWN

The rediscovery in the twentieth century of verses by seventeenth-century writers has produced a rich harvest of hymns. We have already come across George Herbert's 'King of Glory, King of Peace' (no. 70) and 'Let all the world in ev'ry corner sing' (no. 74). This fine poem, which is now an extremely popular hymn much in demand at weddings and on other occasions, was written more than 300 years ago, but has only been widely sung in church in the last 50 years or so. Its enormous popularity in our own times must be very largely attributable to the haunting tune which John Ireland composed for it shortly after the First World War.

The author of 'My song is love unknown' was Samuel Crossman (1624–83), an Anglican clergyman who spent most of his adult life at Bristol Cathedral. Born in Bradfield Monachorum in Suffolk, he was educated at Cambridge University, and after a long period as prebendary of Bristol Cathedral, he became Dean just a few months before his death. He is buried in the south aisle of the cathedral.

The verses printed here first appeared in a small pamphlet containing nine poems by Crossman that was published in 1664 with the title *The Young Man's Meditation, or some few Sacred Poems upon Select Subjects and Scriptures*. It is possible that they were sung as a hymn in the author's own lifetime, set to a tune composed by Henry Lawes (1596–1662) for Psalm 47, but this is unlikely. 'My song is love unknown' does not appear in any hymn collections published during the eighteenth or the first half of the nineteenth century. It is first found as a hymn in the *Anglican Hymn Book* of 1868, where it was set to Lawes's tune, and then in the *Congregational Hymnal* of 1887. It subsequently appeared in the first edition of the *Public School Hymn Book* in 1903 and has been a firm favourite in school chapels ever since.

It was not, however, until Crossman's words were married with the tune Love Unknown by John Ireland (1879–1962) that the hymn achieved widespread popularity. Geoffrey Shaw, the music editor of *Songs of Praise*, asked Ireland if he could supply a tune for Crossman's verses which Percy Dearmer wished to include in the new hymnal. The story goes that Ireland obliged almost immediately and seemingly without effort, writing out the melody on a scrap of paper in less than a quarter of an hour. His tune first appeared in the 1919 edition of the *Public School Hymn Book* and then in the first edition of *Songs of Praise* (1925).

John Ireland was born at Bowden in Cheshire. His father, Alexander Ireland, was editor of the *Manchester Examiner* and a friend of Thomas Carlyle. John was educated at Leeds Grammar School and at the Royal College of Music where he studied under Sir Charles Stanford. He was successively organist of All Saints', Tufnell Park; St Jude's, Upper Chelsea; Holy Trinity, Sloane Square; and St Luke's, Upper Chelsea, where he remained for 22 years. Love Unknown, as it is called, is the only one of his hymn-tunes which is regularly used today.

Several of Samuel Crossman's other poems became hymns, but none has survived in modern hymnals. They include 'My life's a shade, my days', 'Sweet place, sweet place, alone' and 'Farewell, poor world, I must be gone'.

My song is love unknown,
My Saviour's love to me,
Love to the loveless shown,
That they might lovely be.
O, who am I,
That for my sake
My Lord should take
Frail flesh, and die?

2   He came from his blest throne,
Salvation to bestow:
But men made strange, and none
The longed-for Christ would know.
But O, my Friend,
My Friend indeed,
Who at my need
His life did spend!

3   Sometimes they strew his way,
And his sweet praises sing;
Resounding all the day
Hosannas to their King.
Then 'Crucify!'
Is all their breath,
And for his death
They thirst and cry.

4   Why, what hath my Lord done?
What makes this rage and spite?
He made the lame to run,
He gave the blind their sight.
Sweet injuries!
Yet they at these
Themselves displease,
And 'gainst him rise.

5   They rise, and needs will have
    My dear Lord made away;
    A murderer they save,
    The Prince of Life they slay.
    Yet cheerful he
    To suffering goes,
    That he his foes
    From thence might free.

6   In life no house, no home,
    My Lord on earth might have;
    In death no friendly tomb,
    But what a stranger gave.
    What may I say?
    Heav'n was his home;
    But mine the tomb
    Wherein he lay.

7   Here might I stay and sing,
    No story so divine;
    Never was love, dear King,
    Never was grief like thine!
    This is my Friend,
    In whose sweet praise
    I all my days
    Could gladly spend.

NEARER, MY GOD, TO
THEE

Like 'Mine eyes have 'seen the glory of the coming of the Lord'
(no. 84), this hymn comes from the pen of a Unitarian lady. Mrs
Sarah Adams, *née* Flower (1805–48), was born in Harlow, Essex,
the daughter of a Radical journalist who was imprisoned for
criticizing the politics of the Bishop of Llandaff. She had a
distinguished literary career and was a close friend of Robert
Browning.

'Nearer, my God, to Thee' was one of thirteen hymns which
Sarah Adams contributed to a Unitarian collection published in
1841 for use in the South Place Religious Society in Finsbury,
London. It is based on the story of Jacob's dream at Bethel
recounted in Genesis 28.10–22. When the hymn first appeared
there were complaints that it did not mention Christ and that it
was not suitable for public worship in Trinitarian churches.
Several editors composed an additional verse before including it
in their hymnals, and William Walsham How, the author of 'For
all thy saints who from their labours rest' (no. 35) rewrote Mrs
Adams's verses with the purpose of 'expressing more definitely
Christian faith'. It was, however, in its original form that the
hymn achieved widespread popularity in the latter part of the
nineteenth century.

Perhaps the best-known tune for the hymn, at least in Britain,
is Horbury, which John Bacchus Dykes (1823–76) wrote for the
first edition of *Hymns Ancient and Modern* in 1861. He named it
after the town in Yorkshire which he had visited two years earlier
to make his first confession. In the USA the tune most often used
has been Bethany, which was composed in 1856 by Dr Lowell
Mason (1792–1872), a bank clerk from Savannah who founded
the Boston Academy of Music. Other melodies specially
composed for this hymn include *Propior Deo* by Sir Arthur

Sullivan (1842–1900), Liverpool by John Roberts (1822–77), and Nenthorn by Thomas Legerwood Hately (1815–67).

The great question about 'Nearer, my god, to Thee' is, of course, whether it was the hymn that the band struck up on the *Titanic* as that ill-fated liner sank after hitting an iceberg on 14 April 1912. Mrs Eva Hart, one of the longest-living survivors of the disaster, was adamant that it was. 'I am as certain about that as I am sitting here', she is quoted in *The Times* of 13 April 1987 as saying. 'Whether it was the last hymn, I don't know.'

Others, however, are sceptical about the tradition that it was Mrs Adams's hymn that was played as the ship went down. They base their doubts on the fact that contemporary press reports quoted the ship's radio operator, Harold Bride, a former choirboy who survived the disaster, as saying that what he heard being played from the sinking vessel as he was in the sea waiting to be rescued was the hymn-tune Autumn. There are, in fact, three different tunes with this name to be found in early twentieth-century hymnbooks, set respectively to Robert Bridges' 'Joy and triumph everlasting', George Horne's 'See the leaves around us falling' and William Walsham How's 'The year is swiftly waning'. If it was one of these that the band played, the last is the most likely candidate. The lines which close its first verse would certainly have been appropriate to the melancholy occasion:

> And life, brief life, is speeding;
> The end is nearing fast.

Sir Ronald Johnson, who made a special study of the whole question of the *Titanic* hymn and with whom I corresponded at some length on the subject, believed that the tune heard by Bride and wrongly transcribed by reporters was, in fact, Aughton, which accompanied W.B. Bradbury's hymn, 'He leadeth me! O blessed thought'. Its closing verse would certainly have been apt:

> And when my task on earth is done
> When by Thy grace the victory's won
> E'en death's cold wave I will not flee
> Since God through Jordan leadeth me.

Nearer, my God, to Thee,
Nearer to Thee!
E'en though it be a cross
That raiseth me,
Still all my song would be,
'Nearer, my God, to Thee,
Nearer to Thee!'

2   Though, like the wanderer,
The sun gone down,
Darkness be over me,
My rest a stone,
Yet in my dreams I'd be
Nearer, my God, to Thee,
Nearer to Thee!

3   There let the way appear
Steps unto heaven,
All that Thou send'st to me
In mercy given,
Angels to beckon me
Nearer, my God, to Thee,
Nearer to Thee!

4   Then, with my waking thoughts
Bright with Thy praise,
Out of my stony griefs
Bethel I'll raise,
So by my woes to be
Nearer, my God, to Thee,
Nearer to Thee!

5   Or if on joyful wing
      Cleaving the sky,
      Sun, moon, and stars forgot,
      Upwards I fly,
      Still all my song shall be,
      'Nearer, my God, to Thee,
      Nearer to Thee!'

NEW EVERY MORNING IS
THE LOVE

This inspiring morning hymn is the work of John Keble (1792–1866). It was written in 1822 while he was a tutor at Oriel College, Oxford, and published five years later in his book, *The Christian Year*.

John Keble was one of the leading figures in the Oxford Movement which sought to take the Church of England back to its Catholic roots. Indeed, the assize sermon which he preached in the University Church of St Mary the Virgin in Oxford in July 1833 on the theme of national apostasy is generally taken to mark the start of the movement. Unlike other Tractarians, such as Newman, he remained loyal to the Church of England and did not become a Roman Catholic. Commemorated today in Keble College, Oxford, he was revered in his lifetime as a saintly parish priest.

Keble was born at Fairford where his father was vicar. After obtaining a double first at Oxford, he became a fellow of Oriel College at the age of 18 and was ordained six years later. He became a curate of East Leach and Bunthorpe. From 1831 to 1841 he was Professor of Poetry at Oxford University, and in 1836 he became vicar of Hursley, in Hampshire, where he remained for 30 years until his death.

'New every morning' is a small section of a much longer poem. It is made up of verses 6, 7, 8, 9, 13, 14 and 16 of a poem entitled 'Morning', which appeared at the beginning of *The Christian Year* with the text 'His compassions fail not. They are new every morning' (Lam. 3. 22–23). The first five verses of the poem are as follows:

> Hues of the rich unfolding morn,
> That, ere the glorious sun be born,

By some soft touch invisible
Around his path are taught to swell;

Thou rustling breeze so fresh and gay,
That dancest forth at opening day,
And brushing by with joyous wing,
Wakenest each little leaf to sing;

Ye fragrant clouds of dewy steam,
By which deep grove and tangled stream
Pay, for soft rains in season given,
Their tribute to the genial heaven;

Why waste your treasures of delight
Upon our thankless, joyless sight;
Who day by day to sin awake,
Seldom of heaven and you partake?

Oh! timely happy, timely wise,
Hearts that with rising morn arise!
Eyes that the beam celestial view,
Which evermore makes all things new!

Several nineteenth- and early twentieth-century hymnals included the above stanzas, or a selection of them, as a separate hymn in addition to 'New every morning is the love'. Others made a hymn by beginning with the tenth verse of the original poem in *The Christian Year*:

As for some dear familiar strain
Untir'd we ask, and ask again,
Ever, in its melodious store,
Finding a spell unheard before.

The tune to which 'New every morning is the love' is almost always sung, known variously as Melcombe, Granton and St Philip's, is by Samuel Webbe (1740–1816), a cabinet-maker who became organist at the Sardinian Chapel in London. It first appeared in 1792 in an essay which he wrote on church plainchant, where it was written in plainsong notation and set to the words '*O salutaris hostia*'.

Morning

New every morning is the love
Our wakening and uprising prove;
Through sleep and darkness safely brought,
Restored to life, and power, and thought.

2   New mercies, each returning day,
Hover around us while we pray;
New perils past, new sins forgiven,
New thoughts of God, new hopes of heaven.

3   If on our daily course our mind
Be set to hallow all we find,
New treasures still, of countless price,
God will provide for sacrifice.

4   Old friends, old scenes will lovelier be,
As more of heaven in each we see:
Some softening gleam of love and prayer
Shall dawn on every cross and care.

5   We need not bid, for cloister'd cell,
Our neighbour and our words farewell,
Nor strive to find ourselves too high
For sinful man beneath the sky:

6   The trivial round, the common task,
Will furnish all we ought to ask;
Room to deny ourselves – a road
To bring us, daily, nearer God.

7   Only, O Lord, in thy dear love
Fit us for perfect rest above;
And help us, this and every day,
To live more nearly as we pray.

NOW THANK WE ALL
OUR GOD

This great hymn of rejoicing, so popular at weddings and other festive occasions, is translated from a German grace which was written around 350 years ago and designed to be sung after meals in devout Lutheran households in the dark days of the Thirty Years War. It is based on Ecclesiasticus 50.22–23: 'Now bless the God of all, who in every way does great things; who exalts our days from birth, and deals with us according to his mercy. May he give us gladness of heart, and grant that peace may be in our days in Israel, as in the days of old.'

The author, Martin Rinkart (1586–1649), was the son of a coppersmith. Educated at the University of Leipzig, he became precentor at the church in Martin Luther's home town of Eisleben and then, in 1617, returned to his own native Saxon village of Eilenburg as pastor. For the next 30 years rival armies from across Europe roamed through the parish pillaging and plundering everything in their way. To make matters worse, the village was struck with plague in 1637. More than 8,000 of the inhabitants perished, and Rinkart himself buried 4,000 of his parishioners, some days conducting mass funerals for as many as 50 at a time.

In the midst of this terrible plague, and the severe famine that came in its wake, the Swedish forces that were occupying Eilenburg demanded a tribute of 30,000 thalers from the stricken inhabitants. Rinkart appealed to them and managed to have the sum reduced to 2,000 thalers. He also appealed to the Almighty, telling his parishioners, 'We can find no mercy with men; let us take refuge with God.'

The story is often told that it was in these grim circumstances that Rinkart wrote his great hymn of thanksgiving and praise. However, the exact date of its composition is uncertain. Some historians suggest that it was written as early as 1630 while others maintain that Rinkart composed it in 1648 having heard of the impending peace settlement at Westphalia that was to end the three decades of fighting in Germany. The latter view has now been almost wholly discredited. What is certain is that the hymn was widely sung when the Treaty of Westphalia was signed in 1648. Since then it has been a kind of German *Te Deum*, sung on occasions of national thanksgiving.

It has had something of the same status in Britain over the last 130 years, thanks to the translation in 1858 by Catherine Winkworth (1827–78). Catherine lived most of her life in Manchester and was a prolific and highly accomplished translator of German hymns into English – she was also responsible for 'Praise to the Lord, the Almighty, the King of Creation' (no. 110). Her translation of Rinkart's '*Nun danket alle Gott*' first appeared in her *Lyra Germanica*, published in 1855. In his *Dictionary of Hymnology* John Julian lists eleven other translations of the hymn, but none approached Miss Winkworth's in quality nor came anywhere near it in popularity.

The tune *Nun Danket* which has always been associated with this hymn is often ascribed to Johann Crüger (1598–1662), cantor of St Nicholas Church in Berlin and composer of numerous hymn-tunes. It was in a book edited by Crüger that the tune and the hymn made their first appearance in 1647. But there is no direct evidence that he composed the tune and some have suggested that the melody came to Rinkart when he was writing the words. This is quite possible, as he was himself a noted musician.

Grace

Now thank we all our God,
With heart and hands and voices,
Who wondrous things hath done
In whom his world rejoices;
Who from our mother's arms
Hath blessed us on our way
With countless gifts of love,
And still is ours today.

2   O may this bounteous God
Through all our life be near us,
With ever joyful hearts
And blessed peace to cheer us;
And keep us in his grace,
And guide us when perplexed,
And free us from all ills
In this world and the next.

3   All praise and thanks to God
The Father now be given,
The Son, and him who reigns
With them in highest heaven,
The one eternal God,
Whom earth and heaven adore,
For thus it was, is now,
And shall be evermore.

O COME, O COME, EMMANUEL

This Advent hymn is based on the Latin antiphons which were sung in the Early Church during the week leading up to Christmas Day. The origins of these short verses is uncertain although they probably date from the sixth or seventh century and were certainly in use at Rome before the ninth century. There were originally seven antiphons and in monastic institutions they were chanted at the evening service of Vespers by obedientiaries (officers), both before and after the Magnificat.

Originally the antiphons were never sung together but only one on each of the seven days leading up to Christmas. However, some time in the twelfth century five of them were put together to form the verses of a single hymn beginning '*Veni, veni, Emmanuel*', and with the refrain '*Gaude, gaude, Emmanuel, nascetur pro te, Israel*' sung at the end of each verse.

In their original Latin form, as in translation, the verses all began with a long drawn out 'O' to express longing for the Saviour. Each described Christ in a different way – as *Emmanuel* (God with us), as in Isaiah 7.14; *Jesse virgula* (the Root of Jesse), as in Isaiah 11.10; *Oriens* (the Dayspring), as in Malachi 4.2; *Clavis Davidica* (the Key of David), Isaiah 22.22; and *Adonai* (the Lord of Might), as in Exodus 3.15.

The first translation of the Latin antiphons into English was made by John Henry Newman (1801–90: see no. 34) in 1836 for his *Tracts for the Times*. In 1851 John Mason Neale (1818–66: see no. 22) translated the five verses which had been turned into a hymn. He produced a hymn which began 'Draw nigh, draw nigh, Emmanuel', and which first appeared in his book *Mediaeval Hymns*. The following year he revised his translation to produce the version which is printed here. It was first published in his *Hymnal Noted*. Several other translations have been made of the

Latin hymn, but none is as faithful to the original or as fresh as Neale's.

This hymn undoubtedly derives much of its powerful sense of longing from the tune *Veni Immanuel*, which has accompanied Neale's revised translation since 1854. It seems to derive from a tune in a French missal in the National Library of Portugal in Lisbon, which itself was an adaptation of a plainsong Kyrie. Some authorities say that Neale himself copied the tune from the missal, others that it was copied by Bishop Jenner during a visit to Lisbon in 1853. The tune was arranged by Thomas Helmore (1811–90), an Anglican clergyman who was one of the pioneers in the revival of the use of Gregorian chant in the services of the Anglican Church.

Veni, veni, Emmanuel

O come, O come, Emmanuel,
And ransom captive Israel,
That mourns in lonely exile here,
Until the Son of God appear:

Rejoice! Rejoice! Emmanuel
Shall come to thee, O Israel.

2   O come, thou Rod of Jesse, free
    Thine own from Satan's tyranny;
    From depths of hell thy people save,
    And give them vict'ry o'er the grave:

3   O come, thou Day-spring, come and cheer
    Our spirits by thine advent here;
    Disperse the gloomy clouds of night,
    And death's dark shadows put to flight:

4   O come, thou Key of David, come,
    And open wide our heav'nly home;
    Make safe the way that leads on high,
    And close the path to misery:

5   O come, O come, thou Lord of Might,
    Who to thy tribes, on Sinai's height,
    In ancient times didst give the law
    In cloud, and majesty, and awe:

O FOR A CLOSER WALK
WITH GOD

This strikingly honest depiction of the waning of the initial
fervour and joy of Christian belief and longing for its recovery
stands alongside Newman's 'Lead, kindly light' as one of the
greatest poetic expressions of doubt-tinged faith. It was, indeed,
chosen as the first item in a section entitled 'Faith and Doubt'
proposed for the 1983 Methodist collection *Hymns and Psalms*,
but both the hymn and the section were dropped from the final
book – a pity, as we could do with more hymns expressing
honest doubt.

Like 'God moves in a mysterious way' (no. 45: see notes for
biographical details), 'O for a closer walk with God' was written
by William Cowper (1731–1800) during one of the comparatively rare periods of sanity that punctuated his almost
continuous mental torment. He wrote it on 9 December 1769
at a time when he was considerably agitated about the illness of
his housekeeper, Mrs Unwin, on whom he relied almost totally
to keep him going. He was deeply worried at what might happen
to him in the event of her death. He attached to the hymn the
biblical quotation 'Enoch walked with God, and he was not, for
God took him' (Gen. 5.24).

In a letter to a friend the following day, he wrote of these
verses: 'I began to compose them yesterday morning, but fell
asleep at the end of the first two lines. When I awakened again
the third and fourth were whispered to my heart, in a way which
I have often experienced.' The hymn was first published in 1776
in the form printed here and appeared thus in the *Olney Hymns*
of 1779. The second and third verses, with their note of deep
sadness and sense of loss, are often omitted from modern
hymnbooks, giving a rather different feel to the hymn than that
conveyed in Cowper's original composition.

It was shortly after writing these verses that Cowper composed his hymn, 'There is a fountain filled with blood', which is full of strong evangelical imagery of sin and depravity. Its first two verses, which are generally toned down in modern hymnals, originally ran:

There is a fountain filled with blood
Drawn from Immanuel's veins;
And sinners, plunged beneath that flood,
Lose all their guilty stains.

The dying thief rejoiced to see
That fountain in his day;
And there have I, as vile as he,
Washed all my sins away.

'O for a closer walk with God' is generally sung to one of two Scottish tunes: Caithness, a melody from the 1635 Scottish Psalter; or Stracathro, written in the late 1840s by Charles Hutcheson (1792–1860) to be sung in the church where he worshipped, St George's in Glasgow. This latter tune was named after a village on the banks of the North Esk where a fellow member of the congregation, Sir James Campbell, had just bought a property. Hutcheson gave it the name Stracathro as a tribute to Campbell, a former Lord Provost of Glasgow. The tune fell out of use during the next 50 years but was revived in the twentieth century, thanks to the somewhat unlikely combination of the *Public School Hymn Book*, which included in its 1919 edition a version harmonized by Geoffrey Shaw and the Glasgow Orpheus Choir, whose conductor Sir Hugh Roberton arranged a faux-bourdon setting (i.e. alternate verses passing to the tenor) of Stracathro for Cowper's hymn.

Cowper's words of wistful yearning are also perfectly complemented by John Campbell's tune Orlington which provides for the third line in each verse to be repeated. Personally, I find it the most moving and appropriate melody for this hymn.

Walking with God

O for a closer walk with God,
A calm and heavenly frame,
A light to shine upon the road
That leads me to the Lamb!

2   Where is the blessedness I knew
When first I saw the Lord?
Where is the soul-refreshing view
Of Jesus and his word?

3   What peaceful hours I once enjoy'd!
How sweet their mem'ry still!
But they have left an aching void
The world can never fill.

4   Return, O holy Dove, return,
Sweet messenger of rest;
I hate the sins that made thee mourn
And drove thee from my breast.

5   The dearest idol I have known,
Whate'er that idol be,
Help me to tear it from thy throne,
And worship only thee.

6   So shall my walk be close with God,
Calm and serene my frame;
So purer light shall mark the road
That leads me to the Lamb.

93

O FOR A THOUSAND
TONGUES TO SING

Arguably the greatest and certainly the most popular of the many hymns by Charles Wesley (1707–88: see no. 11), this long had pride of place as the first entry in every edition of the Methodist hymnbook.

It is, in fact, only part of a longer hymn which Wesley wrote in May 1739 to celebrate the first anniversary of his conversion to evangelical Christianity. As first published in his *Hymns and Sacred Poems* the following year it ran to eighteen stanzas, beginning:

> Glory to God, and praise and love
> be ever, ever given;
> By saints below, and saints above,
> The Church in earth and heaven.
>
> On this glad day the glorious Sun
> Of Righteousness arose,
> On my benighted soul he shone,
> And filled it with repose.
>
> Sudden expired the legal strife,
> 'Twas then I ceased to grieve,
> My second, real, living life
> I then began to live.

For the *Wesleyan Hymn Book* of 1780 John Wesley selected the ten stanzas printed here, beginning with the seventh verse of his brother's original hymn, which is thought to have been inspired by a remark made by Peter Böhler, a Moravian preacher, to the effect that 'Had I a thousand tongues, I would praise Him with them all.' The phrase 'cancelled sin' in the first line of the fourth verse has offended a number of hymnal editors, and it has been variously changed to 'death and sin' and 'reigning sin', but most modern hymnbooks are happy to stick to the original. Several verses are omitted nowadays, including the ninth with its unfortunate reference to washing the Ethiop white.

A large number of tunes are associated with this hymn. Probably the most commonly used nowadays is Richmond by Thomas Haweis (1734–1820: see no. 24). Methodists have traditionally favoured Lydia by Thomas Phillips (1735–1805), while Anglicans long preferred a melody by Henry Harington (1727–1816), a physician at Bath and Wells, which goes under the names of Landsdowne, Harington, Orlingbury, Bath or Retirement. Other alternatives are Oxford New (from Isaac Smith's collection of c. 1770), Selby by A.J. Eyre (1853–1919) and O God of Love (from the *Divine Companion* of 1709).

I myself am particularly fond of the vigorous Lyngham by Thomas Jarman (1782–1862) which divides the second half of each verse contrapuntally between men and women in a very effective way. For some reason it is known as Desert in Scotland. I am glad to say that it is increasingly being used and appears in a number of recently published hymnbooks as the favoured tune.

Exhorting and beseeching to return to God

❧

O for a thousand tongues to sing
My dear Redeemer's praise!
The glories of my God and King,
The triumphs of his grace.

2   My gracious Master, and my God,
Assist me to proclaim,
To spread through all the earth abroad
The honours of thy name.

3   Jesus, the name that charms our fears,
That bids our sorrows cease;
'Tis music in the sinner's ears,
'Tis life and health and peace!

4   He breaks the power of cancell'd sin;
He sets the prisoner free;
His blood can make the foulest clean;
His blood availed for me.

5   He speaks, and listening to his voice
New life the dead receive,
The mournful, broken hearts rejoice,
The humble poor *believe*.

6   Hear him, ye deaf, his praise, ye dumb,
Your loosen'd tongues employ,
Ye blind, behold your Saviour come,
And leap, ye lame, for joy.

7   Look unto him, ye nations, own
Your God, ye fallen race!
Look, and be saved through faith alone,
Be justified by grace!

8   See all your sins on Jesus laid;
The Lamb of God was slain,
His soul was once an offering made
For every *soul* of man.

9   Awake from guilty nature's sleep.
And Christ shall give you light,
Cast all your sins into the deep,
And wash the *Ethiop* white.

10   With me, your Chief, you then shall know,
Shall feel your sins forgiven;
Anticipate your heaven below
And own, that love is heaven.

O GOD OF EARTH AND ALTAR

This is the only hymn ever written by the great Catholic writer G.K. Chesterton (1874–1936), best known today, perhaps, for his *Father Brown* stories. It first appeared in 1906 in *The Commonwealth*, a Christian socialist magazine edited by Henry Scott Holland, author of 'Judge eternal, throned in splendour' (no. 68), and was included by Percy Dearmer in the first edition of the *English Hymnal*.

Chesterton was 32 when he wrote it, and already an accomplished poet, although he knew little about hymns or music. He later told Percy Dearmer that he had written it with the tune Aurelia in mind (see no. 124), since he assumed that its metre was the norm for hymns. In fact, it is generally sung to King's Lynn, a traditional English melody adapted by Ralph Vaughan Williams. In 1906 Chesterton was a lapsed nonconformist and still sixteen years away from becoming a Roman Catholic, but he had deep religious instincts. He was also strongly committed to social reform and political radicalism. Both of these strands come across in these verses, which must be counted as one of the greatest expressions of the Christian social gospel in English hymnody.

Erik Routley had a particular admiration for this hymn, which he regarded as 'catholic in every good sense, soaring above sectionalism and yet firmly based on the earth', and it is worth quoting at some length what he wrote about it in his book, *Hymns Today and Tomorrow*:*

* Erik Routley, *Hymns Today and Tomorrow* (London: Darton, Longman & Todd, 1964).

There are many hymns – good but commonplace – whose argument could be summed up in a sentence. But the condensation of so much into twenty-four lines in this hymn is unparalleled in the history of the form ... It is the only hymn which exclusively deals with politics in terms of sin and wickedness and confession, not at all in terms of sorrow and healing. It may also be observed how Chesterton uses words in a strictly contemporary sense. He is at heart a militant medievalist – hence his insistence on 'sword': but he is also a modern, for none of any other age could have put quite this sense into the word 'drift'. And none of any other age would have thought of writing 'lies of tongue and pen'. Chesterton was a newspaperman and knew what the pen had lately found itself able to do in the way of corrupting men's minds.

It is interesting to compare 'O God of earth and altar' with other hymns written around the same time with a similar social and political message. We have already encountered Henry Scott Holland's 'Judge eternal, throned in splendour', which was written just four years earlier than Chesterton's hymn. 'Son of God, eternal Saviour', written in 1893 by Somerset Corry Lowry (1855–1932), an Anglican clergyman, contains the powerful plea:

> By the patient years of toiling,
> By thy silent hours of pain,
> Quench our fevered thirst of pleasure,
> Shame our selfish greed of gain

'Father eternal, ruler of creation', a fine hymn written by Laurence Housman in 1919, makes a similar point equally tellingly:

> Lust of possession worketh desolations;
> There is no meekness in the sons of earth.
> Led by no star, the rulers of the nations
> Still fail to bring us to the blissful birth.

Another hymn expressing similar sentiments is Clifford Bax's 'Turn back, O man, forswear thy foolish ways', written in 1916 at the behest of the composer Gustav Holst and now sadly falling out of favour with hymnal editors. A number of us tried to keep it in the latest edition of the Church of Scotland's *Church Hymnary*, but were outvoted by those who feel it is now past its sell-by date. Although its tone, like that of 'O God of earth and altar' is essentially penitential, it is also a wonderful expression of human yearning and idealism:

> Earth might be fair, and all her people one:
> Nor till that hour shall God's whole will be done.
> Now, even now, once more from earth to sky,
> Peals forth in joy man's old undaunted cry—
> 'Earth shall be fair, and all her folk be one!'

O God of earth and altar,
Bow down and hear our cry,
Our earthly rulers falter,
Our people drift and die;
The walls of gold entomb us,
The swords of scorn divide,
Take not thy thunder from us,
But take away our pride.

2   From all that terror teaches,
From lies of tongue and pen,
From all the easy speeches
That comfort cruel men,
From sale and profanation
Of honour and the sword,
From sleep and from damnation,
Deliver us, good Lord!

3   Tie in a living tether
The prince and priest and thrall,
Bind all our lives together,
Smite us and save us all;
In ire and exultation
Aflame with faith, and free,
Lift up a living nation,
A single sword to thee.

O JESUS, I HAVE
PROMISED

A consistent high scorer in the BBC *Songs of Praise* poll – it was ranked 22nd in 2002 – this hymn was written in 1866 by the Revd John Ernest Bode (1816–74) for the confirmation of his three children. Although the opening lines are clearly intended to refer to the promises made by candidates at confirmation, there is nothing in the hymn to restrict its use to this particular service and it is sung widely in churches of all denominations in ordinary Sunday worship.

Bode was born in St Pancras, London, his father being head of the foreign department of the General Post Office. Educated at Eton, Charterhouse and Christ Church, Oxford, he was ordained in 1841. From 1847 to 1860 he was rector of Westwell, Oxfordshire, and for the remaining fourteen years of his life he held the living of Castle Camps in Cambridgeshire. A considerable poet, he published several volumes of verse and was runner up in the election for the Poetry Professorship at Oxford in 1857, coming just one vote behind the victorious Matthew Arnold.

Although he wrote hymns for every Sunday and for each of the festivals in the Christian year, this is the only one to have survived in regular use. It was first published as a leaflet by the Society for the Propagation of Christian Knowledge in 1868 with the title 'A Hymn for the newly confirmed'.

Of the many tunes to which this hymn is sung probably the best known and the most fitting is Wolvercote, which was composed around 1910 by the Revd William Harold Ferguson (1874–1950) for use in the chapel of Lancing College where he was then teaching. He went on to become Warden of St Edward's School, Oxford, and of St Peter's College, Radley, and finally Precentor of Salisbury Cathedral. In recent years, however, Wolvercote, which first appeared publicly in the *Public School Hymn Book* of 1919, has fallen out of favour in certain quarters. In common with other strong unison tunes written around the same period, among them Ferguson's Ladywell (used for 'Lift up your voice, ye Christian folk'), it is regarded as being too much a product of the Establishment and the public school chapel, suggesting a superficial camaraderie rather than anything more profound. Donald Webster, who suspects that this feeling lies behind the exclusion of both Ferguson's tunes from the third edition of the *Church Hymnary*, has some cutting remarks on such 'dismissive dogmatism' in his book *Our Hymn Tunes* (1983). It does certainly seem rather unfair if a fine tune like Wolvercote is being heard less often than it might because of essentially sociological and political objections.

Still, there are plenty of other tunes to which Bode's hymn has been set. They include Thornbury by Basil Harwood (1859–1949), which is unfortunately open to the same objections as Wolvercote; Day of Rest by J.W. Elliott, originally written for 'O day of rest and gladness' but set to Bode's hymn in the 1875 edition of *Hymns Ancient and Modern*; and Komm, Seele by J.W. Franck (1641–?) which was written for Elmenhorst's poem *Komm, Seele, Jesu Leiden soll mein Ergotzung sein* in 1681. Franck, who was a doctor in Hamburg, is said to have been poisoned in Spain. There is also the wonderfully soupy and syncopated Hatherop Castle by Geoffrey Beaumont (1903–70), along with Camberwell for 'At the name of Jesus' (see no. 14), one of the more enduring tunes to come out of the Twentieth Century Light Music Group. Not everyone's cup of tea, but it does undoubtedly go with a swing.

A Hymn for the Newly Confirmed

O Jesus, I have promised
To serve thee to the end;
Be thou for ever near me,
My Master and my Friend;
I shall not fear the battle
If thou art by my side,
Nor wander from the pathway
If thou wilt be my Guide.

2   O let me feel thee near me:
The world is ever near;
I see the sights that dazzle,
The tempting sounds I hear;
My foes are ever near me,
Around me and within;
But, Jesus, draw thou nearer,
And shield my soul from sin.

3   O let me hear thee speaking
In accents clear and still,
Above the storms of passion,
The murmurs of self-will;
O speak to reassure me,
To hasten or control;
O speak, and make me listen,
Thou Guardian of my soul.

4   O let me see thy features,
    The look that once could make
    So many a true disciple
    Leave all things for thy sake;
    The look that beam'd on Peter
    When he thy name denied;
    The look that draws thy loved ones
    Close to thy piercèd side.

5   O Jesus, thou hast promised
    To all who follow thee,
    That where thou art in glory
    There shall thy servant be;
    And, Jesus, I have promised
    To serve thee to the end;
    O give me grace to follow,
    My Master and my Friend.

6   O let me see thy footmarks,
    And in them plant mine own;
    My hope to follow duly
    Is in thy strength alone;
    O guide me, call me, draw me,
    Uphold me to the end;
    And then in heaven receive me,
    My Saviour and my Friend.

O LORD MY GOD, WHEN
I IN AWESOME WONDER

According to the 2002 BBC *Songs of Praise* poll, this is now Britain's favourite hymn, having overtaken 'The day, thou gavest' and 'Dear Lord and Father of mankind' in the nation's affections. Readers of Catholic weekly, *The Tablet*, voted it third in their list of Top Ten hymns in 2004. Like 'Great is thy faithfulness', it owes much of its popularity to its extensive use in the Billy Graham crusades of the 1950s. The result of a triple translation from Swedish into English via German and Russian, 'How Great Thou Art', as this hymn is often known, is the work of the British missionary and evangelist Stuart K. Hine (1899–1989).

The original Swedish poem on which the hymn is based was written by Carl Boberg (1859–1940), an evangelist, journalist and for fifteen years a member of the Swedish parliament. Born at Monsteras on the south-east coast of Sweden, the son of a shipyard worker, Boberg was converted to evangelical Christianity at the age of 19 and went to Bible School at Kristinehamn. He returned to his native town as a preacher and it was there in 1886 that he wrote his nine-verse poem beginning *O store Gud*. He was moved to hymn God's greatness one summer evening as he stood looking across the calm waters of the Monsteras inlet. A rainbow had formed, following a storm in the afternoon, and the church bell was tolling in the distance. The first verse of his poem, translated fairly literally into English, reads:

> O Thou great God! When I the world consider
> Which Thou hast made by Thine almighty Word;
> And how the web of life Thy wisdom guideth,
> And all creation feedeth at Thy board:
> Then doth my soul burst forth in song of praise:
> O Thou great God! O Thou great God!

Boberg's verses were set to music in 1891 and appeared in several Swedish hymnbooks around the turn of the century. An English translation was published in 1925 under the title 'O Mighty God', but never really caught on. Earlier, in 1912, a Russian version by Ivan Prokhanoff had appeared. Prokhanoff's translation, which was almost certainly made from a German translation of the original Swedish hymn, was published in several hymnbooks. It made a deep impression on Stuart Hine, who heard it being sung in the western Ukraine, where he had gone as a missionary in 1923.

After singing the hymn in Russian for many years, Hine translated the first three verses into English while engaging in evangelistic work in the 1930s in the Carpathian mountains on the borders of Russia and Romania. The scenery there inspired his second verse which draws little from Boberg's original poem while remaining true to its general spirit of wonder at God's creation.

Hine wrote the fourth verse of his hymn when he was back in Britain in 1948. In that year more than 100,000 refugees from Russian and other parts of Eastern Europe streamed into the United Kingdom. The question uppermost in many of their minds was 'When are we going home?' In an essay on the story of the hymn Hine writes, 'What better message for the homeless than that of the One who went to prepare a place for the "displaced", of the God who invites into his own home those who will come to him through Christ.'

Stuart Hine published both the Russian and the English versions of the hymn in his gospel magazine *Grace and Peace* in 1949. 'O Lord my God' rapidly caught on in evangelical circles in both Britain and the USA. George Beverly Shea, the leading vocalist in Billy Graham's evangelistic team, was given a copy of the hymn during the London crusade at the Haringey Arena in 1954. It became a favourite of Shea, the team's choir director, Cliff Barrows and Graham himself, who wrote of it: 'The reason I liked "How great Thou art" was because it glorified God: it turned a Christian's eyes toward God rather than upon himself, as so many songs do.'

The hymn is sung to the Swedish folk-melody to which Boberg's verses were set in 1891.

O store Gud

O Lord my God, when I in awesome wonder
Consider all the works Thy hand hath made,
I see the stars, I hear the mighty thunder,
Thy power throughout the universe displayed:

Then sings my soul, my Saviour God, to Thee,
How great Thou art! How great Thou art!
Then sings my soul, my Saviour God, to Thee,
How great Thou art! How great Thou art!

2   When through the woods and forest glades I wander
And hear the birds sing sweetly in the trees:
When I look down from lofty mountain grandeur,
And hear the brook, and feel the gentle breeze;

3   And when I think that God His Son not sparing,
Sent Him to die – I scarce can take it in:
That on the cross, my burden gladly bearing,
He bled and died to take away my sin:

4   When Christ shall come with shout of acclamation
And take me home – what joy shall fill my heart!
Then shall I bow in humble adoration
And there proclaim, my God, how great Thou art!

O LOVE THAT WILT NOT
LET ME GO

I regard this as one of the most moving and profound hymns in the English language. It is one of very few hymns which tackles that most difficult area of human experience for the Christian believer, the reality of suffering, and does so not in a sentimental or cloying way but in a spirit of Christian hope and with an intense sense of the mystery of life. I am glad to say that the great British public seems to agree with me – this hymn came ninth in the 2002 *Songs of Praise* poll.

The author, George Matheson (1842–1906), was a Church of Scotland minister. Born and educated in Glasgow, he spent eighteen years as minister in the Argyllshire parish of Innellan on the north bank of the Clyde and then moved on to a charge in Edinburgh. As well as being a devoted parish minister, Matheson was a considerable scholar, theologian and scientist. Despite the fact that he was almost totally blind from the age of 18, he wrote several books of poems and meditations and a number of serious theological works. He is responsible for two other hymns which are still sung today: 'Make me a captive, Lord', which explores the paradox of Christian freedom through surrender and service; and 'Gather us in, Thou love that fillest all', with its wonderfully inclusive message that God embraces all faiths.

There are various stories about the circumstances which prompted Matheson to write this hymn. One version suggests that he was in a state of abject grief after the girl whom he had hoped to marry had broken off their engagement. Another recounts that it was written after his sister Jane, who had been his housekeeper and constant companion, left to be married. Matheson himself did not specify the precise circumstances which lay behind its composition. He wrote:

The hymn was composed in the manse of Innellan on the evening of 6 June 1882. I was at that time alone. Something had happened to me which was known only to myself and which caused me the most severe mental suffering. The hymn was the fruit of that suffering. It was the quickest bit of work I ever did in my life. I am quite sure the whole work was completed in five minutes, and equally sure it never received at my hands any retouching or correction. I had the impression of having it dictated to me by some inward voice.

In fact, he did subsequently make one correction. When the hymn first appeared in print, in the January 1883 issue of the Church of Scotland magazine *Life and Work*, the third line of the third verse was as printed here: 'I climb the rainbow through the rain'. However, at the request of the editors of the *Scottish Hymnal*, he changed 'climb' to 'trace'. This alteration has been incorporated in all subsequent hymnals.

One of the great strengths of 'O love that wilt not let me go' is that it can be appreciated at so many different levels. It speaks directly and simply to those weighed down with cares and grief and particularly to those approaching death. Yet it also has considerable philosophical depth and some complex mystical allusions. The imagery in the first verse of the soul returning to the ocean depths is in some ways closer to Hindu thought or to the ideas of contemporary 'process' theologians than to orthodox Christianity. Matheson himself explained the significance of the puzzling imagery in the two closing lines of the hymn. White blossoms, he said, represented prosperity and red ones self-sacrifice: 'I took red as the symbol of that sacrificial life which blooms by shedding itself.'

The power and intensity of the hymn is greatly enhanced by the tune St Margaret, written specifically for it by Dr Albert Peace (1844–1912), organist of Glasgow Cathedral. It too was a work of sudden inspiration. Peace recalled that he read Matheson's hymn while staying at Brodrick Manse on the Isle of Arran, and then 'I wrote the music straight off, and I may say that the ink of the first note was hardly dry when I had finished the tune.' There is another tune to which the hymn has been sung by male voice choirs.

Self-surrender

O Love that wilt not let me go,
I rest my weary soul in Thee:
I give Thee back the life I owe,
That in Thine ocean depths its flow
May richer, fuller be.

2   O Light that followest all my way,
I yield my flickering torch to Thee:
My heart restores its borrowed ray,
That in Thy sunshine's blaze its day
May brighter, fairer be.

3   O Joy that seekest me through pain,
I cannot close my heart to Thee:
I climb the rainbow through the rain,
And feel the promise is not vain,
That morn shall tearless be.

4   O Cross that liftest up my head,
I dare not ask to fly from Thee:
I lay in dust life's glory dead,
And from the ground there blossoms red
Life that shall endless be.

O PRAISE YE THE LORD!
PRAISE HIM IN THE
HEIGHT

The author of this hymn, Sir Henry Williams Baker (1821–77), will always have a prominent place in the history of English hymnody as the driving force behind *Hymns Ancient and Modern*.

The eldest son of a vice-admiral, Baker was educated at Trinity College, Cambridge, and ordained in 1844. Seven years later he became vicar of Monkland, near Leominster, on the English–Welsh borders. In the same year he succeeded to his father's baronetcy – hence his title. He remained at Monkland for the rest of his life. The light duties of this small country parish enabled him to devote most of his time to hymnody and specifically to the preparation of *Hymns Ancient and Modern*, which did much to promote the practice of hymn-singing throughout the Church of England.

Baker was present at the meeting, held in 1858 at the clergy house of St Barnabas, Pimlico, which resolved to produce a new hymnal. He was appointed secretary of the committee charged with the book's preparation and effectively became editor-in-chief of the whole project which extended over the next seventeen years, involving an enormous amount of work choosing hymns and commissioning translations, new verses and tunes. Baker was particularly keen to restore to the devotion of the Church of England the treasures of early Latin hymnody and was instrumental in securing the many fine translations by J.M. Neale which appeared in the first volume of the new work, published in 1861. He also supervised the preparation of an appendix, published in 1868, and a revised edition of the hymnal which came out in 1875 and contained 33 of his own hymns and translations, of which this was one.

'O praise ye the Lord' is based on Psalms 148 and 150. The first verse echoes the first two verses of Psalm 148:

> Praise ye the Lord.
> Praise ye the Lord from the heavens:
> Praise him in the heights.
> Praise him, all his angels:
> Praise him all his hosts.

The third verse echoes verses 3–6 of Psalm 150:

> Praise him with the sound of the trumpet:
> Praise him with the psaltery and harp.
> Praise him with the timbrel and dance:
> Praise him with stringed instruments and organs.
> Praise him upon the loud cymbals:
> Let everything that hath breath praise the Lord.

Among Baker's other hymns which are still regularly sung today are 'Lord, thy word abideth' and 'The King of love my Shepherd is' (no. 130).

The tune originally composed for 'O praise ye the Lord' in the 1875 edition of *Hymns Ancient and Modern* was *Laudate Dominum* by H.J. Gauntlett (1805–76). In 1894 Sir Charles Hubert Parry (1848–1918) produced a magnificently affirmative and positive melody, which goes under the same name and has become the standard tune for the hymn. It was originally written as the concluding section of an anthem, 'Hear my words, O ye people' for a Salisbury Diocesan Festival. To avoid confusion, Gauntlett's tune is now known as Gauntlett.

O praise ye the Lord! Praise him in the height;
Rejoice in his word, ye angels of light;
Ye heavens, adore him, by whom ye were made,
And worship before him, in brightness arrayed.

2 O praise ye the Lord! Praise him upon earth,
In tuneful accord, ye sons of new birth;
Praise him who hath brought you his grace from above,
Praise him who hath taught you to sing of his love.

3 O praise ye the Lord, all things that give sound;
Each jubilant chord re-echo around;
Loud organs, his glory forth tell in deep tone,
And, sweet harp, the story of what he hath done.

4 O praise ye the Lord! Thanksgiving and song
To him be outpoured all ages along:
For love in creation, for heaven restored,
For grace of salvation, O praise ye the Lord!

O SACRED HEAD, SORE
WOUNDED

This powerful Passiontide hymn comes to us from a Latin original via German, and is now to be found in three quite distinct English translations as well as several hybrid versions.

It is based on a long medieval poem *Salve mundi salutare* which in turn addresses the various parts of Christ's body hanging on the Cross. The last part of the poem, from which the hymn is taken, is an invocation of the Saviour's head and begins '*Salve caput cruentatum*'. The poem is often attributed to Bernard of Clairvaux (1091–1153), but this seems unlikely, as its earliest known appearance is in fourteenth- and fifteenth-century manuscripts.

In the mid-seventeenth century the last section of the poem was translated into German by Paul Gerhardt (1607–76) and printed in Frankfurt in 1656 as a hymn beginning '*O Haupt voll Blut und Wunden*'. Gerhardt, who spent much of his life as a Lutheran pastor in Berlin, wrote 123 hymns and is regarded as second only to Luther in his contribution to German hymnody.

The first English translation of Gerhardt's hymn was made in 1752 by John Gambold (1711–71), who was vicar of Stanton Harcourt in Oxfordshire but later resigned his living to join the Moravians. His version began 'O Head so full of bruises'. In 1830 Dr James Waddell Alexander (1804–59), a Presbyterian minister who also held the chairs of rhetoric and church history at Princeton University, New Jersey, produced a translation which forms the basis of the version of the hymn found in several modern hymnbooks. Its first verse goes as follows:

> O sacred head, now wounded,
> With grief and shame weighed down!
> Now scornfully surrounded,

With thorns, thy only crown:
O sacred Head! what glory,
What bliss till now was thine!
I read the wondrous story!
I joy to call thee mine!

A further translation was made by Sir Henry Baker for *Hymns Ancient and Modern* in 1861. The first verse of this version, which can be found in the 'New Standard' edition of *Hymns Ancient and Modern* is

O sacred head, surrounded
By crown of piercing thorn!
O bleeding head, so wounded,
So shamed and put to scorn!
Death's pallid hue comes o'er thee,
The glow of life decays;
Yet angel-hosts adore thee,
And tremble as they gaze.

In 1899 Robert Bridges (1844–1930, see no. 6) returned to the original Latin to produce the version that is printed here. It is the one most commonly found in modern hymnbooks.

All these English translations of the hymn are generally sung to the tune Passion Chorale which accompanied Gerhardt's German version. It was written around 1600 by Hans Leo Hassler (1564–1612) for a love-song, *Mein Gmüt ist mir verwirret*. Hassler served as musical director both to the wealthy Fugger family in Augsburg and to the Elector of Saxony. The tune was a favourite of J.S. Bach who used it five times in his *St Matthew Passion*.

O sacred Head, sore wounded,
Defiled and put to scorn;
O kingly Head, surrounded
With mocking crown of thorn:
What sorrow mars thy grandeur?
Can death thy bloom deflower?
O countenance whose splendour
The hosts of heaven adore!

2   Thy beauty, long-desirèd
Hath vanished from our sight;
Thy power is all expirèd,
And quenched the Light of light.
Ah me! For whom thou diest,
Hide not so far thy grace:
Show me, O Love most highest,
The brightness of thy face.

3   I pray thee, Jesus, own me,
Me, Shepherd good, for thine;
Who to thy fold hast won me,
And fed with truth divine.
Me, guilty me refuse not,
Incline thy face to me,
This comfort that I lose not,
On earth to comfort thee.

4   In thy most bitter passion
My heart to thee doth cry,
With thee for my salvation
Upon the Cross to die.
Ah, keep my heart thus movèd
To stand thy Cross beneath,
To mourn thee, well-belovèd,
Yet thank thee for thy death.

5   My days are few, O fail not,
With thine immortal power,
To hold me that I quail not
In death's most fearful hour:
That I may fight befriended,
And see in my last strife
To me thine arms extended
Upon the Cross of life.

O THOU WHO CAMEST
FROM ABOVE

This hymn by Charles Wesley (1707–88) first appeared in the form of two eight-line verses in his *Short Hymns on Selected Passages of Scripture*, published in 1762. The Scripture passage attached is Leviticus 6.13: 'The fire shall ever be burning upon the altar; it shall never go out.' It refers to the Jewish practice of burnt offerings, where the fire is kept blazing until the offering is completely consumed. Wesley portrays the faith of the Christian believer in similar terms.

Like all Wesley's hymns it is packed with biblical references. The first verse draws on images from John 3.31, Acts 2.3, Luke 12.49 and 1 Chronicles 21.26; the third from Romans 10.1 and 2 Timothy 1.6; and the fourth from Romans 12.2, 1 Thessalonians 1.3 and Philippians 2.17. It has been suggested that Wesley may have borrowed the phrase 'celestial fire' in the second line from Alexander Pope, who used it in *An Essay on Criticism*, and that the line 'And still stir up thy gift in me' may have been inspired by Matthew Henry's commentary on 2 Timothy 1.6–14 which notes 'We must not only not quench the Spirit, but we must stir up the gift that is in us.' Wesley would also have been familiar with the phrase 'stir up' from the collect for the 25th Sunday after Trinity in the Book of Common Prayer, which begins: 'Stir up, we beseech thee, O Lord, the wills of thy faithful people.'

Several attempts have been made to alter the second line of the second verse to replace the word 'inextinguishable' which some hymnal editors have regarded as too difficult for congregations to sing. Several editions of *Hymns Ancient and Modern* sought to avoid this particular tongue-twister by substituting the words 'With ever-bright, undying blaze'. In his *Hymnal Companion* of 1872, Edward Henry Bickersteth, Bishop of Exeter, changed the offending line to 'Unquenched, undimmed in darkest days'. He also sought to give the great Wesley a posthumous lecture on hymn-writing. 'Words of five syllables must be admitted into hymns sparingly', he wrote, 'but for a whole congregation to be poised on six practically leads for a hymn to be passed by.'

Charles Wesley's brother John was much taken with this hymn but somewhat uneasy about the personal note at the end. In the *Wesleyan Hymn Book*, which he edited in 1780, he changed the last verse to

> Still let me prove thy perfect will,
> My acts of faith and love repeat;
> Till death thy endless mercies seal,
> And make the sacrifice complete.

The tune most often associated with this hymn is Hereford by Samuel Sebastian Wesley (1810–76), grandson of Charles. After singing as a boy in the Chapel Royal, he became an organist at 16 and served in five parish churches and four cathedrals – Hereford, Exeter, Winchester and Gloucester. One of 130 hymn-tunes which he composed, Hereford first appeared in his *European Psalmist* in 1872. It was first set to Charles Wesley's hymn in the 1909 edition of *Hymns Ancient and Modern*.

For Holiness, and for Earnestness in Work

O Thou who camest from above,
The pure celestial fire to impart,
Kindle a flame of sacred love
On the mean altar of my heart.

2　There let it for thy glory burn
With inextinguishable blaze,
And trembling to its source return
In humble prayer, and fervent praise.

3　Jesus, confirm my heart's desire
To work, and speak, and think for thee;
Still let me guard the holy fire,
And still stir up thy gift in me.

4　Ready for all thy perfect will,
My acts of faith and love repeat,
Till death thy endless mercies seal,
And make my sacrifice complete.

101

O VALIANT HEARTS,
WHO TO YOUR GLORY
CAME

This is a controversial hymn and I fear that its inclusion in this anthology will not please those who regard it as glorifying war and detracting from the sole sufficiency of Christ's sacrifice on Calvary. For me, however, it is one of the most powerful hymns in the English language and one of the few which directly links human suffering and sacrifice with Christ's suffering and sacrifice on the Cross.

'O valiant hearts' was written in the middle of the First World War by Sir John Arkwright (1872–1954), who had been Conservative MP for Hereford from 1900 to 1912, and published in 1917 in leaflet form with the epigraph 'Greater love hath no man than this, that a man lay down his life for his friends.' It appears first to have been sung at a service of solemn intercession attended by King George V in Westminster Abbey on 5 August 1917 to mark the third anniversary of the outbreak of the war. Two days before the service, *The Times* printed the first five verses of the hymn. 'O valiant hearts' appeared in a collection of Arkwright's verse entitled *The Supreme Sacrifice*, published in 1919, and in the same year it was included in *Laus Deo*, a collection of hymns compiled by Walford Davies. It was brought to wider notice with its inclusion in *Songs of Praise* in 1925. Many denominational hymnals published in the first half of the twentieth century included it, but it has been purged from more recent editions. The compilers of the 1997 *BBC Songs of Praise* hymnal were taken to task for including it by the reviewer in the *Bulletin* of the Hymn Society who expressed dismay at seeing it – in full – in a modern hymnbook.

Despite the vociferous protests of its many critics, 'O valiant hearts' continues to be sung at Remembrance Day services and parades up and down the land and has many fans among members of the British Legion. The Revd Michael Saward, one of its strongest critics, and a hymn-writer himself, describes it as 'a poem to the dead and not a Christian hymn'. He regards it as 'virtually unsingable for a Christian congregation' and says, 'I would in no circumstances be a willing party to using it in church.' I have the greatest respect for his views and understand his unease about aspects of the language in this hymn, but I beg to differ with him as to its overall tone and suitability for use in church. Indeed, I confess to having asked for it to be sung in a number of Remembrance Sunday services which I have conducted. I have also used it in two three-hour Good Friday devotions which I have led on the theme of Jesus's sacrifice. It does seem to me to speak very powerfully of the 'lesser Calvaries' which suffering and sacrificing humanity experiences and of the mysterious way in which human suffering is linked to the sacrifice of Christ.

I had better rest my case there. I could say a great deal more about this hymn – indeed, I have preached about it on a number of occasions, not least in the chapel of my old school, Tonbridge, which is where I was first introduced to it and where, I am glad to say, it is still sung. (I fear that the public school connection will simply confirm several of its critics in their dislike of it, so I had better shut up now.) There is an alternative version, written by the leading twentieth-century hymn writer Fred Kaan (b. 1929) which begins:

> God! As with silent hearts we bring to mind
> How hate and war diminish humankind,
> We pause, and seek in worship to increase
> Our knowledge of the things that make for peace.

Both Kaan's hymn and Arkwright's original verses are now sung to the wonderfully majestic and sonorous tune The Supreme Sacrifice which was written for 'O valiant hearts' by Charles Harris and which accompanied it in its first appearance in print in 1917. Harris (1865–1936) was rector of Colwall and later went on to become Prebendary of Hereford. It is not, however, the only tune with which this hymn has been associated. When it was sung at the Westminster Abbey service in 1917, it was to E.J. Hopkins's tune Ellers, which was also used on 11 November 1920 when the Unknown Warrior was buried in the Abbey. In *Laus Deo*, and in the 1923 *A Student's Hymnal* 'O valiant hearts' was set to Andrew Freeman's tune Limpsfield.

O Valiant Hearts

❧❧

O valiant hearts, who to your glory came
Through dust of conflict and through battle-flame;
Tranquil you lie, your knightly virtue proved,
Your memory hallowed in the land you loved.

2 Proudly you gathered, rank on rank to war,
As who had heard God's message from afar;
All you had hoped for, all you had, you gave
To save mankind – yourselves you scorned to save.

3 Splendid you passed, the great surrender made,
Into the light that nevermore shall fade;
Deep your contentment in that blest abode,
Who wait the last clear trumpet-call of God.

4 Long years ago, as earth lay dark and still,
Rose a loud cry upon a lonely hill,
While in the frailty of our human clay
Christ, our Redeemer, passed the self-same way.

5 Still stands His Cross from that dread hour to this
Like some bright star above the dark abyss;
Still, through the veil, the Victor's pitying eyes
Look down to bless our lesser Calvaries.

6 These were His servants, in His steps they trod,
Following through death the martyr'd Son of God.
Victor He rose; victorious too shall rise
They who have drunk His cup of Sacrifice.

7 O Risen Lord, O Shepherd of our Dead,
Whose Cross has brought them and whose Staff has led –
In glorious hope their proud and sorrowing land
Commits her children to Thy gracious hand.

O WORSHIP THE KING,
ALL-GLORIOUS ABOVE

This much-loved paraphrase of Psalm 104 ('Bless the Lord, O my soul') is the work of Sir Robert Grant (1785–1838), who in a distinguished public career was successively a barrister, MP, Privy Councillor and colonial governor.

Much of the imagery which Grant employed in his hymn is taken directly from the psalmist's words. The phrase in the third verse, 'Who maketh the clouds his chariot', becomes 'whose chariot of wrath the deep thunder clouds form', and the statement in the sixth verse, 'Thou coveredst it with the deep as with a garment: The waters stood above the mountains', becomes 'and round it has cast like a mantle the sea'.

Grant modelled 'O worship the king' on an earlier paraphrase of Psalm 104 made by William Kethe (?–1594), author of 'All people that on earth do dwell' (no. 7). The first two verses of Kethe's hymn are as follows:

My soul praise the Lord!
O God, Thou art great:
In fathomless works
Thyself Thou dost hide.
Before Thy dark wisdom
And power uncreate,
Man's mind, that dare praise Thee,
In fear must abide.

This earth where we dwell,
That journeys in space,
With air as a robe
Thou wrappest around:
Her countries she turneth

> To greet the sun's face,
> Then plungeth to slumber
> In darkness profound.

Grant, whose father was MP for Inverness, was educated at Magdalen College, Oxford, and called to the Bar. He sat in the House of Commons as a Tory from 1808 to 1834, successively representing the constituencies of Elgin, Inverness, Norwich and Finsbury. Perhaps his most important political action was to carry the Bill which emancipated Jews in Britain. In 1834, shortly after writing this hymn, he was appointed Governor of Bombay.

Grant is the sole representative in this book of a distinguished band of Victorian and Edwardian MPs who were also hymn-writers. Others included Thomas Hughes, the author of *Tom Brown's Schooldays*, who was successively Liberal MP for Lambeth and Frome and who wrote 'O God of Truth, whose living word'; Sir John Bowring, a Radical who represented first Kilmarnock and then Bolton ('Watchman, tell us of the night'); Philip Pusey, Conservative MP for Berkshire from 1835 to 1852 ('Lord of our life, and God of our salvation'); Charles Silvester Horne, a Congregational minister who was Liberal MP for Ipswich from 1910 to 1914 ('For the might of thine arm we bless thee'); and Britain's only hymn-writing prime minister, William Ewart Gladstone ('O lead my blindness by the hand').

'O worship the King' was first published in Grant's *Christian Psalmody* (1833). It is normally sung to the tune Hanover, which first appeared in print in 1708 and which used to be attributed to George Frideric Handel. It is now more usually regarded as the work of Dr William Croft (1678–1727), organist of Westminster Abbey.

Psalm civ

O worship the King, all-glorious above;
O gratefully sing his power and his love:
Our Shield and Defender, the Ancient of Days,
Pavilioned in splendour, and girded with praise.

2   O tell of his might, O sing of his grace,
Whose robe is the light, whose canopy space;
His chariots of wrath the deep thunder-clouds form,
And dark is his path on the wings of the storm.

3   The earth with its store of wonders untold,
Almighty, thy power hath founded of old;
Hath stablished it fast by a changeless decree,
And round it hath cast, like a mantle, the sea.

4   Thy bountiful care what tongue can recite?
It breathes in the air, it shines in the light;
It streams from the hills, it descends to the plain,
And sweetly distils in the dew and the rain.

5   Frail children of dust, and feeble as frail,
In thee do we trust, nor find thee to fail;
Thy mercies how tender, how firm to the end,
Our Maker, Defender, Redeemer, and Friend.

6   O measureless Might, ineffable Love,
While angels delight to hymn thee above,
Thy humbler creation, though feeble their lays,
With true adoration shall sing to thy praise.

O WORSHIP THE LORD
IN THE BEAUTY OF
HOLINESS

This Epiphany hymn is the work of John Samuel Bewley Monsell (1811–75), whom we have already come across as the author of 'Fight the good fight (no. 33: see there for biographical notes). It was first published in his *Hymns of Love and Praise* in 1863.

The hymn rather effectively takes two of the objects which the Magi brought with them to present to the infant Jesus and turns them into symbolic gifts which all of us can bring to Christ in our lives and worship – the gold of obedience and the incense of lowliness. Although specifically written and particularly suited for use during the season of Epiphany, 'O worship the Lord in the beauty of holiness' is a general call to worship God and can appropriately be sung at any time in the Christian year.

The opening line of the hymn is taken directly from the ninth verse of Psalm 96, 'O sing unto the Lord a new song.' The 'mornings of joy' and 'evenings of tearfulness' in the fourth verse also have a scriptural derivation, coming as they do from the fifth verse of Psalm 30: 'Weeping may endure for a night, but joy cometh in the morning.'

This hymn was a particular favourite of the novelist D.H. Lawrence, who wrote movingly of the lasting impact of the hymns to which he was introduced in the Congregational chapel where he worshipped as a boy. Looking back many years later to his nonconformist hymn-singing childhood, he wrote:

I don't know what the 'beauty of holiness' is, exactly. It easily becomes cant, or nonsense. But if you don't think about it – and why should you? – it has a magic. The same with the whole verse. It is rather bad, really, 'gold of obedience', and 'incense of lowliness'. But in me, to the music, it still produces a sense of splendour.*

Altogether, Monsell wrote some 300 or so hymns. The two included in this collection are probably the most widely sung today. Others which are found in currently used hymnbooks include 'Sing to the Lord a joyful song', 'Sing to the Lord of harvest' and 'Rest of the weary, Joy of the sad'.

The soaring tune *Was lebet, was schwebet*, to which 'O worship the Lord in the beauty of holiness' is invariably sung, comes from a German manuscript of 1754, *Choral-Buch vor Johann Heinrich Reinhardt*, where it provided the setting for the song '*Was lebet, was schwebet*'.

---

* D.H. Lawrence, 'Hymns in a Man's Life', *Evening News*, 13 October 1928.

O worship the Lord in the beauty of holiness,
Bow down before him, his glory proclaim;
With gold of obedience and incense of lowliness,
Kneel and adore him: the Lord is his name.

2　Low at his feet lay thy burden of carefulness,
High on his heart he will bear it for thee,
Comfort thy sorrows, and answer thy prayerfulness,
Guiding thy steps as may best for thee be.

3　Fear not to enter his courts in the slenderness
Of the poor wealth thou wouldst reckon as thine;
Truth in its beauty, and love in its tenderness,
These are the offerings to lay on his shrine.

4　These, though we bring them in trembling and fearfulness,
He will accept for the name that is dear;
Mornings of joy give for evenings of tearfulness,
Trust for our trembling, and hope for our fear.

5　O worship the Lord in the beauty of holiness,
Bow down before him, his glory proclaim;
With gold of obedience and incense of lowliness,
Kneel and adore him: the Lord is his name.

ON JORDAN'S BANK THE BAPTIST'S CRY

This popular Advent hymn, which has been much altered from the original version printed here, was first presented to the British public in somewhat false colours. John Chandler (1806– 76), who translated it from the Latin, published it in 1837 in his *Hymns of the Primitive Church*. In fact, the original Latin hymn *'Jordanis oras praevia'*, far from being of the Early Church dates only from the eighteenth century.

'Jordanis oras praevia' was the work of Charles Coffin (1676– 1749), and first appeared in the *Paris Breviary* of 1736. Born in Buzancy in the Ardennes, Coffin became principal of the College of Doirmans-Beauvais in the University of Paris. He wrote more than a hundred Latin hymns, several of which have been translated and found their way into English hymnbooks. Among other hymns popular today which are based on Coffin's Latin originals are 'O Holy Spirit, Lord of grace', 'Happy are they, they that love God' and 'Great mover of all hearts, whose hand'.

John Chandler was educated at Corpus Christi College, Oxford, and succeded his father as vicar of Witley in Surrey. He collected and translated many hymns from the Early Church, including 'Blessed City, heavenly Salem' and 'Christ is our Corner Stone'.

'On Jordan's bank' has been considerably altered by various hymnal editors, partly to bring the English words more into conformity with the original Latin text than was the case in Chandler's rather free translation. There are various different renderings of the last two lines of the first verse. Perhaps the most common is:

> Awake, and hearken, for he brings
> Glad tidings from the King of Kings.

Some hymn-books carry the following alternative version of the second verse:

> Then cleansed be every Christian breast,
> And furnished for so great a guest!
> Yea, let us each our hearts prepare
> For Christ to come and enter there.

Nearly all modern hymnals print an amended version of the fourth verse which was first produced by the compilers of *Hymns Ancient and Modern* in an effort to get closer to Coffin's original Latin words:

> To heal the sick stretch out Thine hand,
> And bid the fallen sinner stand;
> Shine forth, and let Thy light restore
> Earth's own true loveliness once more.

The tune Winchester New, or Frankfurt, first appeared in Hamburg in 1690, set to a German hymn, '*Wer nur den lieben Gott lasst walten*'. John Wesley seems to have introduced it into England. It appeared in his *Foundry Tune Book* of 1742 where it was described as a 'swift German tune'.

Jordanis oras praevia

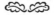

On Jordan's bank the Baptist's cry
Announces that the Lord is nigh;
Come then and hearken, for he brings
High tidings of the King of kings.

2   Then cleansed be every breast from sin;
Make straight the way for God within;
Prepare we in our hearts a home,
Where such a mighty Guest may come.

3   For thou art our salvation, Lord,
Our refuge, and our great reward;
Without thy grace we waste away,
Like flowers that wither and decay.

4   Stretch forth thine hand, to heal our sore,
And make us rise to fall no more;
Once more upon thy people shine,
And fill the world with love divine.

5   To him who left the throne of heaven
To save mankind, all praise be given;
Like praise be to the Father done,
And Holy Spirit, Three in One.

ONWARD, CHRISTIAN SOLDIERS

Widespread unease about its supposedly militaristic message has led this classic Victorian anthem to the Church militant to be dropped from several modern hymnbooks. It is still hugely popular, particularly among the great unchurched majority, standing 26th in the latest *Songs of Praise* poll, but a growing number of clergy will not allow it to be sung in its original form.

There have been several attempts to rewrite it in a more acceptable contemporary idiom. Derek Rawcliffe, former Bishop of Glasgow in the Scottish Episcopal Church, produced a version for the 20th anniversary festival of the Lesbian and Gay Christian Movement at Southwark Cathedral in November 1996 which began 'Onward, Christian homos' and David Wright offered a pacifist version in the aftermath of the Falklands War:

> Onward, Christian pilgrims,
> Working hard for peace,
> Day by day we're praying
> That all wars may cease.
> Christ our royal master
> Bids us love our foes;
> Do good to those who harm us,
> And violence oppose!

Another much-changed version, beginning 'Onward Christian pilgrims, Christ will be our light', which appears in *New Hymns and Worship Songs*, was substituted by the Rector of Newark, Vivian Enever, at a special service held in the town in June 2004 on the 60th anniversary of D-Day, much to the annoyance of many in the congregation who simply ignored the new words and sang the old ones from memory.

The trouble with these attempts, however worthy and well-intentioned, is that they ignore and distort the message and integrity of the original. 'Onward, Christian soldiers' is a great poetic expression of the (highly orthodox and biblical) idea of the Church militant. It is about moving onward in faith rather than standing still, engaging in the world rather than withdrawing from it, and proclaiming the unity of Christians rather than parading their differences. It is firmly Christological in focus and puts the Cross of Jesus at the centre of the Christian life. As such, one might have thought that it would appeal to those committed to an active, progressive faith and attached to the social gospel. Its language is not so much directly militaristic as carefully and calculatedly allegorical and metaphorical – '*like* a mighty army' and 'marching *as* to war'. It also speaks very directly and positively to those many souls in our fractured and broken society who do have to contend with evil forces and demonic influences.

Despite its title, 'Onward, Christian soldiers' is far from being a glorification of war. It is rather a stirring call to Christians to follow the Cross of Christ and a powerful plea for Christian unity. Admittedly its language is a little naïve and its confidence rather misplaced, but we should remember that it was written for children taking part in an outdoor procession. It may not be a hymn of great depth or subtlety, but set to Sullivan's march tune St Gertrude, it has a tremendous capacity to stir, excite and unite those who are singing it – and that surely can be no bad thing.

'Onward, Christian soldiers' comes from the prolific pen of the Revd Sabine Baring-Gould (1834–1924: see notes to no. 138). He wrote it in 1864 while a curate at Horbury Bridge near Wakefield in Yorkshire to be sung by local children on their Whit Tuesday procession through the village. It was very much a last-minute operation – he only sat down to write the hymn on the Saturday, 'knocked it off', to use his own words, 'in about ten minutes', and had it printed and practised so it could be sung by the children on the Tuesday. The hymn was first published in the *Church Times* on 15 October 1864, under the title 'Hymn for Procession with Cross and Banners'.

During his lifetime Baring-Gould was persuaded by hymn-book compilers to sanction various changes to the words. *The Fellowship Hymn Book* obtained his permission to change the phrase 'one in hope and doctrine' in the penultimate line of the third verse to 'one in hope and purpose'. To please the editors of the 1904 edition of *Hymns Ancient and Modern* he also changed the fifth line of that verse from 'We are not divided' to 'Though divisions harass'. But although these alterations may more accurately have expressed the sadly divided state of the Church in the world, Baring-Gould's original words have generally been restored in such modern hymnals as still include the hymn. There is a story that when an evangelical Archbishop of York objected to the Cross being carried in a procession at Dalton at which Baring-Gould was present, he promptly changed the last line of the refrain to 'With the Cross of Jesus / Left behind the door'. However, a letter written after his death suggests that this episode was invented by his son to satisfy an American newspaper reporter avid for anecdotes about the hymn.

There have been many parodies of this hymn. One of the most heartfelt expresses the frustrations of those who seek to reform the Church:

> Like a mighty tortoise,
> Moves the Church of God;
> Brothers, we are treading
> Where we've always trod.

Sabine Baring-Gould originally wrote 'Onward, Christian soldiers' to fit a tune called Haydn which was an adaptation of the slow movement from Haydn's Symphony No. 53. It was set to this tune in the 1868 appendix to the first edition of *Hymns Ancient and Modern* and also in the 1906 *English Hymnal*. It is hard to imagine how this melody would have put much of a spring into the step of the children making their way up the steepish hill on which Horbury is built. In the enlarged edition of *Hymns Ancient and Modern* which appeared in 1875, the hymn was accompanied by a much more jaunty tune by H.J. Gauntlett.

Even more jaunty was the infectiously vulgar march St Gertrude which Sir Arthur Sullivan (1842–1900) wrote for this hymn in 1871 and which is now its inseparable companion. Like Baring-Gould's words, Sullivan's tune was almost certainly dashed off in a few minutes while he was staying at Hanford, a country house near Blandford in Dorset and named after his hostess there, Mrs Gertrude Clay-Ker-Seymer. It appeared in *The Hymnary*, a collection of new hymn-tunes brought out by Novello, and was an instant hit, ensuring 'Onward, Christian soldiers' a much longer life than it would almost certainly otherwise have had and being taken up by brass bands, street hurdy-gurdies and fairground organs, as well as by enthusiastic congregations up and down the land.

Musical purists are scathing about Sullivan's lazy use of repeated notes and his static marching bass, just as politically correct clergy are scathing about Baring-Gould's words, but the fact remains that this is a cracking good hymn with a cracking good tune which energizes, enthuses and inspires those who sing it when they are given the chance.

A Hymn for Procession with Cross and Banners

Onward, Christian soldiers,
Marching as to war,
With the cross of Jesus
Going on before.
Christ, the royal Master,
Leads against the foe;
Forward into battle,
See, his banners go!

> *Onward, Christian soldiers,*
> *Marching as to war,*
> *With the cross of Jesus*
> *Going on before.*

2   At the sign of triumph,
Satan's legions flee;
On, then, Christian soldiers,
On to victory.
Hell's foundations quiver
At the shout of praise;
Brothers, lift your voices,
Loud your anthems raise.

3   Like a mighty army,
Moves the Church of God;
Brothers, we are treading
Where the saints have trod;
We are not divided,
All one body we,
One in hope and doctrine,
One in charity.

4   Crowns and thrones may perish,
    Kingdoms rise and wane,
    But the Church of Jesus
    Constant will remain:
    Gates of hell can never
    'Gainst that Church prevail;
    We have Christ's own promise,
    And that cannot fail.

5   Onward then ye people,
    Join our happy throng;
    Blend with ours your voices
    In the triumph-song;
    'Glory, laud, and honour
    Unto Christ the King!'
    This through countless ages
    Men and angels sing.

OUR GOD, OUR HELP IN
AGES PAST

This paraphrase of Psalm 90 by Isaac Watts (1674–1748: see no. 27 for biographical details) has been regarded by many as the greatest hymn in the English language. It is said that when Dr Benjamin Jowett, that most eminent Victorian who was Master of Balliol College, asked a group of fellow Oxford dons to note down their list of favourite hymns, all of them independently put down just this one which each felt fulfilled all the conditions of a perfect hymn. In Britain it attained the status almost of a second national anthem, and it is still often sung in services held at New Year and on Remembrance Sunday to commemorate the fallen.

'Our God, our help in ages past' was written in 1714 shortly before the death of Queen Anne and at a time of acute national anxiety about the succession to the throne. It was first published five years later in Watts's *The Psalms of David Imitated in the Language of the New Testament*. But it is much more than a mere metrical version of Psalm 90 (Lord thou hast been our dwelling-place in all generations). It is true that some of Watts's phrases are very close to those of the psalmist, or rather of the psalm as it appears in the Authorized Version. The fifth verse of his hymn, for example, echoes very closely its fourth verse: 'For a thousand ages in thy sight are but as yesterday when it is past, and as a watch in the night.' But more often the hymn amplifies a single line in the psalm and turns it into a piece of inspired poetry with a profound depth and great beauty.

The opening of the fifth verse of the psalm is a good case in point: 'Thou carriest them away as with a flood; they are as a sleep.' Watts takes this simple phrase and turns it in the fifth and sixth verses of his hymn into a profound statement about the nature of time and the transience of our earthly lives. These two verses have, in fact, caused much perplexity among Christian commentators as they seem to conflict with the idea of everlasting life. It has been suggested that the sons of time which fly forgotten as a dream are to be understood as the minutes, hours and days of our temporal existence. But, given the title which Watts chose for his hymn, should we not take them rather as referring to our own frailty and perishability as human flesh and blood, contrasted with the eternal nature of God?

In 1737 John Wesley changed the first word of Watts's hymn from 'Our' to 'O' when he included it in his *Collection of Psalms and Hymns*. This alteration has been taken up in virtually every subsequent hymnbook, although the Baptists and Congregationalists long stuck to Watts's original opening, and the hymn still appears in that form in *Rejoice and Sing*, the hymnbook of the United Reformed Church. Verses 4, 6 and 8 are nowadays almost always omitted, and the phrase 'Under the shadow' in verse 2 is sometimes altered to 'Beneath the shadow' to give a more satisfactory stress.

The tune St Anne, which is now almost universally associated with this hymn, was not, in fact, attached to it until the publication of *Hymns Ancient and Modern* in 1861. St Anne first appeared in the 1708 edition of Tate and Brady's book of psalm tunes, where it was set to Psalm 42 ('As pants the hart for cooling streams'). It was probably composed by Dr William Croft (1678–1727), successively organist of St Anne's Church, Soho, the Chapel Royal and Westminster Abbey.

Man frail, and God eternal

Our God, our help in ages past,
Our hope for years to come,
Our shelter from the stormy blast,
And our eternal home.

2   Under the shadow of thy throne
Thy saints have dwelt secure;
Sufficient is thine arm alone,
And our defence is sure.

3   Before the hills in order stood,
Or earth received her frame,
From everlasting thou art God,
To endless years the same.

4   Thy Word commands our flesh to dust,
Return, ye sons of men;
All nations rose from Earth at first,
And turn to earth again.

5   A thousand ages in thy sight
Are like an evening gone;
Short as the watch that ends the night
Before the rising sun.

6   The busy tribes of flesh and blood,
With all their lives and cares,
Are carried downwards by the flood
And lost in following years.

7   Time, like an ever-rolling stream
     Bears all its sons away;
     They fly, forgotten as a dream
     Dies at the opening day.

8   Like flow'ry fields the nations stand
     Pleas'd with the morning light;
     The flowers beneath the Mower's hand
     Lie withering e'er 'tis night.

9   Our God, our help in ages past,
     Our hope for years to come,
     Be thou our guard while troubles last,
     And our eternal home.

PRAISE, MY SOUL, THE
KING OF HEAVEN

This majestic song of praise is one of Her Majesty the Queen's favourite hymns and she chose it for her wedding in 1947. It came 21st in the 2002 *Songs of Praise* poll.

It is the work of Henry Francis Lyte (1793–1847), the author of 'Abide with me' (no. 2: see there for biographical details). He wrote it for his congregation at Lower Brixham in Devon and it was first published in 1834 in a collection called *Spirit of the Psalms*. This book included metrical versions of the Psalms to fit the calendar of the Church of England. Among other hymns in it which are still sung today were 'God of mercy, God of grace' (based on Psalm 67) and 'Pleasant are thy courts above' (based on Psalm 84).

'Praise, my soul, the King of heaven' is based on Psalm 103: 'Bless the Lord, O my soul: And all that is within me, bless his holy name.' As Watts did with 'Our God, our help in ages past', Lyte created vivid new images from phrases in the original psalm, although in his case it was more through compression rather than amplification. Thus the eighth verse of the psalm, 'The Lord is merciful and gracious, slow to anger, and plenteous in mercy. He will not always chide' became 'Slow to chide and swift to bless' in the hymn. In the same way verses 13 and 14, 'Like as a father pitieth his children, so the Lord pitieth them that fear him. For he knoweth our frame', became: 'Father-like he tends and spares us, well our feeble frame he knows'.

The fourth verse of the hymn is now often omitted, and in many hymnals the refrain 'Praise him, praise him' is replaced by 'Alleluia, Alleluia'. The editors of *Hymns Ancient and Modern* were unhappy with the notion of angels helping mortals to adore God and even more unhappy with the idea of the sun and moon bowing down before Him and for a time changed the last verse to:

Angels, in the height adore him;
Ye behold him face to face;
Saints triumphant, bow before Him,
Gather'd in from every race.
Praise him, praise him,
Praise with us the God of grace.

George Macleod, the founder of the Iona Community, who had no problem with angels helping us to adore God and who also had a huge sense of the cosmic and physical power of Christ and the synthesis of religion and science, was fond of rendering the first line of the final verse as 'Atoms help us to adore him'.

The tune Praise my Soul was written especially for Lyte's hymn by Sir John Goss (1800–80) and first appeared in 1869. Born in Fareham, Hampshire, where his father was the parish church organist, Goss was a chorister at the Chapel Royal and became organist at St Luke's, Chelsea. From 1838 to 1872 he was organist at St Paul's Cathedral.

Psalm ciii

Praise, my soul, the King of heaven;
To his feet thy tribute bring.
Ransomed, healed, restored, forgiven,
Who like me his praise should sing?
　　Praise him! Praise him!
　　Praise the everlasting King!

2　Praise him for his grace and favour
　To our fathers in distress;
　Praise him still the same for ever,
　Slow to chide, and swift to bless.
　　Praise him! Praise him!
　　Glorious in his faithfulness.

3　Father-like, he tends and spares us;
　Well our feeble frame he knows;
　In his hands he gently bears us,
　Rescues us from all our foes.
　　Praise him! Praise him!
　　Widely as his mercy flows.

4　Frail as summer's flower we flourish:
　Blows the wind, and it is gone.
　But, while mortals rise and perish,
　God endures unchanging on.
　　Praise him! Praise him!
　　Praise the high eternal One!

5　Angels, help us to adore him;
　Ye behold him face to face;
　Sun and moon, bow down before him,
　Dwellers all in time and space.
　　Praise him! Praise him!
　　Praise with us the God of grace!

PRAISE THE LORD! YE
HEAVENS, ADORE HIM

Virtually everyone knows who composed the tune to which this hymn is almost always sung, but nobody knows who wrote the words.

It first appeared, as laid out here, in a leaflet produced around 1800 as a supplement to the collection of psalms, hymns and anthems sung at the London Foundling Hospital. The verses were headed 'Hymn from Psalm cxlviii, music by Haydn' which makes clear that from the beginning the hymn was set to Joseph Haydn's majestic tune Austria. Psalm 148, on which it is based, begins 'Praise ye the Lord. Praise ye the Lord from the heavens.'

The Foundling Hospital was established by a retired merchant navy captain, Thomas Coram. On his way to a service at St Andrew's, Holborn, one Sunday morning he found an abandoned baby left on the steps. He felt moved to found an institution that would care for some of the many illegitimate children in the capital who suffered a similar fate. The hospital was established in High Holborn and had its own chapel with a fine organ which was the gift of George Frideric Handel. This became a fashionable place of worship in the eighteenth century largely because of the singing by the children. We have already come across another hymn written especially for the inmates of a similar establishment in James Edmeston's 'Lead us, Heavenly Father, lead us' (no. 72).

Both John Kempthorne (1775–1838), rector of St Michael's, Gloucester, and Richard Mant (1776–1848), author of 'Bright the vision that delighted' (no. 20) have been credited with the authorship of this hymn, but John Julian produces conclusive proof in his *Dictionary of Hymnody* that neither of them wrote it. Most hymnbooks pair the original four verses here to form two stanzas and add a third which was written in 1836 by Edward Osler (1798–1863):

Worship, honour, glory, blessing,
Lord, we offer to thy name;
Young and old, their praise expressing,
Join thy goodness to proclaim.
As the hosts of heaven adore thee,
We would bow before thy throne;
As thine angels serve before thee,
So on earth thy will be done.

Interestingly, Joseph Haydn himself attended a service at the chapel of the Foundling Hospital when he was in London in 1792. He wrote afterwards: 'I was more touched by their innocent and reverent music than by anything I had ever heard.' Little can he have thought that a few years later the children would be singing a hymn to a tune which he was to write for a very different purpose. His Austrian hymn, also known as Haydn, Vienna and Cheadle, was composed at the suggestion of the Austrian prime minister and first performed on the Emperor Franz II's birthday, 12 February 1797, where it was set to the words '*Gott erhalte Franz den Kaiser*'. It became the Austrian and later the German national anthem. The tune is said to have been based on a Croatian national song.

Haydn's melody soon passed into use as a hymn-tune in England, being found in a volume of Isaac Watts's psalms and hymns in 1805 and set to 'Praise the Lord, ye Heavens adore Him' in the 1809 edition of the *Foundling Collection*. The tune was a particular favourite of Haydn's in his old age, and when the French were bombarding Vienna in May 1809, he asked to be led to his piano so that he might play it. It was the last piece of music that he played.

Psalm cxlviii

Praise the Lord! Ye heavens, adore him;
Praise him, angels, in the height;
Sun and moon, rejoice before him;
Praise him, all ye stars and light:

2   Praise the Lord, for he hath spoken;
Worlds his mighty voice obeyed;
Laws, which never shall be broken,
For their guidance hath he made.

3   Praise the Lord, for he is glorious!
Never shall his promise fail;
God hath made his saints victorious;
Sin and death shall not prevail.

4   Praise the God of our salvation;
Hosts on high, his power proclaim;
Heaven and earth, and all creation,
Laud and magnify his name!

PRAISE TO THE HOLIEST
IN THE HEIGHT

This is the third hymn in this book to come from the pen of John Henry Newman (1801–90). Like 'Firmly I believe and truly' (no. 34), it was extracted from his long poem *The Dream of Gerontius*. But in this case, as with 'Lead, kindly Light', Newman's meditative verses were turned into a hymn and sung in churches during his own lifetime. It is the most popular of his hymns, at least on the evidence of the 2002 *Songs of Praise* poll in which it came twenty-third.

The Dream of Gerontius, which traces the journey of an aged monk through the gate of death into the presence of Christ, was written in 1865 and first appeared in the Catholic publication, *The Month*. There is a story that Newman thought so little of the poem that he threw it into a waste-paper basket from whence it was retrieved by a friend.

The lines which make up this hymn come from the last part of a 35-verse 'Hymn to the Angelicals'. There the verse beginning 'Praise to the Holiest in the height' was used at the beginning of each of the hymn's five sections. When in 1868 the editors of *Hymns Ancient and Modern* extracted six stanzas from the poem to make a hymn suitable for congregational singing, they began with this verse and repeated it at the end.

The third edition of the *Church Hymnary* omitted the fourth verse of the hymn on the grounds that there is no higher gift than grace and that its words strongly suggests the doctrine of transubstantiation. This was an unfortunate decision. As Donald Webster points out in his book, *Our Hymn Tunes:** 'In less ecumenical times than our own, Protestants have sung this verse

* Donald Webster, *Our Hymn Tunes: Their Choice and Performance* (Edinburgh: St Andrew Press, 1983).

without strain on their consciences and have interpreted the words as referring to Our Lord's earthly ministry.'

The tune Gerontius was written specifically for Newman's hymn by J.B. Dykes (1823–76), precentor of Durham Cathedral, and appeared with it in 1868 in the appendix to the first edition of *Hymns Ancient and Modern*. The 1908 historical edition carried a new tune specially commissioned by Sir Charles Villiers Stanford (1852–1924) and entitled Alverstone. 'Praise to the Holiest in the height' is also sometimes sung to *Chorus angelorum* or Somervell by Sir Arthur Somervell (1863–1937). Somervell was a professor at the Royal College of Music and then an inspector of music in schools. His tune, which was written for Newman's hymn, first appeared in *Arundel Hymns* in 1902 and was subsequently used in his oratorio, *Passion of Christ*. The hymn is also often sung to Richmond by Thomas Haweis (1734–1820: see no. 25) and occasionally to Hebdomadal by Thomas Banks, Bishop of Oxford. The last tune is so called because it was written during a particularly boring session of the University's Hebdomadal Council.

Praise to the Holiest in the height,
And in the depth be praise;
In all his words most wonderful,
Most sure in all his ways.

2   O loving wisdom of our God!
When all was sin and shame,
A second Adam to the fight
And to the rescue came.

3   O wisest love! that flesh and blood,
Which did in Adam fail,
Should strive afresh against the foe,
Should strive and should prevail;

4   And that a higher gift than grace
Should flesh and blood refine,
God's presence and his very self,
And essence all-divine.

5   O generous love! that he, who smote
In Man for man the foe,
The double agony in Man
For man should undergo;

6   And in the garden secretly,
And on the Cross on high,
Should teach his brethren, and inspire
To suffer and to die.

7   Praise to the Holiest in the height,
And in the depth be praise;
In all his words most wonderful,
Most sure in all his ways.

after the place near Atherstone in Warwickshire where Charles Jennens, the compiler of the words of the *Messiah* lived. The tune is also known as Knaresborough, Caernarvon or Handel's 148th.

An alternative tune is Darwall's 148th, composed around 1770 by John Darwall (1731–89), vicar of Walsall, Staffordshire, and more commonly set to 'Ye holy angels bright' (no. 150).

On the Resurrection

Rejoice, the Lord is King!
Your Lord and King adore;
Mortals, give thanks and sing,
And triumph evermore:

> *Lift up your heart, lift up your voice;*
> *Rejoice, again I say, rejoice.*

2 Jesus, the Saviour, reigns,
The God of truth and love;
When he had purged our stains,
He took his seat above:

3 His kingdom cannot fail,
He rules o'er earth and heaven;
The keys of death and hell
Are to our Jesus given:

4 He sits at God's right hand
Till all his foes submit,
And bow to his command,
And fall beneath his feet:

5 He all his foes shall quell,
Shall all our sins destroy,
And every bosom swell
With pure seraphic joy:

6 Rejoice in glorious hope;
Jesus the Judge shall come,
And take his servants up
To their eternal home:

> *We then shall hear th' Archangel's voice,*
> *The trump of God shall sound, Rejoice!*

RIDE ON! RIDE ON IN MAJESTY!

This fine hymn for Palm Sunday is by Henry Hart Milman (1791–1868), who was successively vicar of St Mary's, Reading, rector of St Margaret's, Westminster, and Dean of St Paul's Cathedral.

Henry Milman was born in Westminster, the son of Sir Francis Milman, physician to George III. He was educated at Eton and Brasenose College, Oxford, where he won the Newdigate poetry prize. He wrote a number of books on the history of the Early Church and a long poem, *The Martyr of Antioch*, which became an oratorio with music by Sir Arthur Sullivan.

'Ride on! ride on in majesty!' was written in 1821, while Milman was at St Mary's, Reading, and just before he was elected Professor of Poetry at Oxford University. Reginald Heber (for whom see notes to no. 21) was at that time preparing a book of hymns to cover all the Sundays and festivals of the Christian Year. Milman sent him a copy of 'Ride on! ride on in majesty!' and received the enthusiastic reply: 'You have indeed sent me a most powerful reinforcement to my projected hymnbook. A few more such hymns and I shall neither need nor wait for the aid of Scott or Southey.'

Along with twelve other hymns by Milman, 'Ride on! ride on in majesty!' was first published in Heber's *Hymns Written and Adapted to the Weekly Church Services of the Year*, which came out in 1827 after its compiler's death. It was there given as the first hymn for Palm Sunday, and it has been a regular feature of worship on that day ever since. For some curious reason, the third line of the first verse was long regarded as unacceptable by several hymnbook editors and was generally changed to either 'O saviour meek, pursue thy road' or 'With joyous throngs pursue thy road'.

The hymn is most commonly sung to Winchester New, adapted by W.H. Havergal (1793–1870) from the *Musikalisches Handbuch*, published in Hamburg in 1690. An alternative tune is St Drostane by J.B. Dykes (1823–76), which was written in 1862 and included in *Hymns Ancient and Modern* in 1875.

Palm Sunday

Ride on! ride on in majesty!
Hark, all the tribes hosanna cry;
Thine humble beast pursues his road
With palms and scattered garments strowed.

2   Ride on! ride on in majesty!
In lowly pomp ride on to die:
O Christ, thy triumphs now begin
O'er captive death and conquered sin.

3   Ride on! ride on in majesty!
The wingèd squadrons of the sky
Look down with sad and wondering eyes
To see the approaching sacrifice.

4   Ride on! ride on in majesty!
Thy last and fiercest strife is nigh;
The Father, on his sapphire throne,
Expects his own anointed Son.

5   Ride on! ride on in majesty!
In lowly pomp ride on to die;
Bow thy meek head to mortal pain
Then take, O God, thy power, and reign.

ROCK OF AGES, CLEFT
FOR ME

In his *Dictionary of Hymnody* John Julian wrote of 'Rock of Ages' that 'no other hymn can be named which has laid so broad and so firm a grasp upon the English-speaking world'. It certainly came high on the Victorians' list of favourite hymns – indeed my research suggests that it was probably their top choice and it occupied the No. 1 position in an extensive poll of favourite hymns undertaken among readers of the *Sunday at Home* magazine in 1897. Prince Albert is said to have repeated it constantly on his death-bed at Windsor Castle, and it was a particular favourite of W.E. Gladstone who translated it into Greek, Latin and Italian. After hearing it sung at Gladstone's funeral, A.C. Benson commented, 'To have written words which should come home to people in moments of high, deep and passionate emotion; consecrating, consoling, uplifting ... there can hardly be anything worth better doing than that.' Oliver Wendell Holmes, one of the hymn's many North American admirers, described it as 'the Protestant *Dies Irae*'.

Its author, Augustus Montague Toplady (1740–78), was born in Farnham, Surrey. The son of an Army officer, he was educated at Westminster School and Trinity College, Dublin. He was converted to evangelical religion at the age of 16 by a mission sermon preached in an Irish barn. Ordained into the Church of England after a brief flirtation with Methodism, he became curate of Blagdon in Somerset in 1762, and after serving as an assistant curate at Hungerford, Berkshire, he obtained the living of Broadhembury in Devon. From there he engaged in a vigorous and often acrimonious pamphlet war with his erstwhile friend John Wesley, whose liberal views and rejection of the doctrine of the elect he strongly opposed. Toplady was a Calvinist of the narrowest kind, almost totally obsessed with the subject of sin.

In 1774, suffering from consumption, Toplady obtained permanent leave of absence from his benefice in Devon and moved to London where he looked after the French Reformed Church in Orange Street. 'Rock of Ages', one of 133 hymns that he wrote, first appeared in the form here in an article he wrote for the March 1776 issue of the *Gospel Magazine*. In it he made the astonishing calculation that the number of sins committed by the average individual during his lifetime amounted to 2,522,880,000. The article concluded with 'Rock of Ages' which the author described as 'a living and dying prayer for the holiest believer in the world'.

There is a nice but wholly fanciful story that this hymn was written at the end of an evening during which Toplady and Charles Wesley had met and engaged in long and heated debate. Finally, long after midnight, the two men retired to their rooms, Toplady to write 'Rock of Ages' and Wesley to write 'Jesu, lover of my soul'. In fact, Wesley's hymn was published in 1740 – the year of Toplady's birth. Equally apocryphal is the story that Toplady wrote the hymn in 1763 after sheltering during a storm in a rocky gorge in the Mendips known as Burrington Combe. The story goes that, lacking a notebook to write down the words that had come to him, he found a playing card lying at his feet and wrote the verses out on the back of it.

In fact, 'Rock of Ages' was almost certainly written in the autumn of 1774 to be sung after a sermon based on Numbers 20.11, which tells of Moses' smiting of the rock in the desert to bring forth water for the children of Israel. The second line of the fourth verse is now normally rendered 'When mine eyelids close in death'.

The tune which usually accompanies this hymn, Petra or Redhead, was composed by Richard Redhead (1820–1901), organist of St Mary Magdalene, Paddington. It first appeared in his *Church Hymn Tunes* in 1853. In the USA, however, it is more often sung to Toplady, a tune by Thomas Hastings (1784–1872). This latter tune, which is wrongly attributed in the recent *BBC Songs of Praise* hymnal to Toplady himself, is becoming increasingly popular in Britain. It is played on a piano accordion during the trial scene in the second act of the musical *Chicago*. A third tune, Rousseau's Dream, was used for the hymn when it was sung in the Moody and Sankey crusades in Britain in 1875.

Rock of Ages, cleft for me

Rock of Ages, cleft for me,
Let me hide myself in Thee;
Let the water and the blood,
From Thy riven side which flowed,
Be of sin the double cure,
Cleanse me from its guilt and power.

2   Not the labours of my hands
Can fulfil Thy law's demands;
Could my zeal no respite know,
Could my tears for ever flow,
All for sin could not atone:
Thou must save, and Thou alone.

3   Nothing in my hand I bring,
Simply to Thy Cross I cling;
Naked, come to Thee for dress;
Helpless, look to Thee for grace;
Foul, I to the fountain fly;
Wash me, Saviour, or I die.

4   While I draw this fleeting breath,
When my eye-strings break in death,
When I soar through tracts unknown,
See Thee on Thy judgment throne,
Rock of Ages, cleft for me,
Let me hide myself in Thee.

SHALL WE GATHER AT
THE RIVER

I find this gospel song one of the best and most moving of its kind, and its inclusion in this collection is very much a matter of personal preference. It is not to be found in many modern British hymnals, although I am glad to say that it does make an appearance in the 1997 *BBC Songs of Praise*, and is still included in a number of North American hymnals.

Both the words and music of 'Shall we gather by the river' are by Dr Robert Lowry (1826–99). Born in Philadelphia, Lowry was educated at Lewisburgh University, Pennsylvania, where after a few years in the Baptist ministry he became Professor of Rhetoric. In 1875 he resigned his chair to return to pastoral work at Plainfield. He edited several collections of hymns and wrote many tunes, including that for the popular Victorian Sunday School hymn by Annie Sherwood Hawks, 'I need thee every hour', for which he also supplied the refrain. Another of Lowry's hymns, 'Low in the grave he lay', was long popular among Methodists at Easter services.

According to Ira Sankey, the words of 'Shall we gather at the river' came to Dr Lowry as he was sitting at his study table in Elliott Place, Brooklyn, on a sultry July afternoon in 1864. An epidemic was raging through the city at the time and he had been pondering the question, 'Why do hymn-writers say so much about the river of death and so little about the pure river of the water of life?' He wrote the words in the space of fifteen minutes and then sat down at his parlour organ to work out the tune. In Lowry's own words, 'It is brass-band music, has a march movement, and for that reason has become popular; though, for myself, I do not think much of it.'

The hymn is based on Revelation 22.1: 'And he showed me a pure river of water of life, proceeding out of the throne of God and of the Lamb.' Some critics have taken Lowry to task for wrongly interpreting this symbolic description of the Holy Spirit proceeding out of God's throne as a literal description of a river flowing by God's throne. Personally, I would not be so hard on him. The imagery of rivers and flowing water is much used in the Bible to suggest the idea of eternal life, and it seems to me to be wholly appropriate to use it in hymns as well.

Lowry's hymn became immensely popular with Sunday Schools both in the USA and in Britain. Its compelling tune also made it a favourite for community singing. Once when he was on a railroad journey between Harrisburg and Lewisburg Lowry heard it being sung over and over again by a group of half-drunken lumber-men. This experience brought from him the characteristic observation: 'I did not think so much of the music then, as I listened to those singers; but I did think that perhaps the spirit of the hymn, the words so flippantly uttered, might somehow survive and be carried forward into the lives of those careless men, and ultimately lift them upward to the realisation of the hope expressed in the hymn.'

When Edwin Scrymgeour, the only British MP elected on a prohibitionist ticket, had unseated Winston Churchill from his Dundee constituency in 1922, he announced that, come prohibition, all ales and spirits in the city would be emptied into the River Tay. The assembled crowd reacted by going into a spontaneous and spirited rendition of 'Shall we gather at the river'.

At a time when many inferior modern choruses are being heard increasingly frequently in churches, it seems a pity that such tried and proven old favourites as this are not also being given an airing. No one would claim it as great poetry or great music, but it has a genuine simplicity and feeling.

Lowry's tune for this hymn is known as Hanson Place.

Shall we gather at the river,
Where bright angel feet have trod,
With its crystal tide for ever
Flowing by the throne of God?

Yes, we'll gather at the river,
The beautiful, the beautiful river;
Gather with the saints at the river
That flows by the throne of God.

2   On the margin of the river
Dashing up its silver spray,
We will walk and worship ever
All the happy, golden day.

3   Ere we reach the shining river,
Lay we every burden down;
Grace our spirits will deliver,
And provide a robe and crown.

4   At the shining of the river,
Mirror of the Saviour's face,
Saints whom death will never sever
Raise their song of saving grace.

5   Soon we'll reach the silver river,
Soon our pilgrimage will cease;
Soon our happy hearts will quiver
With the melody of peace.

SOLDIERS OF CHRIST,
ARISE

This is yet another of Charles Wesley's great hymns, based on the well-known passage in St Paul's Epistle to the Ephesians which begins with the injunction: 'Put on the whole armour of God, that ye may be able to stand against the wiles of the devil' (Ephesians 6.11–18).

When it first appeared in 1742 appended to John Wesley's *The Character of a Methodist*, this hymn ran to sixteen verses, each eight lines long. It was pruned to twelve verses for inclusion in the *Wesleyan Hymn Book* of 1780, and it is that version which appears here. Most hymnals use only three verses of the original: 1, 2 and 12, and divide them into six stanzas to make a common metre hymn. *Hymns and Psalms*, the current Methodist hymnal, provides a more generous selection, using verses 1, 2, 4, 12, 8, 9 and 11 of the original in that order.

Although the hymn is very much based on the imagery of Ephesians 6, like all of Wesley's work, it is packed with other biblical allusions and references. (They include Rom. 8.37; Phil. 4.13; 1 Jn 5.5; 1 Pet. 4.1; Ps. 84.7; Col. 1.13; Rev. 22.17; 1 Thess. 4.16 and 5.17; Ps. 18.3, 100.4, 43.3-4; Josh. 24.15, Ps. 62.8, 95.6; 2 Chron. 6.13; and Ps. 122.6. Also characteristic of Wesley is the use of unusual words such as 'panoply' and the wonderfully evocative 'ingrasping'.

The most commonly used tunes for this hymn are either St Ethelwald by W.H.Monk (1823–89), which was written especially for the first edition of *Hymns Ancient and Modern* in 1861, or From Strength to Strength by Edward Woodall Naylor (1867–1934), which first appeared in the *Public School Hymn Book* in 1919. Naylor was the son of Dr John Naylor, organist at York Minster, and himself became organist of Emmanuel College, Cambridge, where he was also a lecturer in musical history.

The Whole Armour of God

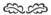

Soldiers of Christ, arise, and put your armour on,
Strong in the strength which God supplies through His eternal
   Son
Strong in the Lord of hosts, and in His mighty power,
Who in the strength of Jesus trusts is more than conqueror.

2   Stand then in His great might, with all His strength endued,
    And take, to arm you for the fight, the panoply of God;
    That, having all things done, and all your conflicts passed,
    Ye may o'ercome through Christ alone and stand entire at last.

3   Stand then against your foes, in close and firm array;
    Legions of wily fiends oppose throughout the evil day;
    But meet the sons of night, and mock their vain design,
    Armed in the arms of heavenly light, of righteousness divine.

4   Leave no unguarded place, no weakness of the soul,
    Take every virtue, every grace, and fortify the whole;
    Indissolubly joined, to battle all proceed;
    But arm yourselves with all the mind that was in Christ, your
      Head.

5   But, above all, lay hold on faith's victorious shield;
    Armed with that adamant and gold, be sure to win the field:
    If faith surround your heart, Satan shall be subdued,
    Repelled his every fiery dart, and quenched with Jesu's blood.

6   Jesus hath died for you! What can His love withstand?
    Believe, hold fast your shield, and who shall pluck you from
      His hand?
    Believe that Jesus reigns; all power to Him is giv'n:
    Believe, till freed from sin's remains; believe yourselves to
      Heav'n.

7   To keep your armour bright, attend with constant care,
      Still walking in your Captain's sight, and watching unto prayer.
      Ready for all alarms, steadfastly set your face,
      And always exercise your arms, and use your every grace.

8   Pray without ceasing, pray, your Captain gives the word;
      His summons cheerfully obey and call upon the Lord;
      To God your every want in instant prayer display,
      Pray always; pray and never faint; pray, without ceasing, pray!

9   In fellowship alone, to God with faith draw near;
      Approach His courts, besiege His throne with all the powers
        of prayer:
      Go to His temple, go, nor from His altar move;
      Let every house His worship know, and every heart His love.

10   To God your spirits dart, your souls in words declare,
      Or groan, to Him Who reads the heart, the unutterable prayer:
      His mercy now implore, and now show forth His praise,
      In shouts, or silent awe, adore His miracles of grace.

11   Pour out your souls to God, and bow them with your knees,
      And spread your hearts and hands abroad, and pray for Zion's
        peace;
      Your guides and brethren bear for ever on your mind;
      Extend the arms of mighty prayer, ingrasping all mankind.

12   From strength to strength go on, wrestle and fight and pray,
      Tread all the powers of darkness down and win the well
        fought day.
      Still let the Spirit cry in all His soldiers, 'Come!'
      Till Christ the Lord descends from high and takes the
        conquerors home.

STAND UP AND BLESS
THE LORD

This hymn is by James Montgomery (1771–1854), the radical journalist who was also responsible for 'Hail to the Lord's Anointed!' (no. 48: see notes for biographical details). It was written for the anniversary of the Sheffield Red Hill Wesleyan Sunday School on 15 March 1824.

When Montgomery published the hymn in the *Christian Psalmist* in 1825, he changed the word 'children' in the second line to 'people', presumably so that it would not be restricted to use in Sunday School, and so it has remained. The fourth verse is now always omitted.

This hymn has strongly Calvinistic overtones, with its clear expression of the doctrine of election in the second line, but it has won a place in the affections of congregations of many denominations. There is plenty of choice in the tunes to which it is set in contemporary hymnbooks, although the favourite seems to be Carlisle by Charles Lockhart (1745–1815). Lockhart, who was blind from childhood, was organist of the Lock Hospital Chapel, and his tune was first published in the *Lock Hospital Collection* in 1792. Alternative tunes for 'Stand up, and bless the Lord' are Doncaster (also known as Bethlehem) by Samuel Wesley (1766–1837) and Kerry from Jowett's *Parochial Psalmody* of 1832.

I myself will always associate this hymn with the soaring and vigorous tune Hillside composed by Alan Bunney, the director of music at Tonbridge School from 1940 to 1967. It deserves to be much more widely known and used.

Stand up, and bless the Lord,
Ye children of his choice;
Stand up, and bless the Lord your God
With heart and soul and voice.

2   Though high above all praise,
Above all blessing high,
Who would not fear his holy name,
And laud and magnify?

3   O for the living flame
From his own altar brought,
To touch our lips, our minds inspire,
And wing to heaven our thought!

4   There, with benign regard,
Our hymns He deigns to hear;
Though unrevealed to mortal sense,
Our spirits feel Him near.

5   God is our strength and song,
And his salvation ours;
Then be his love in Christ proclaimed
With all our ransomed powers.

6   Stand up, and bless the Lord,
The Lord your God adore;
Stand up, and bless his glorious name
Henceforth for evermore.

STAND UP, STAND UP
FOR JESUS

This rousing hymn by George Duffield (1818–88) came out of a tragedy that might stand as a warning to ministers about the dangers of their garb.

It was inspired by the dying words of a leading nineteenth-century American evangelist, Dudley Atkins Tyng. In the summer of 1858 he carried out a particularly successful summer mission in Philadelphia which drew thousands of young men and secured many conversions. Following a particularly success-ful meeting, where he had preached on the text Exodus 10.11 to a crowd of more than five thousand, Tyng was walking alone through the fields of his farm. He stretched out his arm to pat a mule which was working a machine separating corn from the cob. One of the long sleeves of his preaching gown got caught in a cog, and he was drawn into the mill and his arm torn off. It was some time before he was found by his servants and by then he was bleeding to death. He was carried into his house and his friends and associates in the mission gathered to witness his agonizing end.

George Duffield, a Presbyterian minister, who was a helper in Tyng's mission, was one of those who supported him at the end. Moments before he died, Tyng took Duffield's hand and gave his last instruction for the continuance of the mission. 'Tell them', he whispered, 'to stand up for Jesus.' Deeply moved, and with the words ringing in his ears, Duffield went home and wrote his hymn. The following Sunday he preached on the text Ephesians 6.14: 'Stand therefore, having your loins girt about with truth, and having on the breastplate of righteousness.' He concluded the sermon by reading out his hymn. First printed on a single sheet for Sunday School children, it was later published in a Baptist newspaper and soon became immensely popular throughout the USA, being sung by soldiers on both sides of the Civil War.

The fifth line of the third verse takes up the theme of the text on which Dudley Tyng had preached shortly before his terrible accident: 'Come now, ye that are men, and serve the Lord.' Duffield's original fifth verse is now normally omitted:

> Stand up, stand up for Jesus!
> Each soldier to his post;
> Close up the broken column,
> And shout through all the host.
> Make good the loss so heavy
> In those that still remain,
> And prove to all around you
> That death itself is gain.

George Duffield was born at Carlisle, Pennsylvania, and educated at Yale and Union Seminary, New York. He was a minister in New York, New Jersey, Michigan and Illinois. He died in Detroit.

The tune Morning Light, or Stand up, which gives Duffield's hymn so much of its thrilling punch and urgency, was composed by George James Webb (1803–87) in 1837 for a parlour ballad, ''Tis dawn, the lark is singing'. Born in Britain near Salisbury, Wiltshire, Webb emigrated to the USA in 1830, and for nearly 40 years was organist at the Old South Church in Boston. His tune was used for a number of Methodist and Baptist hymns in the 1840s and first appeared attached to Duffield's words in a hymnbook published in 1861.

Stand up! – stand up for Jesus!
Ye soldiers of the Cross;
Lift high his royal banner,
It must not suffer loss.
From victory unto victory
His army he shall lead,
Till every foe is vanquished,
And Christ is Lord indeed.

2   Stand up! – stand up for Jesus!
The solemn watchword hear,
If while ye sleep he suffers,
Away with shame and fear,
Where'er ye meet with evil,
Within you or without,
Charge for the God of battles,
And put the foe to rout.

3   Stand up! – stand up for Jesus!
The trumpet call obey,
Forth to the mighty conflict
In this his glorious day.
Ye that are men now serve him
Against unnumbered foes;
Let courage rise with danger,
And strength to strength oppose.

4   Stand up! – stand up for Jesus!
Stand in his strength alone;
The arm of flesh will fail you,
Ye dare not trust your own.
Put on the Gospel armour,
Each piece put on with prayer;
Where duty calls or danger,
Be never wanting there!

5   Stand up! – stand up for Jesus!
      The strife will not be long;
      This day the noise of battle,
      The next the victor's song.
      To him that overcometh
      A crown of life shall be;
      He with the King of Glory
      Shall reign eternally.

STRONG SON OF GOD,
IMMORTAL LOVE

There was a time when these moving verses by Alfred Tennyson (1809–92) were to be found in virtually every major British hymnbook. Now, I fear, they are much less commonly encountered, although I am glad to say that they do find a place in *The New English Hymnal*. This is a pity – they not only constitute wonderful poetry but a moving and important expression of the truth that faith is very different from certainty.

The verses printed here come from Tennyson's great poem, *In Memoriam*, which was inspired by the death of his great friend Arthur Hallam in 1833 and published anonymously in 1850. The *Congregational Hymnal* of 1887 seems to have been the first to set them as a hymn for congregational singing. Some Christians have found it a shade too liberal for their taste and jibbed at the use of the word 'seemest' in describing Christ's divine and human natures in the third verse. It has none of the confident certainty found in so many Victorian hymns, and in their modern equivalents, but speaks rather with an honesty and sense of perplexity that surely strikes a chord with the mood of our own age.

Alfred Tennyson was the son of the rector of Somersby, Lincolnshire. He succeeded William Wordsworth as Poet Laureate in 1850. While feeling many doubts about the Christian religion and questioning some of its doctrines, he retained a strong faith in God. He once observed: 'A good hymn is the most difficult thing in the world to write. In a good hymn you have to be both commonplace and poetical.'

There was a time when Tennyson made several appearances in most hymnbooks. The *Methodist Hymn Book* of 1933, for example, contains 'Strong Son of God, immortal love', 'Ring out wild bells, across the wild sky' and 'Sunset and Evening Star'.

This last hymn, which Tennyson entitled 'Crossing the Bar' was written in the poet's 81st year. He later explained his reference in it to the Pilot as 'That Divine and Unseen who is always guarding us'.

Tennyson is worthy of at least two entries in an anthology of hymns. So here, as a bonus, is 'Crossing the Bar':

> Sunset and evening star,
> And one clear call for me!
> And may there be no moaning of the bar,
> When I put out to sea,
> But such a tide as, moving, seems asleep,
> Too full for sound and foam,
> When that which drew from out the boundless deep
> Turns again home.
>
> Twilight and evening bell,
> And after that the dark!
> And may there be no sadness of farewell,
> When I embark;
> For though from out our bourne of time and place
> The flood may bear me far,
> I hope to see my Pilot face to face
> When I have crossed the bar.

'Strong Son of God' has been set to a variety of tunes, including St Venantius, a Rouen church melody, Song 5 by Orlando Gibbons (1583–1625) and Rivaulx by John Bacchus Dykes (1823–76).

In memoriam

Strong Son of God, immortal love,
Whom we, that have not seen thy face,
By faith, and faith alone, embrace,
Believing where we cannot prove;

Thou wilt not leave us in the dust:
Thou madest man, he knows not why;
He thinks he was not made to die;
And thou has made him; thou art just.

Thou seemest human and divine,
The highest, holiest manhood, thou;
Our wills are ours, we know not how;
Our wills are ours, to make them thine.

Our little systems have their day;
They have their day and cease to be;
They are but broken lights of thee,
And thou, O Lord, art more than they.

We have but faith: we cannot know;
For knowledge is of things we see;
And yet we trust it comes from thee,
A beam in darkness; let it grow.

Let knowledge grow from more to more,
But more of reverence in us dwell;
That mind and soul, according well,
May make one music as before,

But vaster. We are fools and slight;
We mock thee when we do not fear;
But help thy foolish ones to bear –
Help thy vain worlds to bear thy light.

TAKE MY LIFE, AND LET
IT BE

This hymn was long to be found in that section of hymnbooks / entitled consecration and discipleship. It is still often sung at confirmations and at other services where a commitment, or a rededication is being made to the Christian life.

Its author, Frances Ridley Havergal (1836–79), was born in Astley, Worcestershire, where her father was rector. She showed an early aptitude for both versifying and musical composition, writing her first hymn at the age of 7. A devout evangelical Christian, she led a classic Victorian spinster's life of good works and piety. Her health was delicate and she expressed the hope that 'the angels would have orders to let her alone a bit when she first got to heaven'.

Her output of hymns was considerable and included 'I am trusting thee, Lord Jesus', 'Who is on the Lord's side?' (for both of which she also wrote the music), 'Another year is dawning', 'Standing at the portal', 'Thy life was given for me' and 'Lord, speak to me, that I may speak'.

'Take my life, and let it be' was written on 4 February 1874 at the end of a five-day visit by Frances Havergal to friends at Arley House, Worcestershire. She later described the circumstances that led to its composition:

There were ten persons in the house, some unconverted and long prayed for, some converted but not rejoicing Christians. He gave me the prayer, 'Lord, give me all in this house'. And he just did. Before I left the house every one had got a blessing. The last night of my visit after I had retired, a governess asked me to go to the two daughters. They were crying; then and there both of them trusted and rejoiced; it was nearly midnight. I was too happy to sleep, and spent most of the night in praise and renewal of my own consecration. These little couplets formed themselves and chimed in my heart one after another till they finished with 'ever, only, all for Thee'.

'Take my life, and let it be' was printed as a consecration hymn in Frances Havergal's *Loyal Responses* in 1878. She herself always insisted that it be sung to her father's tune Patmos, which was written specifically for the hymn and was later known as Consecration. The Revd W.H. Havergal (1793–1870), whom we have already come across in connection with the naming of Handel's tune Gopsal (no. 111), was a noted church musician. A carriage accident, in which he sustained concussion and permanent damage to his eyes, forced him to resign his living soon after Frances' birth, and he devoted the rest of his life to improving the quality of church music which was then at a low ebb in England. His best-known work was *English Church Psalmody* (1847).

Other tunes used for this hymn are St Bees by J.B. Dykes (1823–76), Vienna by J.H. Knecht (1752–1817), Innocents, a melody of uncertain origin arranged by W.H. Monk (1823–69) in 1850, Lübeck, from Freylinghausen's *Geistreiches Gesangbuch* of 1704 and Nottingham, often thought to be by Mozart but in fact by Jeremiah Clark (1670–1707).

Self-consecration to Christ

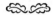

Take my life, and let it be
Consecrated, Lord, to thee;
Take my moments and my days,
Let them flow in ceaseless praise.

2   Take my hands, and let them move
At the impulse of thy love.
Take my feet, and let them be
Swift and beautiful for thee.

3   Take my voice, and let me sing
Always, only, for my King;
Take my lips, and let them be
Filled with messages from thee.

4   Take my silver and my gold;
Not a mite would I withhold.
Take my intellect, and use
Every power as thou shalt choose.

5   Take my will, and make it thine:
It shall be no longer mine.
Take my heart; it is thine own:
It shall be thy royal throne.

6   Take my love; my Lord, I pour
At thy feet its treasure-store.
Take myself, and I will be
Ever, only, all for thee.

TEACH ME, MY GOD AND
KING

Like 'King of glory, king of peace' and 'Let all the world in every
corner sing', this hymn started life as a poem by George Herbert
(1593–1632) and has only been sung in church since the
twentieth century. It is a fine expression of what might rather
grandly nowadays be called incarnational theology. Herbert (for
whose life see notes to hymn no. 70) had a strong sense of the
metaphysical dimension of ordinary material things and mun-
dane tasks. This hymn positively affirms the goodness and
oneness of God's creation and reminds us that the smallest task, if
performed in the right spirit and offered to God, can be a noble
work. This latter theme is taken up in the sixth verse of John
Keble's hymn, 'New every morning is the love' (no. 89).

The verses here were extracted in 1906 by the editors of the
English Hymnal from a poem called 'The Elixir' which was first
published in 1633 in Herbert's posthumous work, *The Temple*.
The poem plays skilfully on the common seventeenth-century
belief in alchemy: the idea that there exists a philosopher's stone
which, in the words of verse 5, 'turneth all to gold'. The
'tincture' referred to in verse 3 is the spiritual principle that can
be infused into matter. The use of the verb 'touch' in the last
verse also continues this metaphor. It was used of the process
whereby the fineness of gold was tested by rubbing it with a
touchstone, and came to be employed metaphorically as in
Shakespeare's *Timon of Athens* (III.iii.6): 'They have all been
touched, and found Base Metal.'

As it originally appeared in *The Temple*, Herbert's poem
contained the following additional stanza, which came between
the first and second verses:

Not rudely, as a beast,
To run into an action;
But still to make thee prepossest,
And give it his perfection.

A manuscript in Dr Williams' Library, London, contains an earlier draft of the poem, which is there entitled 'Perfection'. It begins:

Lord teach me to refer
All things I do to thee,
That I not only may not err
But also pleasing be.

The same manuscript also includes an additional verse after 'A man that looks on glass' (as with the verse above I have modernized the spelling):

He that doth ought for thee,
Marketh that deed for thine;
And When the Devil shakes the tree,
Thou saist, this fruit is mine.

It also has a different version of the last verse:

But these are high perfections:
Happy are they that dare
Let in the Light to all their actions
And show them as they are.

The tune to which the hymn is always sung is Sandys, a traditional air which was set to the carol 'This day a child is born' in *Christmas Carols Ancient and Modern*, by William Sandys (1833). Vaughan Williams set it to 'Teach me, my God and King' in the *English Hymnal*.

The Elixir

Teach me, my God and King,
In all things thee to see;
And what I do in any thing,
To do it as for thee.

2   A man that looks on glass,
On it may stay his eye;
Or if he pleaseth, through it pass,
And then the heav'n espy.

3   All may of thee partake:
Nothing can be so mean,
Which with this tincture, 'for thy sake',
Will not grow bright and clean.

4   A servant with this clause
Makes drudgery divine;
Who sweeps a room, as for thy laws,
Makes that and th'action fine.

5   This is the famous stone
That turneth all to gold;
For that which God doth touch and own
Cannot for less be told.

TELL ME THE OLD, OLD STORY

This is a good old gospel song which still finds a place in several hymnals. Like so many others of the same genre, it comes from the pen of a Victorian spinster who enjoyed indifferent health.

Arabella Catherine Hankey (1834–1911), better known as Kate, was the daughter of Thomas Hankey, a banker and member of the Clapham Sect. While still at school she and her sister began teaching in a Sunday school in Croydon, and at 18 she started a bible class in London for girl assistants in the large West End department stores. Some of her pupils kept in touch with her throughout her life and five met at her funeral, 50 years after the class had ceased. She led a somewhat uneventful life except for an exciting trip to South Africa to nurse and bring home an invalid brother. This involved travelling across the Veldt in bullock waggons and inspired an abiding interest in missions. Her later years were spent in hospital-visiting and other good works.

'Tell me the old, old story' was composed on 29 January 1866 when, in the words of the authoress, 'I was weak and weary after an illness, and especially realizing what most of us realize that simple thoughts in simple words are all that we can bear in sickness.' Her original poem was more than 50 verses long and was published as a leaflet in 1867 entitled 'The Story wanted'. Later it appeared in the form given here, along with other hymns in a collection. Miss Hankey did not object to it being shortened for the purposes of congregational singing, but she did take exception to the insertion of a refrain between each verse.

The hymn was much sung at Moody and Sankey's revival meetings in both Britain and America, where its power as a conversion agent was helped by the catchy tune written for it by William Howard Doane (1832–1915). Doane was the principal of a firm of manufacturers of wood-making machinery in Cincinnati, Ohio, and superintendent of the Baptist Sunday school there. He composed numerous hymn-tunes, including Refuge, for which, at his request, Fanny Crosby wrote 'Safe in the arms of Jesus' in 1868. He gave the following description of the circumstances in which he wrote the tune for 'Tell me the old, old story':

In 1867 I was attending the International Convention of the Young Men's Christian Association in Montreal. Among those present was Major-General Russell, then in command of the English forces during the Fenian excitement. He arose in the meeting and recited the words of this song from a sheet of foolscap paper – tears streaming down from his bronzed cheeks as he read. I wrote the music for the song one hot afternoon while on the stage coach between the Glen Falls House and the Crawford House in the White Mountains. That evening we sang it in the parlours of the hotel. We thought it pretty, although we scarcely anticipated the popularity which was subsequently accorded it.

Tell me the old, old story
Of unseen things above,
Of Jesus and His glory,
Of Jesus and His love.

2   Tell me the story simply,
As to a little child;
For I am weak and weary,
And helpless, and defiled.

3   Tell me the story slowly,
That I may take it in, –
That wonderful redemption,
God's remedy for sin.

4   Tell me the story often,
For I forget so soon;
The early dew of morning
Has passed away at noon.

5   Tell me the story softly,
With earnest tones and grave;
Remember, I'm the sinner
Whom Jesus came to save.

6   Tell me the story always,
If you would really be,
In any time of trouble,
A comforter to me.

7   Tell me the same old story
When you have cause to fear
That this world's empty glory
Is costing me too dear.

8   Yes, and, when that world's glory
      Shall dawn upon my soul,
      Tell me the old, old story,
      'Christ Jesus makes thee whole.'

TELL OUT, MY SOUL,
THE GREATNESS OF THE
LORD

This modern paraphrase of the Magnificat has established itself as one of the most popular hymns of the last 40 years. In a broadcast in 1976 Sir John Betjeman described it as 'one of very few new hymns really to establish themselves in recent years', while in a poll among readers of *Church Times* in 1979 it was voted the most popular new hymn.

It is the work of Timothy Dudley-Smith (b. 1926) who was born and brought up in Derbyshire, where his father was a schoolmaster, and educated at Tonbridge School and Pembroke College, Cambridge. He first felt the call to the ordained ministry when only 11 years old. After serving as a curate in Erith and running the Cambridge University Mission in the East End, he edited *Crusade*, a monthly evangelical magazine established as part of the follow-up to the Billy Graham Crusade of 1955. He then spent thirteen years with the Church Pastoral Aid Society. In 1973 he was appointed Archdeacon of Norwich and since 1981 he has been suffragan Bishop of Thetford in Norfolk.

Timothy Dudley-Smith wrote this hymn in May 1961. While reading a review copy of the New Testament section of the New English Bible he was struck by its rendering of the opening phrase of the Magnificat as 'Tell out, my soul, the greatness of the Lord.' He later wrote, 'I saw in it the first line of a poem and speedily wrote the rest.' He had originally intended his verses simply as a poem but they were included in 1965 in the *Anglican Hymn Book* to which he also contributed 'Lord, who left the highest heaven'. This was the beginning of a prolific career as a hymn writer. In 1967 he produced a metrical version of the *Nunc Dimittis*, 'Faithful vigil ended', as a companion to 'Tell out, my soul'.

Although the first line of this hymn follows exactly the New English Bible's translation of Luke 1.46, the rest is a much more free paraphrase of the Magnificat. It is interesting that several other very popular contemporary hymns, particularly of the chorus type, take their words almost verbatim from the Bible with virtually no alterations. Karen Lafferty's 'Seek ye first the kingdom of God', for example, is made up entirely of direct quotations from the Authorized Version of the Gospels.

The appeal of 'Tell out, my soul' has undoubtedly been greatly enhanced by its setting to Walter Greatorex's grand and sweeping melody Woodlands, which is also used for 'Lift up your hearts!' We lift them, Lord, to thee' (see notes to no. 76 for further details). It is not, however, the only tune to which Timothy Dudley-Smith's hymn has been set – the third edition of the *Church Hymnary* provided Mapperley which was specially composed by Frank Spedding (b. 1929), lecturer and head of department at the Royal Scottish Academy of Music and Drama.

Tell out, my soul, the greatness of the Lord

❧❧

based on the New English Bible translation of the Magnificat, Luke 1.46–55

Tell out, my soul, the greatness of the Lord!
Unnumbered blessings, give my spirit voice;
tender to me the promise of his word;
in God my Saviour shall my heart rejoice.

Tell out, my soul, the greatness of his Name!
Make known his might, the deeds his arm has done;
his mercy sure, from age to age the same;
his holy Name, the Lord, the Mighty One.

Tell out, my soul, the greatness of his might!
Powers and dominions lay their glory by.
Proud hearts and stubborn wills are put to flight,
the hungry fed, the humble lifted high.

Tell out, my soul, the glories of his word!
Firm is his promise, and his mercy sure.
Tell out, my soul, the greatness of the Lord
to children's children and for evermore!

123

TEN THOUSAND TIMES
TEN THOUSAND

This stirring hymn about the Church Triumphant was written by Henry Alford (1810–71), whom we have already encounterd as the author of the harvest hymn, 'Come ye thankful people come' (no. 28).

Alford was born in Bloomsbury, London. His father, also Henry, was rector of Aston Sandford in Buckinghamshire. He was educated at Ilminster Grammar School and Trinity College, Cambridge, where he subsequently became a Fellow. Ordained in 1833, he was curate of Ampton in Suffolk, and incumbent of Quebec Chapel, London, before becoming Dean of Canterbury Cathedral in 1857. He remained there until his death. He wrote a good number of hymns including 'Forward! be our watchword' and the baptismal hymn, 'In token that thou shalt not fear'.

Alford wrote 'Ten thousand times ten thousand' in two parts. The first three verses first appeared in 1867 in his *Year of Praise*. The fourth was added in 1870 and was published that year in *The Lord's Prayer*, illustrated by F.R. Pickersgill, RA, and Henry Alford, DD. The hymn was sung at Alford's funeral on 17 January 1871.

The imagery comes from the Book of Revelation. The opening lines are suggested by the reference in 5.11 to St John the Divine's vision of a mighty throng of angels around the throne of God, 'and the number of them was ten thousand times ten thousand'. The 'rush of Alleluias' and the 'ringing of a thousand harps' in the second verse are taken from Revelation 19.1–6, and 14.2 .

Two tunes have been written for this hymn, Alford by Dr John Bacchus Dykes (1823–76), which first appeared in the 1875 revised edition of *Hymns Ancient and Modern*, and Gresham by

Geoffrey Shaw (1879–1943), inspector of music for London schools, chairman of the schools' music committee of the BBC and organist at St Mary's, Primrose Hill.

Processional for Saints' Days

Ten thousand times ten thousand,
In sparkling raiment bright,
The armies of the ransomed saints
Throng up the steeps of light;
'Tis finished, all is finished,
Their fight with death and sin;
Fling open wide the golden gates,
And let the victors in.

2   What rush of hallelujahs
Fills all the earth and sky!
What ringing of a thousand harps
Bespeaks the triumph nigh!
O day for which creation
And all its tribes were made!
O joy, for all its former woes
A thousandfold repaid!

3   O then what raptured greetings
On Canaan's happy shore,
What knitting severed friendships up,
Where partings are no more!
Then eyes with joy shall sparkle
That brimmed with tears of late;
Orphans no long fatherless,
Nor widows desolate.

4   Bring near Thy great salvation,
Thou Lamb for sinners slain;
Fill up the roll of Thine elect,
Then take Thy power and reign;
Appear, Desire of nations, –
Thine exiles long for home;
Show in the heaven Thy promised sign;
Thou Prince and Saviour, come.

THE CHURCH'S ONE
FOUNDATION

This tremendous hymn was a product of one of those bitter controversies which periodically disturb the generally calm world of the Anglican Church and drive its members into fiercely opposed camps.

In 1863 John Colenso, Bishop of Natal, was deposed by his metropolitan, Bishop Robert Gray of Cape Town, because of his rejection of the doctrine of eternal punishment and his questioning of the traditional authorship of the Pentateuch and the Book of Joshua. Although Gray went on to excommunicate his heterodox junior, Colenso successfully appealed to the Privy Council and remained in his see.

The Colenso affair reopened long-standing divisions between liberals and conservatives within the Anglican Church. One of those most offended by the Bishop of Natal's heretical views was Samuel John Stone (1839–1900), a young curate at Windsor. In 1866, at the age of 27, he wrote this hymn in defence of the orthodox Anglican position. He later said he was moved to write it by admiration for Archbishop Gray's noble stand in defence of the traditional Catholic faith. The hymn is based on the ninth article of the Apostles' Creed: 'I believe in the holy Catholic Church; the communion of saints.'

Stone went on to write a number of hymns, including the Lenten hymn 'Weary of earth and laden with my sin'. In 1874 he succeeded his father as vicar of St Paul's, Haggerston, London, and in 1890 he became rector of the City church of All-Hallows-on-the-Wall.

'The Church's one foundation' was first published in the form printed here in Stone's *Lyra Fidelium* in 1866. It was there given the title 'The Holy Catholic Church: The Communion of Saints. "He is the Head of the Body, the Church."' In 1868 the editors of *Hymns Ancient and Modern* shortened the hymn to five verses by omitting the original third stanza, and the second halves of the sixth and seventh stanzas to give a new composite last verse. It is in that form that the hymn appears in most modern hymnbooks. The third verse, not often sung nowadays, is the only one to give a hint of the schisms and heresies which occasioned its writing. Interestingly, another much-loved Anglican hymn, Sir Henry Baker's 'Lord, thy word abideth', was also written to maintain the cause of biblical orthodoxy during the Colenso affair.

In 1885 the following three extra verses were inserted between the original fifth and sixth stanzas to make a processional hymn for use in Salisbury Cathedral:

> So, Lord, she stands before thee,
> For evermore thine own;
> No merit is her glory,
> Her boasting this alone;
> That she who did not choose thee
> Came, chosen at thy call,
> Never to leave or lose thee
> Or from thy favour fall.
>
> For thy true word remaineth;
> No creature far or nigh,
> No fiend of ill who reigneth
> In hell or haunted sky;
> No doubting world's derision
> That holds her in despite,
> Shall hide her from thy vision
> Shall lure her from thy light.
>
> Thine, thine! in bliss or sorrow,
> As well in shade in shine;
> Of old, today, tomorrow,
> To all the ages, thine!
> Thine in her great commission,

> Baptized into thy name,
> And in her last fruition
> Of all her hope and aim.

The tune universally associated with this hymn is the majestic and unforgettable Aurelia by Samuel Sebastian Wesley (1810–76). It was written in 1864 for 'Jerusalem the golden' (no. 60). The circumstances surrounding its composition were recalled by Dr Kendrick Pyne in his book *English Church Music* (1935):

I was in the drawing room in the Close, Winchester, as a lad of thirteen, with Mrs Wesley, my mother and Mrs Stewart [the mother of the distinguished General Stewart who fell in Egypt]; we were all discussing a dish of strawberries when Dr Wesley came rushing up from below with a scrap of manuscript in his hand, a psalm tune just that instant finished. Placing it on the instrument, he said, 'I think this will be popular.' My mother was the first ever to sing it to the words 'Jerusalem the Golden'. The company liked it, and Mrs Wesley on the spot christened it *Aurelia*.

During the First World War, Allied soldiers kept themselves going with a song to the tune of Aurelia which drew its inspiration from Fred Karno, a comedian famous for his incompetence:

> We are Fred Karno's Army,
> The ragtime infantry;
> We cannot fight, we cannot shoot
> What earthly use are we!
> And when we get to Berlin,
> The Kaiser he will say
> '*Hoch, hoch, Mein Gott,*
> What a bloody fine lot
> Are the ragtime infantry.'

This hymn has also inspired two other parodies, which really deserve quoting in full but for reasons of space and copyright I will restrict myself to extracts. John Betjeman wrote of the Victorians' passion for restoring and improving churches:

> The Church's Restoration
> In eighteen-eighty-three
> Has left for contemplation
> Not what there used to be.

Anglo-Catholicism is celebrated in this parody by an unknown hand:

> Our church is mighty spikey
> With smells and bells and chants
> And Palestrina masses
> That vex the Protestants
> O happy ones and holy,
> Who fall upon their knees
> For solemn Benediction
> And midweek Rosaries.

The Holy Catholic Church: The Communion of Saints

The Church's one foundation
Is Jesus Christ, her Lord;
She is his new creation
By water and the word:
From heaven he came and sought her
To be his holy bride,
With his own blood he bought her,
And for her life he died.

2 Elect from every nation,
Yet one o'er all the earth,
Her charter of salvation
One Lord, one faith, one birth;
One holy name she blesses,
Partakes one holy food,
And to one hope she presses
With every grace endued.

3 The Church shall never perish!
Her dear Lord, to defend,
To guide, sustain and cherish,
Is with her to the end;
Though there be those who hate her,
And false sons in her pale,
Against or foe or traitor
She ever shall prevail.

4   Though with a scornful wonder
Men see her sore oppressed,
By schisms rent asunder,
By heresies distressed,
Yet saints their watch are keeping,
Their cry goes up, 'How long?'
And soon the night of weeping
Shall be the morn of song.

5   'Mid toil and tribulation,
And tumult of her war,
She waits the consummation
Of peace for evermore;
Till with the vision glorious
Her longing eyes are blest,
And the great Church victorious
Shall be the Church at rest.

6   Yet she on earth hath union
With God the Three in One,
And mystic sweet communion
With those whose rest is won;
With all her sons and daughters,
Who by the Master's hand
Led through the deathly waters,
Repose in Eden's land.

7   O happy ones and holy!
Lord, give us grace that we
Like them, the meek and lowly,
On high may dwell with thee;
There past the border mountains
Where, in sweet vales, the Bride
With thee, by living fountains,
For ever shall abide.

('TIS) THE DAY OF
RESURRECTION

This joyful Easter hymn comes from the Greek Orthodox tradition where particular stress has always been laid on Christ's Resurrection and Ascension into heaven, gathering up humanity with him.

It formed the first ode in the Golden Canon for Easter Day written by St John of Damascus (*c.* 675–*c.* 749). Often regarded as the last of the Greek fathers, St John served as chief representative of the Christians in the court of the caliph of Damascus. Apparently forced to leave, he entered the monastery of St Sabas between Jerusalem and the Dead Sea and lived in that remote spot for the rest of his life. He was a powerful defender of the use of icons in the Church, and wrote *The Fount of Wisdom*, which has long been taken as a textbook on doctrinal matters in the Orthodox Church.

St John's original words are still sung in Greek churches at midnight on Easter eve. As the congregation light candles, everyone joins in the cry, 'Christ is risen! He is risen indeed!' His hymn neatly links the Old Testament idea of the Passover with the New Testament. The reference to 'All hail' in verse 2, line 7 is to Matthew 28.9: 'Jesus met them, saying, All hail!'

In 1862 Dr J.M. Neale (1818–66) translated all eight odes of St John's Golden Canon for his *Hymns of the Eastern Church*. This first one appeared there as it is printed here, but when it was first published for congregational use the following year in the *Parish Hymn Book*, Neale changes the first line to 'The day of Resurrection', and this form of opening has been found in nearly all subsequent hymnals. The fifth and sixth lines of the last verse are generally changed to

> Let all things seen and unseen
> Their notes of gladness blend

St John of Damascus also supplies us with the original of another popular Eastern hymn translated by Neale, 'Come ye faithful, raise the strain'. It was the first ode of the canon which he wrote for St Thomas's Sunday, the name given in the Greek calendar to the first Sunday after Easter.

The tune to which 'The day of Resurrection' is most commonly sung, Ellacombe, will be for ever associated in my mind with the film *If*, where it was used for the school hymn, 'Stand up, stand up for college'. The director, Lindsay Anderson, obviously regarded it as epitomizing public school chapel worship with its jaunty confidence and breeziness. In fact, it is an eighteenth-century German melody first found in a songbook published in Würtemberg in 1784.

Although Ellacombe is now almost always used for this hymn, there are alternatives, including Lancashire by Henry Smart (1813–79), Crüger, adapted by William Henry Monk (1823–89) from a melody in Johann Crüger's *Gesangbuch* of 1640, and even a genuine Greek melody to be found in the fourth volume of *Rassegna Gregoriana*.

'Tis the day of Resurrection,
Earth, tell it out abroad!
The passover of gladness,
The passover of God!
From death to life eternal,
From earth unto the sky,
Our Christ hath brought us over
With hymns of victory.

2   Our hearts be pure from evil,
That we may see aright
The Lord in rays eternal
Of Resurrection-light;
And, listening to his accents,
May hear, so calm and plain,
His own 'All hail', and, hearing,
May raise the victor strain.

3   Now let the heav'ns be joyful,
Let earth her song begin,
The round world keep high triumph,
And all that is therein;
Invisible and visible,
Their notes let all things blend,
For Christ the Lord is risen,
Our joy that hath no end.

126

THE DAY THOU GAVEST, LORD, IS ENDED

The tendency for churches to drop evening services means that this hymn is heard less and less often, but that did not stop it from being voted No. 1 in BBC *Songs of Praise* polls throughout the 1980s and 1990s. In 2002 it came in third place, after 'O Lord my God, when I in awesome wonder' and 'Dear Lord and Father of mankind'.

It is the work of John Ellerton (1826–93). Educated at King William's College on the Isle of Man, and Trinity College, Cambridge, where he came under the influence of F.D. Maurice and Christian socialism, he was ordained in 1850 and served as a curate first at Midhurst, West Sussex, and then at Brighton. In 1860 he became vicar of Crewe Green in Cheshire and it was while living there that he wrote some 86 hymns, including two others for evening use, 'Saviour again to thy dear name we raise' and 'Our day of praise is done'. He is said to have composed many of his hymns on his nightly walks to teach classes at the Mechanics' Institute patronized by the workers of the London and North-Western Railway.

'The day thou gavest' was written in 1870 for a liturgy for missionary meetings. Ellerton got the idea for it from an anonymous hymn with an identical first line. It appeared initially in *Church Hymns*, a collection which he put together with William Walsham How (see no. 35) in 1871. The following year Ellerton moved to Hinstock in Shropshire as rector, and after four years there he went to St Mary's in Barnes, west London. He had a major hand in the preparation, in 1875, of the revised version of *Hymns Ancient and Modern*, a work which contained no fewer than 26 of his own hymns. He was also responsible for the *Children's Hymn Book*, *Hymns for Schools and Bible Classes*, the *Temperance Hymn Book* and the *London Mission Hymn Book*. After an attack of pleurisy in 1884 he was transferred to the less onerous parish of White Roding in Essex; there he lived out his days, saintly, courteous, hard-working and beloved by all who met him. While he lay in a state of semi-consciousness on his deathbed in Torquay, hymns flowed almost unceasingly from his lips.

Perhaps more because of its imperialistic overtones than its suggestion of evening, Queen Victoria chose 'The day thou gavest' for her Diamond Jubilee celebrations in 1897 and it was sung at thousands of churches throughout the land on Sunday, 20 June of that year.

The tune St Clement, to which this hymn is almost invariably sung, is always attributed to the Revd Clement Scholefield (1839–1904), who served curacies at St Peter's, Cranley Gardens, South Kensington, and St Luke's, Chelsea, before becoming chaplain of Eton College and later vicar of Holy Trinity, Knightsbridge. The tune first appeared in 1874 in *Church Hymns and Tunes* and was commissioned by Arthur Sullivan, the musical editor and organist at St Peter's, Cranley Gardens, where Scholefield was then serving his curacy.

In an article in the *Hymn Society Bulletin* in 1994 Mervyn Horder, himself a hymn-tune composer, suggested that 'Sullivan almost certainly had a larger hand in St Clement than has been, or can ever definitely be, credited to him.' His starting-point was the fact that this tune stands head and shoulders above the quality of Scholefield's other work. None of the 41 other hymn-tunes penned by this self-taught musician show anything like the craftsmanship, originality or melodic sweep of St Clement. I myself am inclined to agree with Horder and have championed Sullivan's claims to be regarded at least as the co-creator of this tune. It certainly has several distinct Sullivanesque touches, not least its highly sentimental streak and triple-time signature, both of which have come in for a good deal of criticism. When William Walsham How, Bishop of Wakefield and a friend and defender of Sullivan, protested at the decision of the editors of *Hymns Ancient and Modern* to drop St Clement for 'The day, thou gavest' in their 1897 edition, the editor, W.H. Frere, retorted: 'It is quite true that people like waltz tunes but does the Bishop seriously hold that this is a reason for providing them?' Ralph Vaughan Williams, music editor of the 1906 *English Hymnal*, consigned St Clement to the appendix, which he famously dubbed his 'chamber of horrors'. In 1932 Cosmo Gordon Lang, the Archbishop of Canterbury, sparked off a lengthy correspondence to *The Times* by suggesting that it was high time this 'feeble waltz tune' was dismissed from service.

Despite the strictures of its critics, St Clement has continued to remain one of the most popular hymn-tunes. Joldwynds, composed as an alternative by Sir Charles Stanford for the 1909 edition of *Hymns Ancient and Modern*, never caught on and has sunk without trace. It seems to me that the amateur and inexperienced Scholefield was at the very least helped in the composition and harmonization of St Clement by Sullivan, who in the preface to *Church Hymns and Tunes* expressed his hearty acknowledgements of the cordial goodwill shown towards him by composers to whom he had made suggestions for alterations. Sullivan was known for his generosity and I suspect that he may well deserve some of the credit for this wonderful tune. Who else but the composer of 'Poor wandering one' would have dared to set a hymn such as this in waltz time?

The day thou gavest, Lord, is ended,
The darkness falls at thy behest;
To thee our morning hymns ascended,
Thy praise shall sanctify our rest.

2   We thank thee that thy Church unsleeping,
While earth rolls onward into light,
Through all the world her watch is keeping,
And rests not now by day or night.

3   As o'er each continent and island
The dawn leads on another day,
The voice of prayer is never silent,
Nor dies the strain of praise away.

4   The sun that bids us rest is waking
Our brethren 'neath the western sky,
And hour by hour fresh lips are making
Thy wondrous doings heard on high.

5   So be it, Lord; thy throne shall never,
Like earth's proud empires, pass away;
Thy kingdom stands, and grows for ever,
Till all thy creatures own thy sway.

127

THE EARTH BELONGS
UNTO THE LORD

We will shortly be encountering the jewel of Scottish metrical psalmody, 'the Lord's my Shepherd' (no. 131). This hymn, which comes from the same quarry, the Revised Psalter of 1650, is equally precious in the eyes of many Scots. Its last two verses are regularly sung during the bringing up of the elements in communion services in the Church of Scotland.

The first Scottish Psalter was produced in 1564 by John Knox and other Protestants who had returned from exile in Geneva to lead the Scottish Reformation. It was revised in 1650 by a committee of the Westminster Assembly of divines, the body which also drew up the Westminster Confession which remains the doctrinal authority for the Church of Scotland and other reformed churches. It is from that revision that this paraphrase of Psalm 24 comes. The original psalm begins: 'The earth is the Lord's, and the fullness thereof.'

This metrical psalm clearly asserts God's sovereignty over the earth, and has a powerful message in these days of concern about ecology and the destruction being wreaked by man on the natural environment. The concluding lines of the first verse accurately reflect the ancient Israelite view of the cosmos as contained in the book of Genesis, where the earth is seen as floating on the sea out of which it was created when God first moved over the face of the waters.

The ubiquity of MacBrayne's steamers around the west coast of Scotland in the early years of the twentieth century inspired the following parody, which is sadly no longer apt in these days of greatly diminished ferry services:

> The earth belongs unto the Lord,
> And all that it contains

Excepting the West Highland piers
And they are all MacBrayne's.

The last two verses of the hymn, which are so effectively used in Scottish communion services, are closely based on the latter part of Psalm 24. This contains an ancient Hebrew liturgy, possibly dating back to the time of King Solomon, which was used by the Israelites when re-enacting the procession bearing the Ark of the Covenant into the Temple at Jerusalem where Yahweh was acclaimed as king. As the procession reached the entrance to the Holy City, the cry went up 'Lift up your heads, O ye gates.' This powerful command also provided the inspiration for a fine hymn by James Montgomery (on whom see notes to no. 48), 'Lift up your heads, ye gates of brass'.

The first three verses of this hymn are generally sung to the tune St Matthew, which was probably by Dr William Croft (1678–1727), organist of Westminster Abbey. It first appeared in 1708 in a supplement to Tate and Brady's new version of the Psalms, where it was set to Psalm 33. The fourth and fifth verses are sung as a communion hymn to the thrilling tune St George's Edinburgh, written by Andrew Mitchell Thomson (1778–1831) and first published in 1820. Thomson was educated at Edinburgh University and after a period as a schoolteacher in Markinch, Fife, was ordained into the Church of Scotland. After serving as a minister in Kelso and then in Perth he moved to Edinburgh, where he was incumbent first at New Greyfriars and then at St George's. He did much to improve psalmody and congregational singing.

Psalm xxiv

The earth belongs unto the Lord,
And all that it contains;
The world that is inhabited,
And all that there remains.
For the foundations thereof
He on the seas did lay,
And he hath it established
Upon the floods to stay.

2   Who is the man that shall ascend
Into the hill of God?
Or who within his holy place
Shall have a firm abode?
Whose hands are clean, whose heart is pure,
And into vanity
Who hath not lifted up his soul,
Nor sworn deceitfully.

3   He from th' Eternal shall receive
The blessing him upon,
And righteousness, ev'n from the God
Of his salvation.
This is the generation
That after him enquire,
O Jacob, who do seek thy face
With their whole heart's desire.

4   Ye gates, lift up your heads on high;
       Ye doors, that last for aye,
       Be lifted up, that so the King
       Of glory enter may.
       But who of glory is the King?
       The mighty Lord is this;
       Ev'n that same Lord, that great in might
       And strong in battle is.

5   Ye gates, lift up your heads; ye doors,
       Doors that do last for aye,
       Be lifted up, that so the King
       Of glory enter may.
       But who is he that is the King
       Of glory? Who is this?
       The Lord of hosts, and none but he,
       The king of glory is.

THE GOD OF ABRAH'M
PRAISE

Many Christian hymns have been inspired by and closely based on those first songs of praise to God which were sung by the Hebrew people, and which we know today as the Psalms. This particular hymn is interesting in that it derives both its inspiration and its tune from modern Jewish synagogue worship.

Its author, Thomas Olivers (1725–99), was born in Tregynon in Montgomeryshire. His parents died when he was 4 years old and he grew up with little supervision or education. After a somewhat profligate youth he became a cobbler, and was converted to evangelical Christianity by the preaching of George Whitefield, the great itinerant preacher of the early eighteenth century, who is often regarded as the father of the Evangelical Revival. Apparently it was hearing Whitefield preach on the text, 'Is not this a brand plucked out of the fire?' (Zech. 3.2) that changed Olivers' life. He went on to become one of John Wesley's most active itinerant preachers, working first in Cornwall and then throughout England and Wales.

While staying in London in 1770, Olivers visited the Jewish synagogue at Duke's Place in Westminster. There he heard the Yigdal, a paraphrase in metrical form of the thirteen articles of the Jewish faith, sung antiphonally by the congregation and a chorister. He was much affected by the music and resolved to write a Christian text to fit it.

The Yigdal is read at the opening of morning service in all synagogues and is sung to traditional tunes on the eve of the Sabbath and on the evenings of the major Jewish festivals. It is believed to have been composed by Daniel ben Judah early in the fifteenth century. The thirteen articles on which it is based were drawn up by Moses Maimonides (1130–1205), who first formulated the Dogmas of Judaism. The following is a literal translation of the Hebrew original:

Extolled and praised be the living God, who exists unbounded
by time.
He is one of unparalleled unity, invisible and eternal.
Without form or figure – incorporeal, holy beyond conception.
Prior to all created things, the first, without date or beginning.
Lo! He is Lord of all the world and all creation, which evince His
greatness and dominion.
The flow of His prophetic spirit has He imparted to men selected
for His glory.
No one has appeared in Israel like unto Moses; a prophet,
beholding His glorious semblance.
God has given the true law to His people, by the hands of His
trusty prophet.
This law, God will never alter, nor change for any other.
He perceives and is acquainted with our secrets, sees the end of
all things at their very beginning.
He rewards man with kindness according to his work; dispenses
punishment to the wicked, according to his misdeeds.
At the end of days by Him appointed, will He send our Messiah,
to redeem those who hope for final salvation,
God, in His great mercy, will recall the dead to life. Praise be His
glorious name for evermore.

As can be seen, Olivers' hymn is only loosely based on the words of the Yigdal. He himself is reported to have told a friend during a conference in Wesley's City Road Chapel: 'Look at this; I have rendered it from the Hebrew, giving it, as far as I could, a Christian character.' His hymn, which was first published in the form printed below in a pamphlet around 1770, is made up almost entirely either of direct quotations or close paraphrases of passages from the Hebrew Bible, the Christian Old Testament. Olivers thoughtfully produced references for virtually every line of his text.

John Wesley included the hymn in his *Pocket Hymn Book for*

the Use of Christians of All Denominations in 1785 and it became extremely popular in Methodist circles. James Montgomery, the author of 'Hail to the Lord's Anointed' and 'Stand up, and bless the Lord' (nos 48 and 116 in this collection), wrote of Olivers' hymn:

That noble ode, 'The God of Abrah'm praise', though the essay of an unlettered man, claims especial honour. There is not in our language a lyric of more majestic style, more elevated thought, or more glorious imagery; its structure, indeed, is unattractive; and, on account of the short lines, occasionally uncouth; but, like a stately pile of architecture, severe and simple in design, it strikes less on the first view than after deliberate examination, when its proportions become more graceful, its dimensions expand, and the mind itself grows greater in contemplating it.

The striking tune in the minor key to which 'The God of Abrah'm praise' is always sung is a traditional Jewish melody, the origins of which are uncertain. This was the music to which Olivers heard the Yigdal being sung at the Great Synagogue in Duke's Place. He named it Leoni after the chorister who was singing the solo part there – Meyer Lyon, whose liturgical name was 'Leoni'. Meyer Lyon, who also sang publicly at Drury Lane and Covent Garden, went on to become the first qualified *chazan* of the English and German Synagogue in Jamaica.

A Hymn to the God of Abraham

The God of Abrah'm praise	(Ex. 3.6)
Who reigns enthron'd above;	
Ancient of everlasting days,	(Dan .7.22)
And God of Love;	(2 Cor. 13.11)
JEHOVAH, GREAT I AM	(Ex. 6.3; 3.14)
By earth and heav'n confest;	(Rev. 4.8–11)
I bow and bless the sacred Name	(Rom. 1.25)
For ever bless'd.	

2   The God of Abrah'm praise,
At whose supreme command   (Gen. 12.1)
From earth I rise – and seek the joys
At his right hand:
I all on earth forsake,   (Gen 12.4)
Its wisdom, fame and power;
And him my only portion make,   (Gen. 15.1)
My Shield and Tower.   (Ps 18.2)

3   The God of Abrah'm praise,
Whose all-sufficient grace   (Gen. 17.1)
Shall guide me all my happy days   (Gen. 28.15)
In all my ways:
He calls a worm his friend!   (Js 2.23)
He calls himself my God!   (Ex. 3.6)
And he shall save me to the end   (1 Pet. 1.5)
Thro' Jesu's blood.

4   He by himself hath sworn,   (Gen. 22.16–17)
I on his oath depend,   (Rom. 4.20–21)
I shall on eagle's wings up-borne   (Ex. 19.4)
To heaven ascend;
I shall behold his face,   (Jn 17.24)
I shall his power adore,   (Ex. 15.2)
And sing the wonders of his grace   (Ps 145.1; 146.2)
For evermore.

5   Tho' nature's strength decay   (Gen. 15.4, 6; Rom. 4.19)
     And earth and hell withstand,   (Ex. 5.2)
     To Canaan's bounds I urge my way,   (Ex. 14.15)
     At his command:
     The wat'ry deep I pass,   (Ex. 14.22)
     With Jesus in my view;   (Ex. 13.21)
     And through the howling wilderness   (Ex. 13.18)
     My way pursue.

6   The goodly land I see,   (Ex. 3.8)
     With peace and plenty bless'd;   (Deut. 8.7–9)
     A land of sacred liberty,   (Lev. 25.42)
     And endless rest.   (Ex. 33.14)
     There milk and honey flow,   (Ex. 3.8)
     And oil and wine about   (Deut. 32.13–14)
     And trees of life for ever grow,   (Isa. 61.3)
     With mercy crown'd.

7   There dwells the Lord our King,   (Gen. 14.18; Heb. 7.1–2)
     THE LORD OUR RIGHTEOUSNESS   (Jer. 33.16)
     (Triumphant o'er the world and sin)   (Eph. 4.8; Phil. 2.9–11)
     The Prince of Peace: (Isa. 9.6)
     On Sion's sacred height,   (Ps 50.2)
     His kingdom still maintains;
     And glorious with his saints in light   (Isa. 24.23)
     For ever reigns.

8   He keeps his own secure,   (Ps. 12.7)
     He guards them by his side,
     Arrays in garments, white and pure   (Rev. 4.4; 19.7–8)
     His spotless bride;   (Eph. 5.27)
     With streams of sacred bliss   (Rev. 7.17; 22.1)
     With groves of living joys –
     With all the fruits of Paradise   (Rev. 2.7; 22.2)
     He still supplies.

9   Before the great THREE–ONE   (Rev. 7.9–10)
     They all exulting stand;
     And tell the wonders he hath done
     Thro' all their land:
     The list'ning spheres attend,   (Rev. 7.11–12)
     And swell the growing frame;
     And sing, in songs which never end
     The wondrous NAME.

10   The God who reigns on high,   (Rev. 4.8)
     The great arch-angels sing,
     And 'Holy, Holy, Holy,' cry,
     'ALMIGHTY KING!
     Who was and is, the same;
     And evermore shall be;
     JEHOVAH – FATHER – GREAT I AM!
     WE WORSHIP THEE.'

11   Before the Saviour's face   (Rev. 5.8–10; 15.24)
     The ransom'd nations bow;
     O'erwhelmed at his almighty grace,
     For ever new:
     He shews his prints of love –   (Jn 20.27)
     They kindle – to a flame!
     And sound thro' all the worlds above
     The slaughter'd LAMB

12   The whole triumphant host,   (Rev. 5.13; 19.1–7)
     Give thanks to God on high;
     'Hail, FATHER, SON and HOLY GHOST',
     They ever cry;
     Hail, Abrah'm's God – and *mine*   (Ps 89.26; Jn 20.17, 28)
     (I join the heavenly lays)   (Ps 103.1–5)
     All might and majesty are thine   (Rev. 4.11; 5.12; 7.10, 12)
     And endless praise.

THE HEAD THAT ONCE WAS CROWNED WITH THORNS

This Ascensiontide hymn picks up the theme of Christ's two crowns: the crown of thorns placed mockingly on his head by the Roman soldiers (Mk 15.17–19) and the vision of St John the Divine in Revelation 19.12, 'On his head were many crowns.'

The author, Thomas Kelly (1769–1855), was the son of an Irish judge and educated at Trinity College, Dublin, with the intention that he should read for the Bar. He experienced a conversion to evangelical religion and was ordained into the episcopal Church of Ireland in 1792. However, he fell foul of the Archbishop of Dublin on account of his 'Methodistical' leanings and seceded from the episcopal Church to found his own sect. He was by all accounts a magnetic preacher, and also a genuine friend to the poor and oppressed. He was a prolific hymn-writer. His collection, *Hymns on Various Subjects*, first published in 1804, had by its 1853 edition reached 765 entries, all of them from his own pen. He also produced music to go with them. Among his other hymns which are still sung today are 'The Lord is risen indeed!' and 'We sing the praise of him who died'.

'The head that once was crowned with thorns' first appeared in the fifth edition of his hymnbook, issued in 1820. Kelly attached to it the following text from Hebrews 2.10, 'For it became him, for whom are all things, and by whom are all things, in bringing many sons unto glory, to make the Captain of their salvation perfect through sufferings.'

The opening line of this hymn is identical to that of a verse in a poem on the subject of heaven by John Bunyan (1628–88), the author of *Pilgrim's Progress* and of the hymn 'Who would true valour see' (no. 146). It seems highly likely that Kelly drew the inspiration for his hymn from this poem, which was first published in 1688 in Bunyan's *One thing is needful, or serious meditations upon the four last things*. The 39th verse of the poem ran as follows:

> The head that once was crowned with thorns,
>   Shall now with glory shine;
> That heart that broken was with scorns,
>   Shall flow with life divine.

Kelly's hymn is almost always sung to the tune St Magnus (also known as Nottingham, Birmingham or Greenock), which is possibly by Jeremiah Clarke (1670–1707). It is found in the third edition of Playford's *Divine Companion* of 1709 which contains many tunes attributed to Clarke, but this particular one is anonymous. Clarke was organist first at Winchester Cathedral and then at St Paul's, and joint organist with Dr Croft at the Chapel Royal. He met an unhappy end. In a state of deep depression over an unsuccessful love affair, he resolved either to shoot or drown himself. He tossed a coin beside a pond to determine which it should be but the coin fell on its edge, embedded in the mud; he returned to his house by St Paul's and shot himself. In recent times he has been accorded the posthumous honour of being official composer to the short-lived Social Democratic Party, his 'Trumpet tune' having been adopted as the party's theme tune.

Christ perfect through sufferings

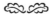

The head that once was crowned with thorns
Is crowned with glory now;
A royal diadem adorns
The mighty Victor's brow.

2   The highest place that heav'n affords
Is his, is his by right,
The King of Kings and Lord of Lords
And heav'n's eternal Light;

3   The joy of all who dwell above,
The joy of all below,
To whom he manifests his love,
And grants his name to know.

4   To them the Cross with all its shame,
With all its grace, is given;
Their name an everlasting name,
Their joy the joy of heav'n.

5   They suffer with their Lord below,
They reign with him above,
Their profit and their joy to know
The mystery of his love.

6   The Cross he bore is life and health,
Though shame and death to him;
His people's hope, his people's wealth,
Their everlasting theme.

THE KING OF LOVE MY SHEPHERD IS

I think I am on safe ground in asserting that more hymns have been based on the 23rd Psalm than on any other. There is space for only two of them in this collection – this fine paraphrase by Sir Henry Baker and the version from the 1650 Scottish Psalter that forms the next entry. Also worthy of mention are Joseph Addison's 'The Lord my pasture shall prepare', Joseph Gelineau's 'The Lord is my Shepherd' and George Herbert's beautiful 'The God of love my shepherd is'.

Biographical notes about Sir Henry Williams Baker (1821–77) can be found in the notes to no. 98, 'O praise ye the Lord! Praise him in the height'. He was chairman of the editorial committee of *Hymns Ancient and Modern*, and it was in the appendix to the first edition of that book that this hymn first appeared in 1869. In his *Notes on English Church Hymns*, published four years after Baker's untimely death at the age of 56, John Ellerton wrote: 'It may interest many to know that the third verse of this lovely hymn, perhaps the most beautiful of all the countless versions of Psalm xxiii, was the last audible sentence upon the dying lip of the lamented author.'

Several commentators have seen this hymn as epitomizing the rather cosy and comfortable complacency of upper-class Victorian Anglicanism. In his important book, *Class and Idol in the Victorian Hymn*,★ Lionel Adey suggests that it expresses the two cardinal principles of Victorian faith – the coherence of God and the certainty of salvation. He draws attention particularly to the lines:

★ Lionel Adey, *Class and Idol in the Victorian Hymn* (Vancouver: University of British Columbia Press, 1988).

> Perverse and foolish oft I strayed,
> And yet in love he sought me,
> And on his shoulder gently laid,
> And home rejoicing brought me.

Adey points to the clear influence here of the words of the General Confession in the Book of Common Prayer: 'We have erred and strayed from thy ways like lost sheep.' He also suggests that to the untold thousands who have sung this hymn in church or school, 'both "home" and "rejoicing" surely denote their present state of life, neither crisis nor consummation, but simply health, cheerfulness, self-acceptance. Home is where the heart has ease. Heaven is a continuance in that state.' It is, he suggests, a hymn written by and for the comfortably off, which suggests that there is no radical discontinuity between this world and the next. Heaven is portrayed as home, and more specifically as an upper-middle-class home.

I wonder, however, whether this is being entirely fair. It is quite true that Baker led the untroubled life of a prosperous squarson and the gentle pastoral imagery of his hymns belongs to the secluded rural world inhabited by so many Victorian hymnwriters. Yet the inspiration for this particular verse, which departs markedly from the 23rd Psalm of which the hymn is otherwise a fairly close paraphrase, is surely the parable of the prodigal son, a theme that recurs again and again in Victorian hymnody. It is not a story that one would expect to appeal to the comfortably off and complacent. After all, it is the nose of the ultra-respectable, God-fearing, eminently Victorian elder brother that is put out of joint by the father's welcome of his feckless ne'er-do-well sibling. I have to say that I find the lines singled out by Adey among the most honest and moving in all English hymnody and I find myself constantly singing them. They are a wonderful evocation of both our erring human condition and the overflowing generosity of God's grace.

The melody universally associated with the hymn is *Dominus Regit Me* which was written especially for it in 1869 by the Revd John Bacchus Dykes (1823–76). The son of a banker and grandson of a well-known evangelical clergyman, he was educated at Wakefield and at St Catharine's College, Cambridge. At the time he wrote this tune Dykes was vicar of St Oswald's, Durham, where his High Churchmanship got him into serious difficulties. He needed two curates to assist him in the work of the large and demanding parish, but the bishop refused to license them unless a pledge was given that they would not be required to wear coloured stoles, have anything to do with incense, or turn their backs on the congregation during the celebration of Holy Communion. Dykes refused to give such a pledge and lost an appeal to the Court of Queen's Bench against the bishop's refusal to issue a licence for the curates. Without any extra help in the church his health gave way and he died at the age of 53.

Dominus Regit Me has rightly won much praise in high places. Ralph Vaughan Williams singled it out for special praise in his preface to the *English Hymnal*, while in his book *The Musical Wesleys*,★ Erik Routley noted:

To speak of a 'Victorian hymn tune' is to set off in any remotely musical mind the strains of John Bacchus Dykes' tune to 'The King of Love'. There is nothing more centrally Victorian in all English religion than those words set to that tune. Probably, without the least consciousness that he was doing anything of the kind, that folk-genius Dykes gathered up there everything that this kind of Victorian music has to say ... The tune does exactly what the words do with Psalm 23. Sir Henry Baker writes, not a pastoral paraphrase like George Herbert's or an eighteenth-century country house paraphrase like Addison's but an English parish church paraphrase ... This is the purest Anglican Herefordshire, and the tune comes flying across the country from Anglican Durham to meet it.

★ Erik Routley, *The Musical Wesleys* (London: Herbert Jenkins, 1968), p. 197.

Psalm xxiii

The King of love my Shepherd is,
Whose goodness faileth never;
I nothing lack if I am his
And he is mine for ever.

2   Where streams of living water flow
My ransomed soul he leadeth,
And where the verdant pastures grow
With food celestial feedeth.

3   Perverse and foolish oft I strayed,
But yet in love he sought me,
And on his shoulder gently laid,
And home rejoicing brought me.

4   In death's dark vale I fear no ill
With thee, dear Lord, beside me;
Thy rod and staff my comfort still,
Thy Cross before to guide me.

5   Thou spread'st a table in my sight;
Thy unction grace bestoweth;
And O what transport of delight
From thy pure chalice floweth!

6   And so through all the length of days
Thy goodness faileth never:
Good Shepherd, may I sing thy praise
Within thy house for ever.

131

THE LORD'S MY
SHEPHERD

Voted 34th in the 2002 BBC *Songs of Praise* poll, and still among the most frequently requested hymn for weddings and funerals, this metrical version of the 23rd Psalm was, rather surprisingly, the work of a committee. Long loved in Scotland, it has only really been popular in England since it was chosen by the Queen for her marriage service in 1947.

'The Lord's my Shepherd' first appeared in the form printed here in the Scottish Psalter of 1650, which was drawn up by the Westminster Assembly. This assembly of divines also drew up the Westminster Confession, which still represents the official doctrinal statement of the Church of Scotland and other reformed churches. An earlier paraphrase of the 23rd Psalm, which began 'The Lord is only my support', had appeared in the earlier Scottish Psalter produced in 1564 by John Knox and others, but it is completely different from the one sung now.

For their version, the divines meeting at Westminster put together lines taken from several different sources. The first line comes from the pen of Zachary Boyd (1585–1654). Born in Kilmarnock and a graduate of St Andrews University, he spent sixteen years in France and was subsequently minister of the Barony Church in Glasgow and vice-chancellor of Glasgow University. In 1646 he wrote a metrical version of the 23rd Psalm which began:

> The Lord's my shepheard, I'le not want.
> He makes me by good will
> Ly in green pastures, he me leads
> Beside the waters still.

The second line comes from a psalter produced in 1643 by Francis Rous (1579–1658), a Cornishman who was a close adherent of Oliver Cromwell and became MP for Truro, Speaker in the Barebones Parliament and provost of Eton College. His version began:

> My shepheard is the living Lord,
> and he that doth me feed:
> How can I then lack any thing
> whereof I stand in need?
> In pastures green and flourishing
> he makes me down to lye:
> And after drives me to the streames
> which run most pleasantly.

Most of the other lines come either from a metrical version of the psalm produced in 1639 by Sir William Mure of Rowallan (1594–?), an Ayrshire soldier who served in Cromwell's forces, or from a revised version of the old 1564 Psalter which was compiled by the Westminster Assembly of divines in 1646. Only the phrases 'He leadeth me the quiet waters by' and the word 'furnished' were original to the compilers of the 1650 edition.

For nearly 300 years this version of the 23rd Psalm was not much sung outside the Church of Scotland, although it entered the *Methodist Hymnal* in 1876 and the *Congregational Hymnal* in 1916. It did not appear in an Anglican hymnbook until 1965, eighteen years after its use at the wedding of Princess Elizabeth and Prince Philip, when it had been set to the tune Crimond. It is with this tune that it has been associated ever since. Crimond is usually attributed to Jessie Irvine (1836–87), whose father was minister of the village of Crimond in Aberdeenshire. It first appeared in 1872 in the *Northern Psalter*, where it was set to the hymn 'I am the Way, the Truth, the Life', and attributed to David Grant, an Aberdeen tobacconist. There continues to be some debate over the circumstances of its composition, but it is now generally agreed by scholars that Jessie Irvine wrote the tune while in her teens as an exercise for an organists' class that she was attending in Banff. Grant was quite possibly responsible for its harmonization and appearance in print. The tune's association with 'The Lord's my Shepherd' undoubtedly owes much to the influence of the Glasgow Orpheus Choir under Sir Hugh Robertson, who frequently broadcast and recorded it in the early twentieth century. Wiltshire, Orlington and Brother James' Air are all excellent alternatives for those who feel Crimond is overused.

Psalm xxiii

The Lord's my Shepherd, I'll not want.
He makes me down to lie
In pastures green; he leadeth me
The quiet waters by.

2   My soul he doth restore again,
And me to walk doth make
Within the paths of righteousness,
E'en for his own name's sake.

3   Yea, though I walk in death's dark vale,
Yet will I fear none ill;
For thou art with me, and thy rod
And staff me comfort still.

4   My table thou has furnishèd
In presence of my foes;
My head thou dost with oil anoint,
And my cup overflows.

5   Goodness and mercy all my life
Shall surely follow me;
And in God's house for evermore
My dwelling-place shall be.

THE SPACIOUS
FIRMAMENT ON HIGH

This fine piece of poetic writing is the work of Joseph Addison (1672–1719), essayist, versifier, dramatist and co-founder, with Richard Steele, of the *Spectator*. It has rightly won high praise from a number of quarters. Lord Selborne, Lord Chancellor in Gladstone's first two governments and a distinguished amateur hymnologist, described it as a 'very perfect and finished composition, taking rank among the best hymns in the English language ... If it be not poetry, I do not know what is; and to prove that it is song, and soul-stirring song too, it is only necessary to hear it, as I often have, heartily sung to an appropriate tune.' The fastidious Scots included it as one of only five hymns authorized to be printed at the end of the Scottish Paraphrases in 1781. Two of the other hymns allowed in were also by Addison.

Addison was born in Milston, Wiltshire, where his father, who later went on to become Dean of Lichfield, was rector. He was educated at Charterhouse, and Queen's College and Magdalen College, Oxford, and was himself originally destined for the Church. However, literature and politics caught his imagination and he served as a minister in several governments before retiring from public life in 1710 to devote himself to writing essays.

'The spacious firmament on high' first appeared at the end of an essay in the *Spectator* of 23 August 1712. It is based on the first four verses of Psalm 19, which begins: 'The heavens declare the glory of God; and the firmament sheweth his handywork.' In his essay Addison observed that the psalm 'furnishes very noble matter for an ode'. His hymn also makes much use of the Platonic idea of the music of the spheres, a theme which was to be taken up again by another hymn-writer 150 years later, when the American Unitarian John White Chadwick wrote his 'Eternal ruler of the ceaseless round of circling planets singing on their way'.

Another of Addison's hymns, 'When all thy mercies, O my God, my rising soul surveys', also originally appeared in a *Spectator* essay and is still found in most modern hymnals. Both hymns gained wide circulation when they were added by the printers to the 1818 edition of Tate and Brady's version of the Psalms.

The best tune by far for this hymn is one specially composed for it by Sir Henry Walford Davies (1869–1941). Born in Oswestry, Shropshire, Davies was successively a teacher at the Royal College of Music, conductor of the London Bach Choir, organist of the Temple Church, Professor of Music at the University College of Wales, Aberystwyth, organist of St George's, Windsor, and Master of the King's Music. His tune for 'The spacious firmament on high' was first published in the *Fellowship Hymn Book Supplement* of 1920 with the name *Laudare Domino*, and is now known as Firmament.

Ode

The spacious firmament on high,
With all the blue, ethereal sky,
And spangled heav'ns, a shining frame,
Their great Original proclaim.
Th'unwearied sun, from day to day,
Does his Creator's power display,
And publishes to every land
The work of an Almighty Hand.

2   Soon as the evening shades prevail,
    The moon takes up the wondrous tale,
    And nightly to the listening earth
    Repeats the story of her birth;
    Whilst all the stars that round her burn,
    And all the planets in their turn,
    Confirm the tidings as they roll,
    And spread the truth from pole to pole.

3   What though, in solemn silence, all
    Move round the dark terrestrial ball?
    What though nor reäl voice nor sound
    Amid their radiant orbs be found?
    In reason's ear they all rejoice,
    And utter forth a glorious voice,
    For ever singing, as they shine,
    'The Hand that made us is Divine'.

THE STRIFE IS O'ER, THE BATTLE DONE

This dignified and measured Easter hymn is a translation by Francis Pott (1832–1909) of a Latin original, '*Finita iam sunt praelia*'. Dr J.F. Neale, who included it in his *Hymni Ecclesiae* of 1851, reckoned that the original Latin verses dated from the twelfth century, but the earliest source in which they have been found is a book published in Cologne in 1695 with the title *Symphonia sirenum* and it may be that they date only from the seventeenth century.

Francis Pott was educated at Brasenose College, Oxford, and ordained in 1856. He held curacies at Bishopsworth in Somerset, and Ardingly and Ticehurst, both in Sussex, before becoming rector of Northill, Bedfordshire, in 1866. In 1891 deafness forced him to retire and he spent the last years of his life in Speldhurst, Kent. He was a keen student of hymnology and was on the original committee which produced *Hymns Ancient and Modern*. 'The strife is o'er' first appeared in his *Hymns fitted to the Order of Common Prayer* in 1861. Among his other hymns which are still widely sung today are 'Angel voices, ever singing' and 'Forty days and forty nights'.

This Easter hymn portrays Christ's death as the victorious end to a battle with the principalities and powers of darkness. The imagery is of battle and the Word of God is seen as having come down from heaven in the person of Christ to do battle with the Devil and slay him. This way of looking at Christ's saving work as essentially doing battle with the Devil (rather than paying a ransom for the sins of men or showing a depth of love which begets love on the part of man) was first developed by Irenaeus and was common in the early Middle Ages. To some extent it was taken up again by Luther at the Reformation.

Two tunes are commonly used for this hymn: Victory,

adapted by W.H. Monk from the *Gloria Patri* of a Magnificat by G.P. da Palestrina (d. 1594) and *Gelobt sei Gott*, harmonized by F. Layriz in 1844 from a tune by Melchior Vulpius (1560–1616), cantor at Weimar, in his 1609 *Gesangbuch*. When this latter tune (which is often known as Vulpius) is used, the word 'Alleluia!' is repeated three times at the end of each verse. In the original Latin version, three Alleluias were sung at the beginning of the hymn. In the medieval Church the word Alleluia, which is a Greek rendering of the Hebrew phrase for 'Praise Yahweh', was banished from worship during Lent, but taken up on Easter Sunday when it was used with great frequency in hymns and psalms of praise.

Finita iam sunt praelia

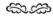

The strife is o'er, the battle done;
Now is the Victor's triumph won;
O let the song of praise be sung:
    Alleluia!

2   Death's mightiest powers have done their worst,
And Jesus hath his foes dispersed;
Let shouts of praise and joy outburst:
    Alleluia!

3   On the third morn he rose again,
Glorious in majesty to reign;
O let us swell the joyful strain:
    Alleluia!

4   He brake the age-bound chains of hell;
The bars from heav'n's high portals fell;
Let hymns of praise his triumph tell:
    Alleluia!

5   Lord, by the stripes which wounded thee,
From death's dread sting thy servants free,
That we may live, and sing to thee:
    Alleluia!

134

THERE'S A WIDENESS IN
GOD'S MERCY

It is a bizarre coincidence that on the two occasions in assembling this collection that I have made a late change of decision as to what to include, a hymn by the same author has been substituted for my original choice. The first hymn by F.W. Faber, 'My God! How wonderful Thou art' (no. 86), was chosen at the last moment in preference over 'My God, I love thee not because I hope for heaven thereby'. Now I find myself inserting another of Faber's hymns in place of Mrs Alexander's 'There is a green hill far away', which was originally destined to occupy this slot.

I have to confess that I find the theology of 'There is a green hill far away' less than satisfactory and, although it is still much loved and sung, I hope readers will excuse me for jettisoning it in favour of this wonderfully inclusive and consoling hymn, one of the most inclusive, I think, in the whole canon of English hymnody. It speaks eloquently of the boundless, overflowing nature of God's grace and forgiveness and reminds us of how our own cramped and narrow perspectives restrict our view of the divine nature.

The verses printed here are part of an eight-verse hymn first published in Faber's *Oratory Hymns* in 1854 and entitled 'Come to Jesus!' This was subsequently expanded to thirteen verses and appeared in his *Hymns* in 1862 under the title 'The Divine Call'. As printed here, the hymn is made up of verses 4–10 and 13 of this longer version which originally began 'Souls of men! Why will ye scatter'. The first three verses of this longer version run as follows:

> Souls of men! Why will ye scatter
> like a crowd of frightened sheep?
> Foolish hearts! why will ye wander
> from a love so true and deep?

455

> Was there ever kinder shepherd
>   half so gentle, half so sweet,
> as the Saviour who would have us
>   come and gather round his feet?

> It is God: his love looks mighty,
>   but is mightier than it seems:
> 'tis our Father: and his fondness
>   goes far out beyond our dreams

The eleventh and twelfth verses of the original are also worth quoting:

> 'Tis not all we owe to Jesus;
>   it is something more than all;
> greater good because of evil,
>   larger mercy through the fall.

> Pining souls! come nearer Jesus,
>   and O come, not doubting thus,
> but with faith that trusts more bravely
>   his huge tenderness for us.

Few modern hymnals contain all of the verses even of the truncated version of 'There's a wideness in God's mercy' printed here. Some change the last two lines of the first verse to 'and forgiveness in his justice / sealed for us on Calvary'. There are also extensive variations in the last two lines of the last verse ('If our love would be more simple') to avoid the rather cloying and simplistic reference to 'sunshine in the sweetness of our Lord'. They include the following permutations:

> and our lives would be all gladness,
>   in the joy of Christ our Lord.

> and our lives be filled with gladness,
>   from the presence of the Lord.

and our lives would be illumined,
by the presence of our Lord.

and our lives would be illumined,
by the glory of the Lord.

and our lives be filled with glory,
from the glory of the Lord.

and our lives would find assurance
in the promise of the Lord.

This hymn is often set to Sussex, the English traditional melody adapted and arranged by Ralph Vaughan Williams in 1906 for 'Father, hear the prayer we offer' in the *English Hymnal*. It also goes well to John Stainer's wonderfully robust yet poignant tune Cross of Jesus composed for his oratorio, *The Crucifixion* in 1887.

There's a wideness in God's mercy,
like the wideness of the sea;
there's a kindness in his justice
which is more than liberty.

2   There is no place where earth's sorrows
are more felt than up in heaven:
there is no place where earth's failings
have such kindly judgement given.

3   There is welcome for the sinner,
and more graces for the good;
there is mercy with the Saviour;
there is healing in his blood.

4   There is grace enough for thousands
of new worlds as great as this:
there is room for fresh creations
in that upper home of bliss.

5   For the love of God is broader
than the measures of man's mind;
and the heart of the Eternal
is most wonderfully kind.

6   But we make his love too narrow
by false limits of our own;
and we magnify his strictness
with a zeal he will not own.

7   There is plentiful redemption
in the blood that has been shed;
there is joy for all the members
in the sorrows of the head.

8   If our love were but more simple,
    we should take him at his word;
    and our lives would be all sunshine,
    in the sweetness of our Lord.

THINE BE THE GLORY

Because of its magnificent eighteenth-century tune, based on a chorus by Handel, this hymn always seems much older than it actually is. It also seems quintessentially British. It comes as something of a surprise to discover that it comes from a Swiss original and that the author died only a little over 70 years ago.

In 1904 the *YMCA Hymn Book*, published in Lausanne, contained a hymn which began:

> A toi la gloire, O Réssuscite,
> A toi la victoire pour l'éternité.
> Brillant de lumière, l'ange est descendu,
> Il roule la pierre de tombeau vaincu.

The author of the hymn was Edmond L. Budry (1854–1932). Educated at Lausanne, he became a minister in the Église Évangélique Libre du Canton de Vaud, an evangelical breakaway from the Swiss National Reformed Church. After serving in Cully and Sainte Croix he spent 35 years as the pastor of Vevey, near Montreux on Lake Geneva. He wrote '*A toi la gloire*' in 1896 following the death of his first wife, Marie de Hayenborg. It was translated into English by Richard Birch Hoyle (1875–1937), a Baptist minister whose last pastorate was at Kingston-upon-Thames and who translated hymns from twelve different languages, all of which he read fluently. The hymn is found in many other languages – I have sung it in Norwegian on Easter Sunday in a small church at the end of a fjord.

The tune which Budry's hymn was written to fit, and to which 'Thine be the glory' is always sung, was written in 1746 by George Frideric Handel (1685–1759) for the chorus 'See the Conquering Hero Comes' in his oratorio *Judas Maccabeus*. Born in Halle, Germany, the son of the surgeon to the Duke of

Saxony, Handel was originally marked out by his father for a legal career. However, he early showed his considerable musical talents, and after studying at Halle, Hamburg and in Italy he became chapelmaster to the Elector of Hanover, later King George I of England. Handel first visited Great Britain in 1710 and liked the country so much that he made it his permanent home from 1713. He became chapelmaster to the Duke of Chandos, a position which gave him the security from which to write more than 40 operas, seven oratorios and numerous psalms and *Te Deum*s, as well as many orchestral and instrumental pieces.

A toi la gloire

Thine by the glory, risen conquering Son,
Endless is the victory Thou o'er death hast won;
Angels in bright raiment rolled the stone away.
Kept the folded grave-clothes, where Thy body lay.

Thine be the glory, risen conquering Son,
Endless is the victory Thou o'er death has won.

2 Lo! Jesus meets us, risen from the tomb;
Lovingly He greets us, scatters fear and gloom;
Let the Church with gladness, hymns of triumph sing,
For her Lord now liveth, death hath lost its sting.

3 No more we doubt Thee, glorious Prince of life;
Life is nought without Thee: aid us in our strife;
Make us more than conquerors, through Thy deathless love;
Bring us safe through Jordan to Thy home above.

THOU, WHOSE ETERNAL WORD

This hymn was written to be sung to the tune of the National Anthem. Its author, John Marriott (1780–1825), was too modest to publish it during his lifetime and it was not sung in any church until after his death.

John Marriott was educated at Rugby and Christ Church, Oxford. Ordained in 1804, he spent four years at Dalkeith Palace near Edinburgh as domestic chaplain to the 4th Duke of Buccleuch and private tutor to his eldest son, Lord George Scott. When his young charge died suddenly at the age of 10, Marriott was presented by the Duke to the living of Church Lawford in Warwickshire. However, ill-health made it impossible for him to live there and instead he served a series of curacies in Devon. In 1824 he was attacked by ossification of the brain. By all accounts he was a saintly individual and was highly thought of by Sir Walter Scott, who got to know him when he was at Dalkeith. Marriott contributed three ballads to Scott's *Minstrelsy of the Scottish Border* and wrote several hymns.

Too modest to publish his hymns during his own lifetime, Marriott would not even allow the words of 'Thou, whose eternal Word', which he wrote around 1813, to be copied by friends. Six weeks after his death, the verses of the hymn were read out to a meeting of the London Missionary Society by the Revd Thomas Mortimer. It was much acclaimed by those who heard it there and was printed later that year (1825) in both the *Evangelical Magazine* and the *Friendly Visitor*.

The hymn is based on Genesis 1.3: 'And God said, Let there by light: and there was light.' It is printed here as it was written by Marriott. The version which is familiar to us today, with 'almighty' substituted for 'eternal' in the first line, is that which appeared in the first edition of *Hymns Ancient and Modern* in 1861.

The editors of that work made two further changes to Marriott's original, reversing the order of 'Blessed and holy' in the first line of verse 4 and changing 'world' to 'earth' in the penultimate line. Most modern hymnals have reverted to Marriott's original version of the fourth verse, but all retain the alteration made to his first line. Perhaps it is time to return to the original here too.

The tune, known variously as Moscow, England, Trinity or Giardini, was written by Felice Giardini (1716–96) and first printed in the *Lock Hospital Collection of Psalm and Hymn Tunes* in 1769. Giardini was a chorister at Milan Cathedral, led the Italian Opera orchestra in London and was himself a composer of operas. He lived for most of his life in London, but after losing favour with the English public he went to Russia and died in Moscow.

Missionary Hymn

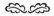

Thou, whose eternal Word
Chaos and darkness heard,
And took their flight,
Hear us, we humbly pray,
And, where the Gospel-day
Sheds not its glorious ray,
Let there be light!

2   Thou, who didst come to bring
On thy redeeming wing
Healing and sight,
Health to the sick in mind,
Sight to the inly blind,
O now, to all mankind,
Let there be light!

3   Spirit of truth and love,
Life-giving, holy Dove,
Speed forth thy flight;
Move o'er the waters' face,
Bearing the lamp of grace,
And, in earth's darkest place,
Let there be light!

4   Blessed and holy Three,
Glorious Trinity,
Wisdom, Love, Might;
Boundless as ocean's tide
Rolling in fullest pride,
Through the world, far and wide,
Let there be light!

THROUGH ALL THE CHANGING SCENES OF LIFE

Like 'As pants the hart for cooling streams' (no. 13), this fine paraphrase of Psalm 34 ('I will bless the Lord at all times; his praise shall continually be in my mouth') comes from the New Version of the Psalter produced in 1696 by Nahum Tate and Nicholas Brady.

This particular paraphrase has generally been credited to Nahum Tate (1652–1715), who must stand as one of the most colourful figures in the history of English hymnody. He was born in Dublin, where his father, Faithful Teate, was a divine. Young Nahum seems to have changed his name to Tate when he came to London. He aspired to be a poet, but to make a living meanwhile he translated French and Latin texts for publishers, including a cautionary treatise on *Syphilis, or a Poetical History of the French Disease*. As well as poems, he wrote plays and altered the works of established dramatists, including Shakespeare. He gave *King Lear* a happy ending by allowing Cordelia to escape death and marry Edgar, and omitted the character of the fool completely. Probably his best-known work besides the version of the Psalms on which he collaborated with his fellow Irishman Nicholas Brady, is his libretto for Purcell's opera, *Dido and Aeneas*. In 1692 he became Poet Laureate and was later appointed Historiographer Royal. However, he turned to drink and died ignominiously in a debtors' refuge housed within the precincts of the Royal Mint.

The text printed here forms the first ten verses of the paraphrase as it appeared in 1696 in Tate and Brady's *New Version of the Psalms of David fitted to the tunes used in the churches*. The spelling has been updated. The original version ran to eighteen verses, but no hymnbook has ever printed the paraphrase in its entirety – most take verses 1–4 and 7–9, plus the following doxology:

> To Father, Son and Holy Ghost,
> The God whom we adore,
> Be glory, as it was, is now,
> And shall be evermore.

The fine tune, Wiltshire, was written by Sir George Smart (1776–1867) when he was only 19 and organist at St James's Chapel, London. When it was first published it was as a setting for Psalm 18. Scots, who long knew the tune as New St Ann, are used to singing other metrical psalms to it including 'The Lord's my Shepherd'. Smart went on to become organist at the Chapel Royal.

Psalm xxxiv

Through all the changing scenes of life,
In trouble and in joy,
The praises of my God shall still
My heart and tongue employ.

2   Of his deliverance I will boast,
Till all that are distress'd
From my example courage take
And soothe their griefs to rest.

3   O magnify the Lord with me,
With me exalt his name;
4   When in distress to him I called,
He to my rescue came.

5   Their drooping hearts were soon refreshed,
Who looked to him for aid;
Desired success in every face,
A cheerful air displayed.

6   'Behold,' say they, 'Behold the man
Whom providence relieved;
The man so dangerously beset,
So wondrously retrieved!'

7   The hosts of God encamp around
The dwellings of the just;
Deliverance he affords to all
Who on his succour trust.

8   O make but trial of his love;
     Experience will decide
     How blest they are, and only they,
     Who in his truth confide.

9   Fear him, ye saints, and you will then
     Have nothing else to fear;
     Make you his service your delight,
     Your wants shall be his care.

10   While hungry lions lack their prey,
     The Lord will food provide
     For such as put their trust in him,
     And see their needs supplied.

THROUGH THE NIGHT
OF DOUBT AND
SORROW

As far as I know, this is the only Danish hymn to find its way into English-language hymnbooks. Its author, Bernhard Severin Ingemann (1789–1862), was a legendary figure in his country, whose influence on children was second only to that of the great Hans Christian Andersen.

Born on the island of Falster, Ingemann, a devout Lutheran, became Professor of Danish Language and Literature at the Academy of Sorö in Zealand. He wrote historical romances which were much influenced by the work of Sir Walter Scott, but it was his stories for children which won him his greatest fame. On his 70th birthday he was presented with a golden horn ornamented with figures from his poems and stories, and paid for by halfpenny donations from every child in the land.

Ingemann wrote his hymn, 'Igjennem Nat og Traengsel', based on the Israelites' journey to the Promised Land, in 1825. It was published in a Copenhagen *Psalmebog* in 1859. Sabine Baring-Gould (1834–1924) came across a copy of the hymn and translated it. His translation was first published in the *People's Hymnal* in 1867 and later, in an altered state, in *Hymns Ancient and Modern* in 1875. It is the earlier version which appears here and is to be found in most modern hymnals.

Baring-Gould, who is best known as the author of 'Onward Christian soldiers' (no. 105), was the son of an Indian cavalry officer who tried to settle in Devon but found the milieu there too conservative and spent the latter part of his life on a perpetual grand tour of the spas and cities of Europe. Young Sabine was not sent to school but succeeded in obtaining a place at Clare College, Cambridge. He was ordained into the Church of England and married a Yorkshire mill-girl half his age who bore him five sons and nine daughters. In 1872 his uncle, who was rector of Lew Trenchard in Devon, died and he presented himself to the living. He spent the rest of his life as parson and squire of the village.

A strong Anglo-Catholic and a considerable scholar, Baring-Gould published a sixteen-volume *Lives of the Saints*. He also wrote novels and collected the folk-songs of Devon and Cornwall, including the immortal 'Widdecombe Fair'. Other hymns by him which are still sung today include 'Daily, daily sing the praises' and 'Now the day is over'.

In the 1980s 'Through the night of doubt and sorrow' got into trouble on account of its sexist language. Fritz Spiegel* revealed that during a rehearsal for BBC Radio 4's morning service a female preacher objected to the line 'Brother clasps the hand of brother': 'According to a friend who was singing in the choir she tried (fortunately in vain) to get it changed to "Person clasps the hand of person". In the end a compromise was reached and the offending verse omitted.'

The hymn has been set to a number of tunes, but by far the best – which is now almost universally used – is Marching, which was specially written for it by Martin Shaw (1875–1958). Shaw wrote it in 1915 for use at St Mary's, Primrose Hill, where he was organist.

* Fritz Spiegel, *Daily Telegraph*, 29 July 1987.

Igjennem Nat og Traengsel

Through the night of doubt and sorrow
Onward goes the pilgrim band,
Singing songs of expectation,
Marching to the Promised Land.

2   Clear before us through the darkness
Gleams and burns the guiding light;
Brother clasps the hand of brother,
Stepping fearless through the night.

3   One the light of God's own presence
O'er his ransomed people shed,
Chasing far the gloom and terror,
Brightening all the path we tread;

4   One the object of our journey,
One the faith which never tires,
One the earnest looking forward,
One the hope our God inspires:

5   One the strain that lips of thousands
Lift as from the heart of one;
One the conflict, one the peril,
One the march in God begun;

6   One the gladness of rejoicing
On the far eternal shore,
Where the one almighty Father
Reigns in love for evermore.

7   Onward, therefore, pilgrim brothers,
     Onward with the Cross our aid;
     Bear its shame, and fight its battle,
     Till we rest beneath its shade.

8   Soon shall come the great awakening,
     Soon the rending of the tomb;
     Then the scatt'ring of all shadows,
     And the end of toil and gloom.

THY HAND, O GOD, HAS GUIDED

This hymn was the work of Edward Hayes Plumptre (1821–91) and first appeared in the 1889 supplement to *Hymns Ancient and Modern*. Its title, 'Church Defence', might suggest that it was written in circumstances similar to those which prompted Samuel Stone to pen 'The Church's one foundation' (no. 124). However, 'Thy hand, O God, has guided' does not seem to have been born out of any particular controversy; it was rather an expression of confidence in the Church in general, and the Church of England in particular, at a time when there was much scepticism and religious uncertainty in the land.

According to W.K. Lowther Clarke★ in his book *A Hundred Years of Hymns Ancient and Modern*, Plumptre's hymn originally contained a verse which began:

> God bless our merry England,
> God bless our Church and Queen,
> God bless our great Archbishop,
> The best there's ever been.

This the editors of the 1889 supplement quite understandably refused to print. I find it slightly hard to believe that Plumptre should have seriously proposed such a verse as the one quoted above, but I suppose it is possible.

E.H. Plumptre (1821–91) was a notable figure in the Victorian Church of England. Educated at King's College, London, and University College, Oxford, he became a fellow of Brasenose and was ordained in 1846. He was successively

---

★ W.K. Lowther Clarke, *A Hundred Years of Hymns Ancient and Modern* (London: William Clowes, 1960).

chaplain of King's College, London, assistant preacher at Lincoln's Inn, Dean of Queen's College, Oxford, prebendary of St Paul's Cathedral and Professor of New Testament at King's College, London. He held the livings of Pluckley and Bickley in Kent before in 1881 becoming Dean of Wells. A considerable scholar, he translated Aeschylus, Dante and Sophocles. His other hymns include 'O Light, whose beams illumine all', 'Rejoice, ye pure in heart' and 'Thine arm, O Lord, in days of yore'. This last hymn would certainly have found a place in this anthology had there been more room. Let me at least give its first verse:

> Thine arm, O Lord, in days of old
> Was strong to heal and save;
> It triumphed o'er disease and death,
> O'er darkness and the grave:
> To thee they went, the blind, the dumb,
> The palsied and the lame;
> The leper with his tainted life,
> The sick with fevered frame.

The tune Thornbury was specially composed for 'Thy hand, O God, has guided' by Basil Harwood (1859–1949), organist at Ely Cathedral and Christ Church Cathedral, Oxford. It was first used at an annual festival of the London Church Choir Association in 1898 but did not come into *Hymns Ancient and Modern* until 1916.

Church Defence

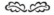

Thy hand, O God, has guided
Thy flock, from age to age;
The wondrous tale is written,
Full clear, on every page;
Our fathers owned thy goodness,
And we their deeds record;
And both of this bear witness:
One Church, one Faith, one Lord.

2   Thy heralds brought glad tidings
To greatest, as to least;
They bade men rise, and hasten
To share the great King's feast;
And this was all their teaching,
In every deed and word,
To all alike proclaiming
One Church, one Faith, one Lord.

3   When shadows thick were falling,
And all seemed sunk in night,
Thou, Lord, didst send thy servants,
Thy chosen sons of light.
On them and on thy people
Thy plenteous grace was poured,
And this was still their message:
One Church, one Faith, one Lord.

4   Through many a day of darkness,
    Through many a scene of strife,
    The faithful few fought bravely,
    To guard the nation's life.
    Their Gospel of redemption,
    Sin pardoned, man restored,
    Was all in this enfolded:
    One Church, one Faith, one Lord.

5   And we, shall we be faithless?
    Shall hearts fail, hands hang down?
    Shall we evade the conflict,
    And cast away our crown?
    Not so: in God's deep counsels
    Some better thing is stored;
    We will maintain, unflinching:
    One Church, one Faith, one Lord.

6   Thy mercy will not fail us,
    Nor leave thy work undone;
    With thy right hand to help us,
    The vict'ry shall be won;
    And then, by men and angels,
    Thy name shall be adored,
    And this shall be their anthem:
    One Church, one Faith, one Lord.

TO GOD BE THE GLORY

This is another rousing evangelical hymn by Frances Crosby (1820–1915), whom we have already come across as the author of 'Blessèd assurance, Jesus is mine' (no. 18).

'To God be the glory' was written in the early 1870s and was popular with Ira Sankey, who used it in his British crusade with fellow American evangelist, Dwight Moody, in 1872. Sankey also included the hymn in his *Sacred Songs and Solos*, which was published in Britain in 1873, but for some reason he did not include it in his *Gospel Hymns*, which appeared in the USA after his return there in 1875. It seems to have lapsed into relative obscurity for the next three-quarters of a century until it was rediscovered by members of the Billy Graham evangelistic organization in the 1950s.

Cliff Barrows, one of the Billy Graham team, included 'To God be the glory' in the song-book for the 1954 London crusade 'because of its strong text of praise and its attractive melody'. It was immediately popular with the audiences in the Haringey Arena and became the theme hymn of the crusade, being repeated every night.

Returning to America in the summer of 1954, the Billy Graham team used Fanny Crosby's hymn in their crusade in Nashville, Tennessee. It was quickly taken up and found its way into several American hymnals, notably the *Baptist Hymnal*, and the *Trinity Hymnal* of the Presbyterian Church. It now finds a place in many modern British and American hymnals.

This is a hymn which is definitely much better heard sung than read on a page. Some of the language in which it expresses its message of salvation by faith alone is less than inspiring, although it does have a certain originality.

Much of the hymn's popularity is undoubtedly attributable to the tune by W.H. Doane (1832–1916), which seems to cry out for tambourines and foot-tapping. For details of Doane's life, see notes to 'Tell me the old, old story' (no. 121).

To God be the glory

To God be the glory! great things He hath done:
So loved He the world that He gave us His Son;
Who yielded His life an atonement for sin,
And opened the Life gate that all may go in.

> *Praise the Lord! Praise the Lord!*
> *Let the earth hear his voice!*
> *Praise the Lord! Praise the Lord!*
> *Let the people rejoice!*
> *Oh, come to the Father through Jesus the Son;*
> *And give Him the glory! great things He hath done!*

2 O perfect redemption, the purchase of blood,
   To every believer – the promise of God;
   The vilest offender who truly believes,
   That moment from Jesus a pardon receives.

3 Great things He hath taught us, great things He hath done,
   And great our rejoicing through Jesus the Son;
   But purer, and higher, and greater will be
   Our wonder, our transport, when Jesus we see.

WAKE, O WAKE! WITH
TIDINGS THRILLING

This powerful Advent hymn is German in origin. It was written at the very end of the sixteenth century by Philipp Nicolai (1556–1608) in circumstances very similar to those that may have inspired another Lutheran pastor, Martin Rinkart, to compose 'Now thank we all our God' a generation or so later (see notes to hymn no. 90).

Nicolai, who was educated at the Universities of Erfurt and Wittenberg, was ordained into the Lutheran Church at the age of 20. At the time of writing this hymn, he was pastor at Unna in Westphalia. In 1597 there was a terrible plague in the town; in just six months over 1,300 people died and Nicolai was regularly burying up to 30 of his parishioners a day. In his despair he reread St Augustine's *City of God*, and then wrote a book of meditations which he called *A Mirror of Joy*. He wrote of it:

There seemed to me nothing more sweet, delightful and agreeable than the contemplation of the noble, sublime doctrine of eternal life ... I gave to my manuscript the name and title of Mirror of Joy and took this thus composed, to leave behind me (if God should call me from the world) as the token of my peaceful, joyful Christian departure, or (if God should spare me in health) to comfort other sufferers whom He should also visit with the pestilence.

'*Wachet auf, ruft uns die Stimme*', to give this hymn its original German title, is one of two hymns in *A Mirror of Joy* which became very popular. The other, '*Wie schön leuchtet uns der Morgenstern*', which became a favourite marriage hymn in Germany, is also found in a number of English hymnals in a translation which begins 'How brightly beams the morning star'.

'*Wachet auf*' makes much of the image of Christ as the

bridegroom which is found in the parable of the wise and foolish virgins in Matthew 25.1–13. The hymn was originally entitled 'Of the voice at midnight and the wise Virgins who meet their heavenly Bridegroom'. The reference to the watchmen in the first and second verses is taken from Isaiah 52.8: 'Thy watchmen shall lift up the voice; with the voice together they shall sing: for they shall see eye to eye, when the Lord shall bring again Zion.' The gates of pearl mentioned in the last verse are found in Revelation 21.21.

Erik Routley describes this as 'one of the perfect hymns of all time'.* He goes on: 'It conveys a single overall impression of pageantry, energy, light, colour and expectancy. This is entirely faithful to the biblical teaching about the relation between the temporal world and the eternal world.'

The translation printed below was made for the *English Hymnal* by Francis Crawford Burkitt (1864–1935), a distinguished biblical and patristic scholar who was Norrisian Professor of Divinity at Cambridge from 1905 to 1935. It appears in the *New English Hymnal*. There are a number of other translations in current use. The New Standard edition of *Hymns Ancient and Modern* uses one by Frances E. Cox (1812–97) which begins: 'Sleepers, wake! the watch-cry pealeth', while the *Church Hymnary* favours a version by Catherine Winkworth (1829–78) which begins: 'Wake, awake! for night is flying'.

Common to all these translations is the majestic tune *Wachet auf*, which Nicolai himself composed for the hymn. It was later adapted and harmonized by J.S. Bach in one of his best-known cantatas. Felix Mendelssohn also made use of the tune.

---

* Erik Routley, *Hymns Today and Tomorrow*, p. 37.

Wachet auf, ruft uns die Stimme

꙾

Wake, O wake! with tidings thrilling
The watchmen all the air are filling,
Arise, Jerusalem, arise!
Midnight strikes! no more delaying,
'The hour has come!' we hear them saying.
Where are ye all, ye virgins wise?
  The Bridegroom comes in sight,
  Raise high your torches bright!
    Alleluia!
  The wedding song
  Swells loud and strong:
Go forth and join the festal throng.

2   Zion hears the watchmen shouting,
Her heart leaps up with joy undoubting,
She stands and waits with eager eyes;
See her Friend from heaven descending,
Adorned with truth and grace unending!
Her light burns clear, her star doth rise.
  Now come, thou precious Crown,
  Lord Jesu, God's own Son!
    Alleluia!
  Let us prepare
  To follow there,
Where in thy supper we may share.

3 Every soul in thee rejoices;
From men and from angelic voices
Be glory giv'n to thee alone!
Now the gates of pearl receive us,
Thy presence never more shall leave us,
We stand with Angels round thy throne.
 Earth cannot give below
 The bliss thou dost bestow.
  Alleluia!
 Grant us to raise,
 To length of days,
The triumph–chorus of thy praise.

WE PLOUGH THE FIELDS,
AND SCATTER

This much-loved harvest hymn which seems to come from the very depths of the English countryside is, in fact, another translation from a German original. '*Wir pflugen und wir streuen/ Den Samen auf das Land*' was written by Matthias Claudius (1740–1815).

Born in Reinfeld near Lübeck, Claudius was the son of a Lutheran pastor and was originally destined for the same calling. However, an affliction of the chest coupled with the rationalist influence of the University of Jena, where he studied, combined to change his course and he became a journalist instead. He edited several newspapers, wrote poetry and was a close friend of the poet Goethe. After a period of atheism, he renewed his Christian faith. At the time he wrote this hymn, he was editor of the local paper in Hesse Darmstadt, where he also served as a Commissioner of Agriculture.

Claudius's harvest hymn first appeared in a play which he wrote in 1783 about a harvest thanksgiving in a north German village. It was closely based on a peasants' song which he heard sung at the home of one of the farmers. In its original version it ran to seventeen four-line verses, with a refrain to each, but when in 1800 the hymn was published in a collection of melodies for schools it was shortened to six verses with a chorus.

It was this shorter version of the hymn which was translated into English in 1861 by Jane Montgomery Campbell (1817–78). The daughter of the vicar of St James's, Paddington, she translated many German hymns and assisted in the compilation of two hymnbooks for children. She lived in Bovey Tracey, Devon, and met an unfortunate death in a carriage accident while driving across Dartmoor.

The tune *Wir pflugen*, or Dresden, is by J.A.P. Schultz (1747–

1800) and first appeared set to Claudius's hymn in 1800. Schultz, who is famous for his *Christmas Cantata*, was *Kapellmeister* to Prince Henry of Prussia and then occupied the same office at the Court of Copenhagen.

Miss Campbell's translation has been altered slightly in most modern hymnals so that the last four lines of the third verse now run:

> Accept the gifts we offer
> For all thy love imparts,
> And, what thou most desirest,
> Our humble, thankful hearts.

It is now quite common for an updated version of the hymn to be sung at harvest festivals. This begins:

> We plough the fields with tractors,
> With drills we sow the land;
> But growth is still the wondrous gift
> Of God's almighty hand.
> We add our fertilizers
> To help the growing grain,
> But for its full fruition
> It needs God's sun and rain.

I have to say that I find this modern version, whose origins I have been unable to trace, all too reminiscent of John Betjeman's splendid parody which begins:

> We spray the fields and scatter
> The poison on the ground.
> So that no wicked wild flowers
> Upon our farms be found.
> We like whatever helps us
> To line our purse with pence;
> The twenty-four hour broiler house
> And neat electric fence.

Another modern parody by Clive Sansom, entitled 'Hymn of
the Scientific Farmers', begins:

> We squirt the fields and scatter
> Our phosphates on the land:
> 'Organic waste' and 'humus'
> We do not understand.
> We slaughter trees in thousands
> To sell for what they're worth;
> No stems to hold the water,
> No roots to bind the earth.

Wir pflugen und wir streuen

We plough the fields, and scatter
The good seed on the land,
But it is fed and watered
By God's almighty hand;
He sends the snow in winter,
The warmth to swell the grain,
The breezes and the sunshine,
And soft refreshing rain.

All good gifts around us
Are sent from heav'n above;
Then thank the Lord, O thank the Lord
For all his love.

2 He only is the Maker
Of all things near and far,
He paints the wayside flower,
He lights the evening star.
The winds and waves obey him,
By him the birds are fed;
Much more to us, his children,
He gives our daily bread:

3 We thank thee then, O Father,
For all things bright and good;
The seed-time and the harvest,
Our life, our health, our food.
No gifts have we to offer
For all thy love imparts,
But that which thou desirest,
Our humble, thankful hearts:

143

WHAT A FRIEND WE
HAVE IN JESUS

Although it is not found in several modern hymnals, this hymn came sixth in the 2002 *Songs of Praise* poll and there is no doubt that it is still held in very great affection by many people – and rightly so, for though it may not be great poetry, it conveys in a simple but sincere and effective way the love that God has for his creatures and the consolation which he can offer them in times of distress.

It was certainly born out of bitter personal experience. Its author, Joseph Medicott Scriven (1820–86), had more than his fair share of misfortune. Born in Dublin, his early hopes for a military career were dashed by ill-health which continued to dog him throughout his life. He emigrated to Canada at the age of 25, after his intended bride had been drowned the evening before their wedding. He settled first at Rice Lake and then at Port Hope, Ontario, where he gained a living as a tutor, while spending most of his time working tirelessly among the poor and destitute. He became engaged again, only to see his second fiancée die after a brief illness. In October 1886 he was found drowned in a water-run near Rice Lake. A monument to his memory was erected near the lake by local people.

Scriven did not publish 'What a Friend we have in Jesus' during his lifetime. A friend who was with him shortly before he died came across the manuscript and was much impressed by it. Scriven told him that he had written the verses for his mother back home in Ireland at a time of particular sorrow. When asked whether he had written it unaided, he replied, 'The Lord and I did it between us.'

The tune Converse is the work of Charles Converse (1832–1918). Having studied music in Germany, where he was friendly with Franz Liszt and Louis Spohr, he went on to become a successful lawyer in his native USA. He was equally at home composing symphonies, oratorios and gospel songs. There is some doubt as to whether he wrote the tune specifically for this hymn or whether it was originally written for another sacred song and put to Scriven's words by Ira Sankey for the first edition of his *Gospel Hymns*.

This hymn was much parodied by soldiers in the First World War. The text below is one of the more salubrious versions, which was used with particular effect in the film *Oh What a Lovely War*; it was sung contrapuntally, against the words of Scriven's original, in an open-air service:

When this lousy war is over,
Oh, how happy I will be!
When I get my civvy clothes on,
No more soldiering for me.
No more church parades on Sundays,
No more asking out for leave,
I shall kiss the Sergeant-Major,
How he'll miss me, how I'll grieve.

There was an outcry when 'What a Friend we have in Jesus' was left out of the third edition of the Church of Scotland's *Church Hymnary* in 1973. To make amends, it was included in the supplement, *Songs of God's People* in 1988. There it was given an alternative tune, the folk-melody Scarlet Ribbons arranged by John Bell.

Pray without ceasing

What a Friend we have in Jesus,
All our sins and griefs to bear!
What a privilege to carry
Everything to God in prayer!
O what peace we often forfeit,
O what needless pain we bear,
All because we do not carry
Everything to God in prayer!

2   Have we trials and temptations?
Is there trouble anywhere?
We should never be discouraged:
Take it to the Lord in prayer.
Can we find a friend so faithful,
Who will all our sorrows share?
Jesus knows our every weakness:
Take it to the Lord in prayer.

3   Are we weak and heavy-laden,
Cumbered with a load of care?
Jesus only is our refuge:
Take it to the Lord in prayer.
Do thy friends despise, forsake thee?
Take it to the Lord in prayer;
In His arms He'll take and shield thee;
Thou wilt find a solace there.

WHEN I SURVEY THE WONDROUS CROSS

These much-loved and much-sung verses by Isaac Watts (1674–1748; see notes to hymn no. 27) have an important place in the history of English hymnody. They introduced a new note of subjective religious experience into a genre which had previously been studiously objective. This is the first known hymn in the English language to include the personal pronoun 'I' and to express the experience of Christian faith rather than simply limiting itself to matters of doctrine.

It has long been acknowledged as one of the finest hymns ever written. It was certainly so regarded by the great Victorian essayist and poet Matthew Arnold, who heard it sung in Sefton Park Presbyterian Church, Liverpool, on the last Sunday of his life, and who was overheard repeating the third verse shortly before his sudden death a few days later. In his *Dictionary of Hymnology*, first published in 1892, John Julian described the hymn as 'one of the four which stand at the head of all hymns in the English language', the others being 'Awake, my soul, and with the sun', 'Hark! the herald angels sing' and 'Rock of Ages, cleft for me'. It was voted nineteenth in the 2002 BBC *Songs of Praise* poll.

Watts wrote 'When I survey the wondrous Cross' as a communion hymn and it first appeared in 1707 in his *Hymns and Spiritual Songs*. He there appended the text on which it is based, from Paul's Epistle to the Galatians 6.14: 'God forbid that I should glory, save in the cross of our Lord Jesus Christ, by whom the world is crucified to me, and I to the world.'

In 1709 Watts changed the second line to 'On which the Prince of Glory died'. It is not clear why he made this alteration. The fourth verse was dropped from many eighteenth- and nineteenth-century hymnals, being considered rather too gory, and it continues to be generally omitted today. In verse 5, line 2 the word 'present' is sometimes changed to 'offering'.

The tune Rockingham (also known as Caton and Communion), to which the hymn is almost invariably sung in Britain, is first found in *The Psalms of David for the Use of Parish Churches*, published in 1790 with music selected and composed by Edward Miller. Dr Miller was organist at Doncaster Parish Church from 1756 to 1807. He took the name Rockingham from his patron and friend the Marquis of Rockingham, the Whig statesman who was three times prime minister. In his book the tune accompanied nine different psalms. It seems to have been adapted from an earlier tune called Tunbridge, which is found in a *Supplement to Psalmody in Miniature* by Aaron Williams (1778). Rockingham was not used for 'When I survey the wondrous Cross' until 1854. Before that, Watts's words were sung to a debased version of Tallis's Canon, known as Suffolk. In the USA the hymn is often sung to Hamburg, arranged by Lowell Mason (1792–1872).

Crucifixion to the world by the Cross of Christ

When I survey the wondrous Cross,
Where the young Prince of Glory died,
My richest gain I count but loss,
And pour contempt on all my pride.

2   Forbid it, Lord, that I should boast
Save in the death of Christ my God;
All the vain things that charm me most,
I sacrifice them to his blood.

3   See from his head, his hands, his feet,
Sorrow and love flow mingled down;
Did e'er such love and sorrow meet,
Or thorns compose so rich a crown?

4   His dying crimson, like a robe,
Spreads o'er his body on the Tree;
Then am I dead to all the globe,
And all the globe is dead to me.

5   Were the whole realm of nature mine,
That were a present far too small;
Love so amazing, so divine,
Demands my soul, my life, my all.

WHEN MORNING GILDS
THE SKIES

This is not, as its title might suggest, a morning hymn but rather a general hymn of praise to Christ which is suitable for use at any time or season. The German original on which it is based is of unknown authorship. Beginning '*Beim frühen Morgenlicht*', and running to fourteen verses, it first appeared anonymously in the *Katholisches Gesangbuch* published in Würzburg in 1828.

The translation printed here was made by Edward Caswall (1814–78). Educated at Marlborough and Brasenose College, Oxford, Caswall was ordained into the Church of England, but in 1847 he became a Roman Catholic. Following the death of his wife, he joined John Henry Newman's Oratory in Birmingham. He wrote a large number of hymns, many of them translations, including the Advent hymn, 'Hark! a thrilling voice is sounding', 'My God, I love thee; not because', and the Good Friday hymn, 'At the Cross her station keeping'.

Caswall's translation was first published in *Catholic Hymns*, a collection edited by the Revd Henry Formby and published in 1854. In 1873 he published a longer translation, covering all fourteen verses of the German original. At the same time he made some alterations to his earlier translation. He changed the first two lines of the second verse to:

> The sacred minster bell,
> It peals o'er hill and dell,

and altered the last line of verse 6 to 'Through all the ages on'. These alterations appear in the version of the hymn contained in the *New English Hymnal*, which also includes the following additional verses from the later translation:

When sleep her balm denies,
My silent spirit sighs,
May Jesus Christ be praised;
When evil thoughts molest,
With this I shield my breast,
May Jesus Christ be praised.

In heaven's eternal bliss,
The loveliest strain is this,
May Jesus Christ be praised;
Let air, and sea, and sky
From depth to height reply,
May Jesus Christ be praised.

The New Standard edition of *Hymns Ancient and Modern* contains Caswall's original six-verse translation, as printed below. The third edition of the *Church Hymnary* and *Hymns for Church and School* print another six-verse translation of the hymn, which has the same first three lines as Caswall's but differs considerably thereafter. It is the work of Robert Bridges (1844–1930).

The tunes normally used for his hymn are either *Laudes Domini* by Joseph Barnby (1838–96) or *O Seigneur*, a tune by Louis Bourgeois (1510–61) set to Marot's version of Psalm 3 in the French Psalter of 1551. 'When morning gilds the skies' also goes particularly well to the tune of Count Danilo's song, 'I'm off to Chez Maxim's' from *The Merry Widow* by Franz Lehár.

Beim frühen Morgenlicht

When morning gilds the skies,
My heart awaking cries,
May Jesus Christ be praised:
Alike at work and prayer
To Jesus I repair;
May Jesus Christ be praised.

2 Whene'er the sweet church bell
Peals over hill and dell,
May Jesus Christ be praised:
O hark to what it sings,
As joyously it rings,
May Jesus Christ be praised.

3 My tongue shall never tire
Of chanting with the choir,
May Jesus Christ be praised:
This song of sacred joy,
It never seems to cloy,
May Jesus Christ be praised.

4 Does sadness fill my mind?
A solace here I find,
May Jesus Christ be praised:
Or fades my earthly bliss?
My comfort still is this,
May Jesus Christ be praised.

5 The night becomes as day,
When from the heart we say,
May Jesus Christ be praised:
The powers of darkness fear,
When this sweet chant they hear,
May Jesus Christ be praised.

6   Be this, while life is mine,
    My canticle divine,
    May Jesus Christ be praised:
    Be this the eternal song
    Through ages all along,
    May Jesus Christ be praised.

WHO WOULD TRUE
VALOUR SEE

This hymn is sung today in two very different versions. It comes from John Bunyan's great spiritual classic, *Pilgrim's Progress*. The verses printed here originally appeared in the book at the point where Mr Greatheart and Mr Valiant-for-truth, near the end of their long pilgrimage, have reached the enchanted ground. It is introduced into the narrative with these words by Mr Valiant-for-truth: 'I believed, and therefore came out, got into the way, fought all that set themselves against me, and, by believing, am come to this place.'

John Bunyan (1628–88) is one of the great figures of English Protestantism. Born in the village of Elstow, Bedfordshire, the son of a tinker, he served in Cromwell's army during the Civil War and then returned to his native village as a brazier and itinerant Independent preacher. Following the imposition of anti-nonconformist laws at the restoration of the monarchy in 1660, Bunyan was imprisoned in Bedford gaol for twelve years. It was during a second much briefer period of imprisonment that he began writing *Pilgrim's Progress*, the first part of which was published in 1678, and the second part, in which these verses appear, in 1684.

As with many other fine examples of seventeenth-century religious verse, it is only in the present century that Bunyan's poem has been sung as a hymn. It owes its popularity to Dr Percy Dearmer (1867–1936), who included a heavily edited version in the *English Hymnal* in 1906. Dearmer's version, which can be found in the *New English Hymnal*, has the following changes from Bunyan's original:

verse 1, lines 1–4:

> He who would valiant be
> 'Gainst all disaster,
> Let him in constancy
> Follow the Master.

verse 2, lines 5–8:

> No foes shall stay his might,
> Though he with giants fight:
> He will make good his right
> To be a pilgrim.

verse 3:

> Since, Lord, thou dost defend
> Us with thy Spirit,
> We know we at the end
> Shall life inherit.
> Then fancies flee away!
> I'll fear not what men say,
> I'll labour night and day
> To be a pilgrim.

In a lengthy passage in his book *Songs of Praise Discussed*,★ Dr Dearmer defended his substantial rewriting of Bunyan's words on the grounds that the original was never meant for congregational singing. In recent years, however, more and more hymnals have reverted to Bunyan's original, hobgoblins and foul fiends notwithstanding, and this is surely right: it has a power and directness which is lost in the more modern version.

The tune Monks Gate was one of the 35 traditional folk-songs which Ralph Vaughan Williams adapted for use in the *English Hymnal*. It is based on a song called 'Our Captain Calls', and was collected by Vaughan Williams from Mrs Verral in the village of Monks Gate, near Horsham in West Sussex.

★ Percy Dearmer, *Songs of Praise Discussed* (Oxford: Oxford University Press, 1933).

Who would true valour see,
Let him come hither;
One here will constant be,
Come wind, come weather;
There's no discouragement
Shall make him once relent
His first avowed intent
To be a pilgrim.

2   Who so beset him round
With dismal stories
Do but themselves confound;
His strength the more is.
No lion can him fright;
He'll with a giant fight;
But he will have a right
To be a pilgrim.

3   Hobgoblin nor foul fiend
Can daunt his spirit;
He knows he at the end
Shall life inherit.
Then fancies fly away,
He'll fear not what men say;
He'll labour night and day
To be a pilgrim.

WILL YOU COME AND FOLLOW ME

The Iona Community, the ecumenical Christian community set up in 1938 by the visionary Church of Scotland minister George Macleod, has greatly reinvigorated and revitalized Christian worship and witness in all kinds of ways. Its Wild Goose Resource Group, based in Glasgow, but in demand all over the world to lead liturgical events and teach new songs to Christians of very varied traditions, has produced a significant body of contemporary hymns and worship-songs as well as promoting the use of material from Africa, Latin America and Asia in churches in Britain, Europe and North America. 'Will you come and follow me' is the work of the two leading song-writers in the Wild Goose group, John Bell and Graham Maule.

Born in 1949, John Bell hails from Kilmarnock in Ayrshire. Educated at Glasgow University, he was ordained into the ministry of the Church of Scotland in 1978 and served in the Scots Kirk in Amsterdam and as youth adviser to Glasgow Presbytery before beginning full-time work with the Iona Community in 1983. He was appointed as the Community's worship resource worker in 1988 and has been working with the Wild Goose group ever since.

It is hardly too much to say that John Bell has almost single-handedly transformed the culture of worship and especially of church music in Scotland, introducing a range of new material, much of it his own but also the work of other contemporary writers and songs from the wider Church. He has convened the Church of Scotland's Panel on Worship and the committee preparing the fourth edition of the *Church Hymnary* (on which he and I have had many a tussle over Victorian hymns which he wants to scrap and I want to keep).

His influence has spread far beyond Presbyterian Scotland.

Passionately ecumenical, he was the driving force behind *Common Ground*, a songbook produced by representatives of all the main Scottish churches and published in 1998. He leads worship workshops throughout the UK, in the USA, Canada, Australia and Japan.

Graham Maule was born in 1958 and studied architecture. After several years in youth work, he joined the Wild Goose worship group. Among the other songs and hymns on which he and John Bell have collaborated, and which are now found in hymnals throughout the world, are 'Christ's is the world in which we move' (A Touching Place), 'Come with me, come wander', 'Before the world began', 'Jesus calls us here to meet him' and 'We cannot measure how you heal'.

'Will you come and follow me' was one of Bell and Maule's earliest collaborations. It was written in 1986 and published the following year in *Heaven Shall Not Wait*. It displays much of the characteristic theology and spirituality of the Iona Community. It is grittily incarnational and both challenging and disturbing. It is also direct, simple and deeply biblical. Like many of the songs from the Wild Goose stable, it is set to a Scottish folk-tune, in this case Kelvingrove.

Will you come and follow me
if I but call your name?
Will you go where you don't know
and never be the same?
Will you let my love be shown,
will you let my name be known,
will you let my life be grown
in you and you in me?

2   Will you leave your self behind
if I but call your name?
Will you care for cruel and kind
and never be the same?
Will you risk the hostile stare
should your life attract or scare,
will you let me answer prayer
in you and you in me?

3   Will you let the blinded see
if I but call your name?
Will you set the prisoners free
and never be the same?
Will you kiss the leper clean
and do such as this unseen,
and admit to what I mean
in you and you in me?

4   Will you love the 'you' you hide
if I but call your name?
Will you quell the fear inside
and never be the same?
Will you use the faith you've found
to reshape the world around
through my sight and touch and sound
in you and you in me?

5   Lord, your summons echoes true
    when you but call my name.
    Let me turn and follow you
    and never be the same.
    In your company I'll go
    where your love and footsteps show.
    Thus I'll move and live and grow
    in you and you in me.

'Will You Come And Follow Me'
Words: John L. Bell + Graham Maule © 1987, WGRG, Iona
Community, G2 3DH.

WILL YOUR ANCHOR
HOLD

This rousing hymn by Priscilla Jane Owens (1829–99) is the official hymn of the Boys' Brigade.

Priscilla Owens was born in Baltimore, but came of Scottish and Welsh descent. For more than 50 years she was active in Sunday School work in her home town, and most of her hymns and songs were written for Sunday School children. She is also remembered for another spirited hymn which begins:

> We have heard the joyful sound –
> 'Jesus saves, Jesus saves!'
> Spread the gladness all around:
> 'Jesus saves, Jesus saves!'
> Bear the news to every land,
> Climb the steeps and cross the waves;
> Onward! – 'tis our Lord's command,
> Jesus saves! Jesus saves!

Miss Owens was not the first to compare Christian faith to an anchor. Hebrews 6.19 speaks of the 'hope we have as anchor of the soul, both sure and steadfast'. It was almost certainly that biblical reference which inspired this particular hymn. Several other popular gospel songs of the nineteenth century also use nautical imagery to powerful effect. The catchy Salvation Army chorus 'Count your blessings' begins: 'When upon life's billows you are tempest tossed'. Philip Bliss (1838–76), author of 'Ho, my comrades', produced at least two songs with a maritime flavour. We have already had cause to quote from one of them, 'Brightly beams our Father's mercy' (see note to no. 51). The other has the following first verse and chorus:

Light in the darkness, sailor, day is at hand!
See o'er the foaming billows fair Heaven's land.
Drear was the voyage, sailor, now almost o'er;
Safe within the lifeboat, sailor, pull for the shore!
Pull for the shore, sailor; pull for the shore!
Heed not the rolling waves, but bend to the oar;
Safe in the lifeboat, sailor, cling to self no more;
Leave the poor old stranded wreck, and pull for the shore.

The tune to which the hymn is sung, Will Your Anchor Hold?, was written by William J. Kirkpatrick (1838–1921). A carpenter from Philadelphia, Pennsylvania, he became much involved in church work and composed many gospel songs. Altogether he compiled 87 books of such songs, the sales of which ran into millions. He is best remembered for his tune Cradle Song, which is universally used for the Christmas carol 'Away in a manger'.

Will your anchor hold in the storms of life,
When the clouds unfold their wings of strife?
When the strong tides lift, and the cables strain
Will your anchor drift, or firm remain?
We have an anchor that keeps the soul
Steadfast and sure while the billows roll;
Fastened to the Rock which cannot move,
Grounded firm and deep in the Saviour's love!

2   Will you anchor hold in the straits of fear?
When the breakers roar and the reef is near;
While the surges rave, and the wild winds blow,
Shall the angry waves then your bark o'erflow?

3   Will your anchor hold in the floods of death,
When the waters cold chill your latest breath?
On the rising tide you can never fail,
While your anchor holds within the veil.

4   Will your eyes behold through the morning light
The city of gold and the harbour bright?
Will you anchor safe by the heavenly shore,
When life's storms are past for evermore?

YE CHOIRS OF NEW
JERUSALEM

This Easter hymn derives from a medieval original, '*Chorus novae Jerusalem*', which was the work of St Fulbert of Chartres (d. 1028). Little is known about the author, who was consecrated Bishop of Chartres in 1007, but his hymn was widely taken up in England during his lifetime and became one of the office hymns in the Sarum, York and Hereford breviaries for the Sundays after Easter.

The hymn was translated in the late 1840s by Robert Campbell (1814–68) and first appeared in his *Hymns and Anthems* (1850). Born at Troehraig, Ayrshire, Campbell became an advocate. He translated a large number of Latin hymns, including 'At the Lamb's high feast we sing' and 'Thy work on earth, O Christ, is done'. In 1852 he moved from Episcopalianism to Roman Catholicism.

The opening words of the second verse are a curious amalgam of the description of Christ as the lion of 'the tribe of Judah' in Revelation 5.5 and God's promise to the serpent in Genesis 3.15 that he will bruise its head because of its beguiling of Eve.

Hymns Ancient and Modern prints Campbell's original first verse but goes on to use its own different version of verses 2–5. There have been several other translations of St Fulbert's hymn. Their first lines include 'Thou New Jerusalem on high', 'Wake, choir of our Jerusalem' and 'Jerusalem, thy song be new'. The compilers of *Hymns Ancient and Modern* also made a translation which preserves the metre of the original. It begins:

> Up, new Jerusalem and sing
> The sweet new song of Christ thy King;
> In sober joy thy children call
> To keep the Paschal festival.

The tune normally used for Campbell's hymn is St Fulbert by H.J. Gauntlett (1805–76). It was actually written for the hymn 'Now Christ our Passover is slain', and first appeared in the *Church Hymn and Tune Book* in 1852.

Chorus novae Jerusalem

Ye choirs of new Jerusalem,
Your sweetest notes employ,
The Paschal victory to hymn
In strains of holy joy.

2   How Judah's Lion burst his chains,
And crushed the serpent's head;
And brought with him, from death's domains,
The long-imprisoned dead.

3   From hell's devouring jaws the prey
Alone our Leader bore;
His ransomed hosts pursue their way
Where he hath gone before.

4   Triumphant in his glory now
His sceptre ruleth all,
Earth, heaven, and hell before him bow,
And at his footstool fall.

5   While joyful thus his praise we sing,
His mercy we implore,
Into his palace bright to bring
And keep us evermore.

6   All glory to the Father be,
All glory to the Son,
All glory, Holy Ghost, to thee,
While endless ages run. Alleluya!

YE HOLY ANGELS
BRIGHT

This is yet another hymn which is derived from the rich storehouse of seventeenth-century devotional verse. It is based on a poem by John Bunyan's near contemporary and fellow Puritan, Richard Baxter (1615-91).

Baxter was born at Rowton in Shropshire and educated at Wroxeter School. He was ordained into the Church of England and served at Bridgnorth and Kidderminster. He developed a strong distrust of episcopacy and during the English Civil War served as one of Oliver Cromwell's chaplains. In 1660 he became chaplain to Charles II who nominated him for the vacant bishopric of Hereford. However, he refused to accept it and, following the passage of the Act of Uniformity in 1662, he left the Established Church. In 1673 he became a nonconformist minister, and in 1685 he was tried before the notorious Judge Jeffreys for sedition and imprisoned for eighteen months. His most famous literary composition is *The Saints' Everlasting Rest*, but he was also a pioneer hymn-writer, believing that singing in church should not be limited to metrical psalms but should also embrace 'hymns more suitable to gospel times'.

In 1672 Baxter published 'a psalm of praise to the tune of Psalm cxlviii'. It ran to sixteen stanzas, the first two of which were

Ye holy angels bright,
Which stand before God's throne,
And dwell in glorious light,
Praise ye the Lord, each one!
You were so nigh,
Fitter than we
Dark sinners be,
For things so high.

You blessed souls at rest,
Who see your Saviour's face,
Whose glory, ev'n the least,
Is far above our grace,
God's promise sound
As in his sight
With sweet delight
You do abound.

In 1838 John Hampden Gurney (1802–62) took Baxter's verses as the basis of a new hymn which was published in his *Collection of Hymns for Public Worship*. It is Gurney's work which appears overleaf and which has become a favourite congregational hymn. Educated at Trinity College, Cambridge, Gurney entered the Church after studying for a legal career. He was for 23 years curate at Lutterworth in Leicestershire, and in 1847 he became rector of St Mary's, Bryanston Square, London. In 1857 he was made a prebendary of St Paul's Cathedral. His other hymns include 'Fair waved the golden corn' and 'Lord, as to thy dear cross we flee'.

In many modern hymnals the word 'light' is erroneously given instead of 'sight' in the sixth line of verse 2.

The best tune for this hymn is surely Darwall's 148th by John Darwall (1731–89), which is first found in Williams's *New Universal Psalmodist* (1770), set to Psalm 148. Darwall, successively curate and vicar of Walsall, Staffordshire, was an enthusiastic musician and composed tunes for all the 150 metrical psalms.

Ye holy angels bright,
Who wait at God's right hand,
Or through the realms of light
Fly at your Lord's command,
Assist our song,
Or else the theme
Too high doth seem
For mortal tongue.

2   Ye blessèd souls at rest,
Who ran this earthly race,
And now, from sin released,
Behold the Saviour's face,
His praises sound,
As in his sight
With sweet delight
Ye do abound.

3   Ye saints, who toil below,
Adore your heavenly King,
And onward as ye go
Some joyful anthem sing;
Take what he gives,
And praise him still
Through good and ill,
Who ever lives.

4   My soul, bear thou thy part,
Triumph in God above,
And with a well-tuned heart
Sing thou the songs of love.
Let all thy days
Till life shall end,
Whate'er he send,
Be filled with praise.

BIBLIOGRAPHY

Collections of hymns

The list below is not exhaustive, but includes some of the most commonly cited hymnals in this text.

Baptist Praise and Worship (Oxford: Oxford University Press, 1991).
BBC Songs of Praise (Oxford: Oxford University Press, 1997).
Celebration Hymnal (Great Wakering: Mayhew-McCrimon, 1978).
The Church Hymnary, 4th edn (Norwich: Canterbury Press, 2005).
Common Praise (Norwich: Canterbury Press, 2000).
The English Hymnal (London: Oxford University Press, 1933).
Hymns Ancient and Modern, New Standard edition (Norwich: Hymns Ancient and Modern, 1984).
Hymns and Psalms (London: Methodist Publishing House, 1987).
Hymns Old and New (Bury St Edmunds: Kevin Mayhew, 1996).
Mission Praise, complete edition (London: Marshall Pickering, 2005).
The New English Hymnal (Norwich: Canterbury Press, 1986).
Rejoice and Sing (Oxford: Oxford University Press, 1991).
Songs and Hymns of Fellowship (Eastbourne: Kingsway, 1987).
Your Favourite Songs of Praise (Oxford and London: Oxford University Press and BBC Books, 1987).

Secondary works

Adey, Lionel, *Hymns and the Christian Myth* (Vancouver: University of British Columbia Press, 1986).
—— *Class and Idol in the English Hymn* (Vancouver: University of British Columbia Press, 1988).
Baker, David and Welsby, Joan, *Hymns and Hymn-Singing* (Norwich: Canterbury Press, 1993).
Barkley, John, *Handbook to the Church Hymnary* (Oxford: Oxford University Press, 1979).

Barnby, Bertram, *In Concert Sing* (Norwich: Canterbury Press, 1993).

Barr, Andrew, *The Nation's Favourite Hymns* (Oxford: Lion, 2002).

Benson, Louis, *The English Hymn – Its Development and Use in Worship* (Richmond, VA: John Knox Press, 1962).

Bradley, Ian, *'Abide With Me': The World of Victorian Hymns* (London: SCM Press, 1997).

Braley, Bernard, *Hymn Writers* (3 vols) (London: Stainer & Bell, 1987, 1989, 1991).

Brooks, Peter Newman, *Hymns as Homilies* (Leominster: Gracewing, 1997).

Castle, Brian, *Sing a New Song to the Lord* (London: Darton, Longman & Todd, 1994).

Colquhoun, Frank, *A Hymn Companion* (Sevenoaks: Hodder & Stoughton, 1985).

—— *Preaching on Favourite Hymns* (London: Mowbrays, 1986).

A Companion to the Baptist Church Hymnal (London: Psalms and Hymns Trust, 1953).

Companion to Hymns and Psalms (London: Methodist Publishing House, 1988)

Davie, Donald, *The Eighteenth-Century Hymn in England* (Cambridge: Cambridge University Press, 1993).

Davis, A.P., *Isaac Watts* (London: Independent Press, 1948).

Dearmer, Percy, *Songs of Praise Discussed* (Oxford: Oxford University Press, 1933).

Frost, M. (ed.), *Historical Companion to Hymns Ancient and Modern* (London: William Clowes, 1962).

Gilman, F.J., *The Evolution of the English Hymn* (London: Allen & Unwin, 1927).

Hancock, C.P., *A Hymn Lovers' Companion* (Leominster: Orphans Press, 1984).

Hodges, M.A. and Allchin, A.M., *A Rapture of Praise* (London: Hodder & Stoughton, 1966).

Jefferson, H.A.L., *Hymns in Christian Worship* (London: Rockcliff, 1950).

Julian, John (ed.), *A Dictionary of Hymnology* (London: John Murray, 1892; 1907).

Lightwood, James, *Hymn Tunes and their Story* (Charles Kelly, 1905).

Moorsom, R.M., *A Historical Companion to 'Hymns Ancient and Modern'* (London: 1889).

Patrick, Millar, *Four Centuries of Scottish Psalmody* (Oxford: Oxford University Press, 1949).

Phillips, C.H., *The Singing Church* (Oxford: Mowbrays, 1979).

Routley, Erik, *Hymns and Human Life* (London: John Murray, 1952).

—— *Hymns Today and Tomorrow* (London: Darton, Longman & Todd, 1964).

—— *The Musical Wesleys* (London: Herbert Jenkins, 1968).

—— *Church Music and the Christian Faith* (London: Collins, 1978).

—— *A Panorama of Christian Hymnody* (Collegeville, MN: The Liturgical Press, 1979).

—— *Christian Hymns Observed* (Mowbray, 1983).

Sankey, Ira, *My Life and Sacred Songs* (London: Hodder & Stoughton, 1906).

Taylor, Cyril, *Hymns for Today Discussed* (Norwich: Canterbury Press, 1984).

Watson, Richard, *The English Hymn* (Oxford: Clarendon Press, 1997).

Webster, Donald, *Our Hymn Tunes: Their Choice and Performance* (Edinburgh: St Andrew Press, 1983).

Whittle, Tyler, *Solid Joys and Lasting Treasures* (Bolton: Ross Anderson Publications, 1985).

INDEX OF FIRST LINES

INDEX OF AUTHORS,
TRANSLATORS AND
COMPOSERS

(This index refers to the hymn numbers printed beside each title in the text)